To Don Thachtenberg,
who works hard keeping
this place on an even keel

all Best
Pete Beye

To Don
our great leader
Deborah

RICHARDSON
DILWORTH

Also by Peter Binzen

Whitetown USA
The Wreck of the Penn Central (coauthor)
The Cop Who Would Be King (coauthor)
Nearly Everybody Read It (editor)

RICHARDSON
DILWORTH
LAST OF THE BARE-KNUCKLED ARISTOCRATS

PETER BINZEN
with
JONATHAN BINZEN

Camino Books, Inc.
Philadelphia

For Virginia Flower Binzen,
transcendent wife and mother

Manufactured in the United States of America

1 2 3 4   17 16 15 14

Library of Congress Cataloging-in-Publication Data

Binzen, Peter.
  Richardson Dilworth: last of the bare-knuckled aristocrats / Peter Binzen with Jonathan Binzen. — 1st Edition.
    pages cm
  Includes bibliographical references and index.
  ISBN 978-1-933822-86-0 (alk. paper) — ISBN 978-1-933822-87-7 (ebook)
  1. Dilworth, Richardson, 1898-1974. 2. Reformers—United States—Biography. 3. Political activists—United States—Biography. I. Binzen, Jonathan. II. Title.
  HN57.B546 2014
  303.48'4092—dc23
  [B]
                                                                            2014005537
  ISBN 978-1-933822-86-0
  ISBN 978-1-933822-87-7 (ebook)

Cover and interior design: Jerilyn Bockorick

This book is available at a special discount on bulk purchases for promotional, business, and educational use.

Publisher
Camino Books, Inc.
P.O. Box 59026
Philadelphia, PA 19102
www.caminobooks.com

Contents

Acknowledgments

Writing this book would not have been possible without the contributions of many people who knew Richardson Dilworth in his years of public service. One invaluable source is the collection of interviews conducted by Walter M. Phillips for his oral history of mid-20th century Philadelphia. Phillips was active in the reform movement of that period, and transcripts of his interviews with more than 60 men and women are available for researchers at Temple University's Urban Archives. They are a historical treasure. Also at Temple in the Special Collections Research Center is an enormous trove of photographs from the Philadelphia *Bulletin*, *The Philadelphia Inquirer*, and the *Philadelphia Daily News*. Librarians there were extremely helpful.

Dilworth's letters and other personal papers and family photographs are housed in the Historical Society of Pennsylvania; his official papers from his years as mayor are preserved in the Philadelphia City Archive.

This book began as an article I wrote in 1989 for *The Inquirer Sunday Magazine*, which was based largely on six long interviews I conducted with Richardson Dilworth in 1972. He came alive in the tapes, and the magazine piece convinced Edward Jutkowitz, publisher of Camino Books in Philadelphia, that Dilworth's career would make for a lively biography. The research and editing of my son, Jonathan, have greatly strengthened the manuscript. Without his help, it might still be unfinished.

Two of Dilworth's sons, Warden and Richardson (Dickie), and two of his daughters, Anne Hackett and Deborah Dilworth Bishop, offered insights into their father as a parent and family man. His late stepson, Louis G. Hill, was generous in sharing his cache of Dilworthiana.

A host of other individuals helped to fill out the portrait; some knew Dilworth well, all knew the city well. They include Michael J. Bradley, Clifford Brenner, William B. Churchman, William T. Coleman, Joseph R. Daughen, Richard H. de Lone, Graham Finney, John Gillespie, Tom Gilhool, John Haas, Frank Hoeber, Harry Kalish, Samuel P. Katz, Harold Kohn, Paul Levy, Claude Lewis, Peter J. Liacouras, Suzanne F. Roberts, Dan Rottenberg, Natalie Saxe, Harry Toland, and Alan Wood.

Introduction

On a steamy day in July 1951, I left my home in northern New Jersey to join the reporting staff of the Philadelphia *Bulletin*. I was familiar with Manhattan, where my father worked, but I knew little about Philadelphia except that it seemed to be a somnolent city on the murky Delaware.

What I found was a town that had earned the sobriquet "the world's greatest workshop" with the most diversified economy of any American city in the 19th and early 20th centuries. It could claim such entrepreneurs as Matthias Baldwin (locomotives), John B. Stetson (hats), William Craig (ships), and John Wanamaker, the "merchant prince." At the time of my arrival, the city was still home to the nation's largest railroad (the Pennsylvania) and America's favorite magazine (*The Saturday Evening Post*). The Bulletin, my new employer, with its daily circulation of more than 700,000, was the largest broadsheet evening newspaper in North America. Walter H. Annenberg, owner of the rival *Philadelphia Inquirer*, was soon to launch *TV Guide* as a national publication, and it would quickly become the largest-circulation magazine in the country. Culturally, the city's symphony orchestra and its art museum were widely acclaimed and Philadelphia continued to dominate its region.

But signs of decline were clearly evident. Major companies were moving out. Manufacturing, the hallmark of Philadelphia's economy, was diminishing precipitously. I discovered that most of Philadelphia's office buildings were second-rate, its hotels were almost uniformly dreadful, and it was hard to find a decent restaurant anywhere downtown.

Although Philadelphia's population had edged over two million in the previous decade, it had already begun what would become a long, steady decline. Middleclass whites had started moving from the city to the suburbs in the 1930s; after World War II, the outward trickle became a torrent. "White flight," as it was called, drained Philadelphia of talent and tax revenue. My Australian-born wife, Virginia, and I were part of the exodus. After living for a year in an apartment in the city, we moved to Bucks County in 1952. For $100 down and $65 a month, we got a $10,000 house on a half-acre lot in Levittown. Thousands of young married couples joined us out there. All were white, because William J. Levitt refused to sell to African Americans. Federal policies actually encouraged the outpouring—by financing highways that made commuting easier, and by underwriting the mortgages of house buyers in "safe" middle-class sections while refusing them in depressed city neighborhoods. The policy of "red-lining" mortgages, which blatantly discriminated against African Americans, went unchallenged for years by the public and the press.

As a newcomer, I was also struck by Philadelphia's spiritual malaise, its lack of civic pride. H.L. Mencken, the sage of Baltimore, had denounced Philadelphia as "the most Pecksniffian" of cities, but some of its locals were just as scathing. Stanley Walker, who edited *The Public Ledger*, one of the city's dailies in the 1940s, termed Philadelphia "duller than seven Sundays in Flatbush." Sociologist Digby Baltzell agreed with Philadelphia novelist Owen Wister that the natives harbored "a deep instinct for self-disparagement." Baltzell believed that the virus had spread from generation to generation among those, like himself, who had been born in Philadelphia. Writer Struthers Burt admired Philadelphia's "Quaker façade" but criticized its conformism, anti-intellectualism, materialism, and lack of enthusiasm. His son, Nathaniel, also a writer, said that next to Brooklyn, Philadelphia was "the most belabored and ridiculed great city in the United States," and he attributed these attacks to the self-satisfaction of its residents. Philadelphians, he wrote, were "born retired."

This was a place where old Wasp money and old Wasp families influenced all phases of life—cultural, civic, and commercial. They ran the banks, the businesses, the law firms, the insurance companies, and the arts institutions. It wasn't just Jews and blacks who were excluded; the role of Catholics was severely limited and, of course, few women were heard from. Most of them stayed at home.

Perhaps the sharpest assessment of Philadelphia came from muckraker Lincoln Steffens, who famously labeled Philadelphia "corrupt and contented," and said that it was saddled with the worst city government in the country. It was also saddled with one-party rule. Steffens was writing in 1902; when I arrived half a century later, Philadelphia was still entirely controlled by the same party—the Republicans—and their dominance had been unchallenged for 67 years. The Democratic organization was a mere appendage of the GOP machine. Offices that were required by law to go to the minority party were actually occupied by collaborators with the Republican clique. They were Democrats in name only. Even during the years of Franklin D. Roosevelt's New Deal, when Democrats were winning elections all over the country, they kept losing in Philadelphia, sometimes by margins of 10 to 1.

Yet, politically, I saw that times were changing. The Republican grip on the city was loosening. And within months of taking my seat in *The Bulletin*'s newsroom, I witnessed a remarkable transformation in November 1951 as the Democrats seized power from the ruling GOP. They seized it and they held it and they still hold it today, more than 60 years later.

CHAPTER ONE

Iron in the Bloodlines
The Dilworths and the Woods

Richardson Dilworth was an outsider in clubby Philadelphia. Born in Pittsburgh and raised there and in New York City, he arrived in Philadelphia at 27 to look for work as a lawyer. It was 1926, and he was just out of law school and just into parenthood. Ancestors on both sides of his family had settled in and around Philadelphia centuries before, but he would never feel fully accepted in the city himself. His wealthy parents were staunchly conservative, but his own political views, awakened by Woodrow Wilson's fight for the League of Nations, had shifted decidedly to the left. In this way, too, he was out of place in a city entirely controlled by a notorious Republican machine in close alliance with conservative businessmen. Yet 25 years later, Dilworth would emerge as the central figure in two decades of progressive leadership that shook the city to its foundations and lifted it to national prominence as an exemplar of vigorous reform.

Two liberal Democrats led the assault on the Republican bastions. Though never close friends, they were loyal running mates. Joseph S. Clark was a Philadelphia-born, Harvard-educated intellectual who served one term as mayor

1

after being elected in 1951 and then realized his boyhood ambition of winning a seat in the United States Senate. After his four years in the mayor's office, Joe Clark virtually vanished from the city's political scene.

Dick Dilworth, who won the race for district attorney in 1951, poured all of his energies in the next two decades into making Philadelphia a better place. As DA, then mayor, and then school board president, he became the defining Philadelphian of his era.

The broad strokes of Dilworth's agenda were lauded in the national press and adopted in other cities. Senator John Kennedy, who admired Dilworth, kept a wary eye on him as a potential challenger for the 1960 Democratic presidential nomination. In Philadelphia, opinion was often divided over Dilworth's more innovative policies, but all Philadelphians could agree that the city had never seen the like of him before.

Dilworth was a man of disparate parts, some of them mystifying but all of them fascinating. In a cynical age, he cut a romantic figure: handsome and hard-working, well-bred and witty, a dashing, sometimes reckless politician who was remarkably open to the press and deeply committed to his adopted city. His running mate, Joe Clark, once spoke of him as "D'Artagnan in a double-breasted suit."

Indeed, there was an Old World chivalry about Dilworth that friends found beguiling. "What surprised me most about him," said Tom Gilhool, who came to Philadelphia from the Yale Law School at Dilworth's behest, "was his shyness.... He was truly a gentle man in every sense of the word." And Dilworth's stepson, Louis G. Hill, said that "a lot of his beliefs were rooted in his Victorian upbringing.... He placed fierce emphasis on manhood and manners."

Those who campaigned against Dilworth, however, didn't find him either gentle or mannerly. Often angry, sometimes wrong, he never shied from a fight or ducked an issue. Thacher Longstreth, who ran against him for mayor in 1955, called him "the last of the bare-knuckled aristocrats." And a Philadelphia *Bulletin* reporter described one campaign event that year as the "wildest, most vicious political debate in the city's recent history." At streetcorner rallies, Dilworth could slug it out with the toughest ward politicians. Not infrequently, his slashing style on the stump boiled over into baseless charges against his opponents. Longstreth said Dilworth displayed a "reckless indifference to the truth." Republican Party chairman William F. Meade called him a "psychopathic liar." And county commissioner Mort Witkin termed him "crazy as a bedbug—with apologies to the bedbug." Few politicians have ever served Philadelphia with such passion.

It was the sheer force of his personality that made Richardson Dilworth so memorable. He never relied on media spokesmen or public relations handouts. If he wanted to make a point, he did it bluntly and with relish. Showing fine impartiality, he alienated numerous individuals and entire groups without regard for race, creed, or social class—and still got elected.

Dilworth coined the phrase "white noose" to describe restrictive suburban zoning meant to exclude blacks, and he once suggested that it might do wealthy white Main Liners some good to get mugged—they might learn the facts of city life. He said it was difficult to find police officers "without tendencies toward brutality," and accused Frank Rizzo, whom he despised, of having him shadowed when Rizzo was police commissioner and Dilworth headed the school board. Just before a referendum on a public school bond issue, Dilworth disparaged the parochial schools in heavily Catholic Philadelphia, declaring their quality "even lower than our public schools."

Dilworth outraged traditionalists by recommending that Philadelphia's ornate, Victorian-era City Hall be torn down. And he took delight in skewering his fellow patricians. "The rich seem to want the city to be a compound where the poor will be kept clean, orderly, and well-policed," he remarked. Yet the rich, he pointed out, also relied on the city to provide them with services like airports and subways. "And they expect all this to be paid for by the same people they would have as household servants."

Although Dilworth never ran for national office, his clash with Senator Joseph R. McCarthy made headlines in 1953. The Wisconsin Republican had alleged widespread Communist infiltration of the State Department after the perjury conviction of Alger Hiss, an ex-employee of the department. When the senator produced no names of conspirators, Dilworth, who was Philadelphia's district attorney at the time, declared that one McCarthy was more dangerous than a thousand Hisses. Challenged by the lion of anti-Communism, Dilworth repeated the statement in a confrontation with McCarthy on national television, adding the pointed admonition that while lawbreakers are punished, "demagogues remain too long above and beyond the processes of the law."

Courage and patriotism were instinctual for Dilworth. He left Yale in his freshman year early in 1918 to fight in France, where, as a 19-year-old Marine rifleman, he was wounded in one of the climactic battles of World War I. Shortly after Pearl Harbor, he volunteered again at 43. Leaving behind a thriving law practice and a wife and eight children (two of them stepchildren), he shipped over to the South Pacific and won a Silver Star at Guadalcanal.

There were rough patches in Dilworth's personal life. He scandalized proper Philadelphians in the 1930s with a messy divorce that left him persona non grata in social circles for many years and triggered a vendetta by his prominent former father-in-law. And bouts of heavy drinking were a recurrent problem, one that threatened his career in the 1940s. The excitement and engagement of politics, however, proved helpful in keeping his demons at bay, and the wider public was never aware of his struggle with alcoholism.

With a dimpled smile and a nasal twang, Dilworth had a mischievous sense of humor and could be an outrageous gossip. He had many friends but few confidants. "There was always an air chamber between us that neither he crossed nor we crossed," said his longtime law partner, Harold E. Kohn. One of Dilworth's great strengths was his ability to attract talented men and women to public service. And once they arrived, he inspired them to perform at the highest possible level.

When Dilworth became Philadelphia DA in 1952, the office was a sleepy, spiritless preserve for part-timers; he quickly transformed it into a place that hummed with young, bright, energetic people, many of whom would go on to distinguished careers. Samuel Dash, who would later teach law at Georgetown and serve as co-chief counsel for the Senate Watergate Committee, was an assistant district attorney under Dilworth. "When Dick was DA, we hated it when it was time to go home," Dash recalled. "He made you feel 10 feet tall."

Dilworth hired blacks and women for a DA's office that had previously been staffed almost exclusively by white men. Until Dilworth became district attorney, no black lawyer had ever argued on behalf of the Commonwealth of Pennsylvania in the Court of Common Pleas. One of the first to do so was A. Leon Higginbotham, a Dilworth hire who went on to become Chief Judge of the United States Court of Appeals for the Third Circuit, a professor at Harvard's Kennedy School of Government, and a recipient of the Presidential Medal of Freedom for his work in civil rights. Higginbotham remembered Dilworth as "an inspiring and imposing boss who was always in charge. He was also a humanitarian. I doubt I will ever meet either a public or private figure whom I admire more."

Dilworth's inspiring leadership was equally evident when he was mayor. Edmund N. Bacon, Philadelphia's legendary city planner, served under both Clark and Dilworth. He admired both mayors but found that in Clark's staff meetings the atmosphere got "gloomier and gloomier—'We've got to do better.' " In a Dilworth meeting, by contrast, the feeling was " 'We're all in this together, and we're going to do great.' You'd go in there and you'd feel, 'My God, this is marvelous. I would die for this guy.' "

As president of Philadelphia's Board of Education during the turbulent 1960s, Dilworth attracted another remarkably talented group to work with him. Bernard C. Watson left a teaching position at the University of Chicago to become associate superintendent of schools in Philadelphia. Why? "It was Dilworth that drew a bunch of us," Watson explained. "He was a mythic figure. Smart as hell and not afraid of anything. It was a special time and he was absolutely fearless."

What was perhaps most striking about Richardson Dilworth was his indomitable spirit, his steely determination. He lost three elections before finally winning his first one, and by then he was over 50. While campaigning for mayor in 1955, Dilworth was criticized for his bellicose rhetoric. Far from apologizing, he replied, "Yes, I am an emotional man. And a fighter—do you think there would be any cities if there were not men to fight for them?" Dilworth, who died at the age of 75 in 1974, loved his adopted city, but he shunned the cautious "Philadelphia style," which was once described as "drowning without making waves." He made waves.

*   *   *

Richardson Dilworth was the second son of Joseph Dilworth and Annie Hunter Wood, whose marriage in McKeesport, near Pittsburgh, in 1888 brought together two Pennsylvania families prominent in manufacturing. The Woods, who settled in eastern Pennsylvania in 1726, made a fortune in metals. Annie's great-grandfather, James Wood, established a village smithy in Pigeontown in 1792, and within a decade was operating a tilt-hammer forge, becoming one of the first in the United States to produce cast steel. In 1818, he and two partners bought and rebuilt a disused forge on the banks of the Valley Creek, 26 miles from Philadelphia. The old forge, previously owned by Colonel William Dewees, was one of a pair on Valley Creek that had given the place its name: Valley Forge.[1] James Wood managed the new business, overseeing the production of sickles, scythes, shovels, saws, and files, and becoming one of the first Americans to produce crucible steel. Wood's productivity was not limited to ironwork. Between 1797 and 1832, he fathered 20 children—11 boys and nine girls—by two wives. Most of his boys joined him in business. Wood's second son, Alan, born on Christmas Day in 1800, helped him at Valley Forge. Alan learned the trade there, and also met and married Ann Hunter Dewees, granddaughter of Colonel Dewees. Alan and Ann were married in Philadelphia in 1826 with the city's mayor officiating, and their first

---

[1] Colonel Dewees was a contemporary of George Washington and a supporter of the rebellion. He and his partner, Isaac Potts, committed nearly their entire iron production to the anti–British cause, and Potts rented the army a house near the forge for Washington's headquarters while the general and his 12,000 troops were encamped there in 1777. Dewees must have profited from the arrangements, but working in the shadow of an army had its risks. In the spring of 1788, Washington issued this order: "Complaints having been made by Mr. Dewees, the proprietor of the Valley Forge…the Commander–in–Chief strictly forbids all persons from further damages to the said buildings and works, which he hopes will be particularly attended to, especially when they consider the great loss that Mr. Dewees has already suffered by the great waste which our army has been under the necessity of committing upon the wood and other improvements."

child, Waters Dewees Wood (Richardson Dilworth's grandfather), was born that
same year.

Alan and Ann moved to Delaware so that he could run a forge his father
bought on the Red Clay Creek outside Wilmington. Thanks to processes for rolling iron and steel that James Wood patented, the Delaware Iron Works was quite
successful. One year, the 10-man shop turned out 40 tons of sheet iron, 110 tons
of rolled steel, 150 hoes, and 9,000 shovels. But James Wood was always looking
for the next opportunity, and in 1832, he and Alan built a new and far larger plant
in Conshohocken, 14 miles upstream from Philadelphia. They moved the whole
Delaware operation 40 miles to the new site—anvils, shears, raw metal stock, roll-
ers, even employees. The Schuylkill Iron Works specialized at first in rolling iron
and steel for shovels. And the plant did a booming business producing shovels and
other implements for 50 years, but the real growth in the business was in sheet iron
and sheet steel. In 1841, at the age of 70, James Wood was awarded his third patent, this one for a process of planishing, or lightly hammering, sheet iron, which
gave it a distinctive sheen. At the time he received the patent, the most lucrative
application for planished iron was just around the bend: railroad steam engines.
They needed weatherproof insulating jackets on their boilers, and as steam engines
proliferated in the second half of the 19th century, the demand for planished iron
skyrocketed.

When James Wood died at 80 in 1851—just three years retired—Alan was
running the Conshohocken business with help from various brothers, half-broth-
ers, sons, and nephews. Over the ensuing decades, members of the Wood family
formed and dissolved partnerships with each other, built new plants, started new
companies, and renamed old ones. One thing remained constant: the enormous
quantity of iron and steel moving through their mills. The Wood ironworks
remained an industrial powerhouse for a century and a half, making the family
enormously rich.

Alan Wood had six sons, but two of them died as young men. The four surviv-
ing sons all worked in the family business. In 1844, at just 18, Alan's eldest, Dewees,
took charge of the reopened ironworks in Wooddale, Delaware. At 22, he married
Rosalind Gilpin of Wilmington, and the couple would have four sons and three
daughters, including Richardson Dilworth's mother, Annie.

In 1851, Dewees left the Wood family business to form a partnership with his
wife's father, Richard B. Gilpin. Moving his young family to far western
Pennsylvania, Dewees helped found an ironworks in McKeesport. Over the following half-century, he built the McKeesport Iron Works, later known as the W.
Dewees Wood Company, into a firm that employed at its peak more than 1,000
workmen in the manufacture of planished sheet iron.

By all accounts, Dick Dilworth's grandfather was a paternalistic employer in the very best sense. Dewees Wood paid high wages, trained his men well, helped them buy houses, and treated them with a solicitude they never forgot. After Wood died in 1899, one former worker in the mill related that when he first hired on, "I was astonished at the kindness with which Mr. Wood treated all of his employees. He would pass through the plant every few hours, looking keenly about him, praising a man here, advising another there, and always having a joke or a pleasant word for us. He knew all of us by name, and liked to learn about our families." Another former worker in the plant recalled, "If a man looked ill, he would tell him to take a few days off. He didn't take vacation out of the man's time, either."

M.G. Cunniff, writing in 1901 about the rise of the U.S. Steel Corporation, said of McKeesport, whose population was then 35,000: "In that city, the best-known and best-liked man was W. Dewees Wood. In that city, too, which has prided itself on having more home-owning workmen than any other city of its size in the country, the employees of the Wood mill, the greater number of whom own their own homes, are regarded as the highest type of skilled steel workers."

Dewees Wood's sons all joined him in the business, and when one of them married, Wood invited every man in the workforce, with their wives and families—a group that would have numbered several thousand—to an oyster supper in celebration. "It made a tremendous crowd when we were all gathered together," one employee was quoted as saying years later, "and it must have cost enormously. But it paid well, if you want to measure its worth to the firm, for it gave every man, woman and child who was supported by the income from the Dewees Wood mill a sense of gratitude which nothing could shake."

At the time of Dewees Wood's death, Andrew Carnegie was quietly buying up many of the most significant iron and steel works in the country to form the monopolistic Carnegie Steel Company, which was soon acquired by J.P. Morgan's U.S. Steel Corporation. When Carnegie Steel approached Dewees Wood's sons with an offer to buy, they were disinclined to sell out. But they were convinced by a combination of cash and coercion. A friend of Richard Wood quoted him as saying at the time: "I don't want to go into the trust; I have to. If I hold out, I can't get supplies for my mill; I must go in." The total amount paid for the company was not made public, but at a director's meeting on May 1, 1900, the U.S. Steel Corporation resolved to spend seven million dollars on stock and bonds of the W. Dewees Wood Company (which was known thereafter as The Wood Works of U.S. Steel). By some reports, it was the largest amount U.S. Steel paid for any plant.

With the sudden influx of cash, two of Dewees Wood's sons each invested about $700,000 in the original family company outside Philadelphia. Other Wood heirs provided additional funds. The Alan Wood Company, which had been run for 50 years by Dewees Wood's younger brothers, was in need of expansion, and the capital infusion financed construction of a new plant along the river a mile west of Conshohocken.[2]

J. Wood & Sons and the Hecksher Iron Company, incorporated as the Alan Wood Iron & Steel Company. Fortified and reorganized, for the next two decades the company continued to generate enormous profits for the Wood family. Richard Gilpin "R.G." Wood, the oldest of Dewees's sons, moved east and became second in command at the firm. In 1901, he bought his uncle Alan's estate, a 300-acre hilltop property with a 25,000-square-foot French Gothic chateau overlooking the family steel mills. Alan Wood Jr. had reportedly spent $1,000,000 to build the house, which was designed by the prominent Philadelphia architect William Price and completed in 1894.

After Dick Dilworth's uncle R.G. Wood took the helm of the company in 1911, it continued to generate enormous revenues as the steel industry boomed. By the time Dilworth arrived to practice law in Philadelphia 15 years later, however, the Wood family empire was breaking apart. An inheritance struggle led to protracted litigation that wound up in the Pennsylvania Supreme Court, and along the way, the Internal Revenue Service obtained a judgment for $1,000,000 in unpaid taxes. In 1928, the company was sold, and a year later, R.G. Wood sold his estate.[3]

---

[2] The experience of Dewees Wood's second son, Alan W. Wood, in the aftermath of the buyout proved to be a cautionary tale. Declining to join his brothers in investing in the old family business outside Philadelphia, the 51–year–old widower took his share of the U.S. Steel payment and moved to New York City. Once in Manhattan, he bought a motorcar and a mansion on Riverside Drive, and he married a much younger woman. When he died in August 1905, the fight over his will became a tabloid sensation. The papers were primed for the story, since he had made headlines earlier that year when his eight children threatened legal action after discovering that he had secretly married Goldie Mohr, an actress and onetime performer in the Barnum & Bailey Circus. Initially, the papers calculated his estate at $15 million and reported that his will provided for its division in nine equal shares to his eight children and his "beloved, lawful wife." *The New York Times* later adjusted its estimate of the Wood estate to five million dollars and explained that Goldie Mohr would contest the will "to seek her one–third dower right." By the end of August, *The Times* wrote that the family had reached a compromise and Goldie Mohr would receive one–fourth of the estate, which was now said to have shrunk during Wood's years in New York to three million dollars or so. A month later, a special to *The Times* reported that Wood's executors had "failed to find the large fortune which it was supposed he left.... [The] children have told their friends that their father's estate seems to have dwindled to a few pieces of mortgaged property." The article closed with a note: "Mr. Wood's widow was Goldie Mohr, an actress formerly with Weber & Fields. It was announced on Broadway last night that Mrs. Wood was to return to the stage soon."

[3] R.G. Wood sold 100 acres to the Philadelphia Country Club and sold the house and some 70 acres around it to a corporate lawyer and horseman named J. Hector McNeal. After McNeal's death, his wife, a follower of the evangelist Father Divine, sold the house to his Universal Peace Mission for $75,000. It remains the property of the Peace Mission and has been designated a National Historic Landmark.

Alan Wood Iron and Steel remained a force in the industry, however, and by 1957, with a workforce of 3,800, the company broke into the Fortune 500 with profits of three million dollars on revenues of $69 million. Despite continuing to post robust numbers, it took on a heavy load of debt, and after reporting a record profit of $8.2 million in 1974, the bottom fell out. The company lost $9.4 million in 1975 and $15 million in 1976. It lost $5.1 million in the first quarter of 1977, and could not meet its debt obligations. In June 1977, the company filed for bankruptcy, and on September 15, 1977, Alan Wood Iron & Steel closed its doors.

Some years later, the facilities were acquired by the multinational Mittal Steel, and today the plant is bustling again. It produces half a million tons of steel plate each year for bridges, ships, and railroad cars, and is the largest supplier of armored plate to the U.S. military.

*   *   *

James Dilworth arrived in Pennsylvania from Liverpool on the ship *Lamb* in 1682, two months before William Penn stepped ashore. Dilworth and his family settled north of Philadelphia in Bucks County, where they purchased 1,000 acres for a farm in 1692. A century later, William Dilworth, of the fifth American generation of the family and the great-grandfather of Richardson Dilworth, was born on May 20, 1791, in a Chester County hamlet 25 miles west of Philadelphia that is still known as Dilworthtown.

In 1795, William and his two younger sisters traveled with their parents, Samuel and Elizabeth, over the Allegheny Mountains to western Pennsylvania. Their conveyance was a team of oxen. That same year, the Lancaster Pike was completed, the nation's first long-distance paved road. Twenty-four feet wide and paved with broken stone and gravel, it linked Philadelphia with Lancaster, 62 miles to the west. If the Dilworths traveled on the new turnpike as they began their journey west, they would have shared the road with a stream of Conestoga wagons, the tractor-trailers of the day. From Lancaster to the western end of the state—another 250 miles—the primary road was a far rougher affair, essentially a wagon track hewn through the wilderness. The Dilworths and their team of oxen would have needed three weeks or more to make the trek.

Among the family's possessions on the trip were a bull calf and a salt pan. Salt, essential at the time for preserving food as well as seasoning it, was scarce and expensive. But with a salt pan one could produce salt by evaporating brine— salty water obtained by digging a shallow well. Samuel Dilworth found that his large iron salt pan was so highly coveted by other pioneers in western Pennsylvania that in exchange for it and his bull calf, he was reportedly offered "all of East Liberty Valley," an area that would later become one of the wealthiest suburbs of Pittsburgh, home to Mellons and Fricks. Not liking the moistness of the soil, however, Samuel Dilworth turned down the deal and settled instead on higher ground overlooking the Ohio River just northwest of the town then called Pittsborough.

Samuel Dilworth bought nearly 1,000 acres in a place now known as Bellevue, and settled down to farm it. The log house he built was four miles from Fort Pitt, which stood on a wedge of land where the Allegheny and Monongahela Rivers join to form the Ohio—the heart of the fledgling town. The fort's location had long been seen as militarily strategic, but it turned out to be an ideal site as well for a manufacturing city. Pittsburgh's easily navigable rivers, which connected it to New Orleans to the south and the St. Lawrence River to the north and provided access to all the Great Lakes, simplified bringing goods and raw materials in and getting the city's manufactured goods out to market. In addition, by the middle of the 19th century, Pittsburgh had canals and railroads tying it directly to the East Coast. The region also had a wealth of natural resources, including a seemingly inexhaustible supply of soft, accessible bituminous coal. The great Pittsburgh coal seam provided inexpensive fuel for the scores of foundries, ironworks, glass works, and rolling mills that would make Pittsburgh one of the great industrial engines of the country. And to top it off, oil was discovered just north of Pittsburgh, adding another enormous driver to the city's economy.

In 1790, five years before the Dilworths arrived by ox cart, Pittsburgh's population was just 376. By the time Samuel and Elizabeth's son William turned 10 in 1801, the population had risen to 1,600 and the town was beginning to bustle, having some 60 shops. Before William was out of his teens, the population had tripled, rising to nearly 4,800 in 1810. And by 1820, it had jumped again, to over 7,000. It would reach 20,000 by 1840, and 50,000 by 1860.

When William was 21, he served in the War of 1812 with the "Pittsburg Blues" under General William Henry Harrison, commander of the Army of the Northwest. He saw action along the Sandusky River in Ohio, fighting against the British and their Native American allies. Returning home a colonel, he became a building contractor, and as Pittsburgh grew, so did his business and his reputation.

In 1817, while still in his twenties, William Dilworth superintended construction of the Smithfield Bridge, the first ever built across the Monongahela River at Pittsburgh. Two years later, he oversaw construction of the St. Clair Street Bridge, the first to span the Allegheny River at Pittsburgh. With his firm, Coltart & Dilworth, he built Pittsburgh's original waterworks and many of the finest buildings in the city.

His crowning achievement was the Allegheny County Courthouse, which Coltart & Dilworth built in 1834. Sherman Day, in his 1840 book, *Historical Collections of the State of Pennsylvania*, said of the courthouse, "This edifice, one of the most elegant in the United States, occupied five years in being built and cost nearly $200,000." The Greek Revival courthouse, capped by a glazed cupola, was built with polished gray sandstone and featured fluted Doric columns six feet in diameter. Inside the three-story building, the courtrooms were arrayed around a central rotunda that was 60 feet across and 80 feet high. This in a town that had been little more than a collection of log cabins just three decades before.

An early history of Pittsburgh states that William Dilworth was recognized not only as "a master builder," but "an important figure in business and religious circles." It described him as "a devout Christian...noted for his charity."

William and his wife, Elizabeth, had 12 children. As the children were growing up, the Dilworths built a schoolhouse on their land and hired a teacher. According to a neighbor who wrote a letter to the editor some 50 years later, "Mr. Dilworth requested the residents...of the near country around to send their children to the school. He not only requested the children of the poor to attend free of charge, but he also bought them necessary books. I was one of that class, and nearly all the school training I ever received was from books bought by him, and in a school house built at his expense."

William Dilworth also made a foray into politics, foreshadowing his great-grandson's career a century later at the other end of the state. Elected to serve in the Pennsylvania state legislature in 1834, he was determined to be a reformer. But he could make no headway. According to Richardson Dilworth, his great-grandfather discovered that major manufacturers and corrupt politicians "absolutely dominated the situation," controlling the levers of power and having "no desire for good government." William Dilworth served just one term before returning to private life. The corruption he encountered in Pennsylvania politics would endure. Half a century later, journalist Henry Demarest Lloyd, in a scathing article about the monopolistic practices of John D. Rockefeller, wrote that Rockefeller's Standard Oil Company "has done everything with the Pennsylvania legislature except refine it."

Of William Dilworth's seven sons, one died as a young man, one became a doctor, and the other five all prospered in business, involving themselves in a range of pursuits that might have defined Pittsburgh's thriving economy. Separately, the various brothers were engaged in oil, gas, coal, iron, steamboats, gunpowder, railroads, sugar, and lumber. And together, in partnerships that shifted between the brothers over the years, they founded and ran Dilworth Brothers, Pittsburgh's largest wholesale grocery business, which continued to operate into the 1930s.

Joseph Dilworth, Richardson Dilworth's grandfather, was born in 1826, the sixth of William Dilworth's 12 children. After working in the family grocery business, Joseph Dilworth teamed up with George Porter in 1852 and founded Dilworth, Porter & Company, a manufacturer of railroad spikes and other railroad supplies. The plant occupied more than two acres on Pittsburgh's south side and employed, at its peak, about 200 workers.

Dilworth, Porter opened just as train tracks began crisscrossing the country, and the new mode of transport passed from infancy to adulthood seemingly overnight. The first U.S. railway, a three-mile line on which the trains hauling granite were pulled by horses, had been launched in Quincy, Massachusetts, in 1826. One year later, a nine-mile, coal-carrying railroad began running in Carbon County, Pennsylvania. The Pennsylvania Railroad opened for business in 1849 with 61 miles of track, two locomotives, two passenger cars, and one baggage car. By 1858, six years after the founding of Dilworth, Porter & Company, the PRR inaugurated travel between Philadelphia and Pittsburgh—a 300-mile trip. Soon the railroad was connecting Philadelphia with Chicago, St. Louis, and Cincinnati. And less than 30 years after its founding, the Pennsylvania Railroad became what the *London Economist* termed the world's largest corporation, twice over.

Many of Dilworth, Porter's products—and some of its machines and processes—were invented in-house. A machine designed by James H. Swett, an early partner in the firm, made Dilworth, Porter the first company to produce railroad spikes automatically by machine. An 1879 book called *Industries of Pittsburgh* reported that at Dilworth, Porter, "ingenious machinery and labor-saving and perfecting devices have been gradually introduced...until at present the firm is justly regarded as the largest and most thoroughly equipped of any similar concern in the country."

Like his father, Joseph Dilworth made a foray into elective politics, serving as an Allegheny County commissioner. Pittsburgh historian Joseph Rishel writes that as a commissioner, Dilworth "strictly supervised the granting of saloon licenses," and that "his zeal in office led to the trial and conviction of two fellow commissioners for corrupt practices."

Joseph Dilworth married Louisa Mendenhall Richardson in 1850, and the couple had five children. The fifth, Dick's father, Joseph Richardson Dilworth, was born in 1860. Joseph Jr. went to Yale and returned home after graduation in 1883 to join his father at Dilworth, Porter. Just two years later, Joseph Sr. died, and Joseph Jr. was soon running the company.

Dilworth, Porter continued to flourish under his leadership. In 1896, the firm invented tie plates—iron fittings for attaching a railroad track's metal rails to its wooden ties, or sleepers. Previously, rails had been spiked directly to the ties. Workers would drive in pairs of spikes on an angle, one from either side of the rail. That method was fast but not foolproof. As locomotives grew larger and train traffic increased, the rails could shift on the sleepers and cause derailments. Tie plates provided a simple and far stronger solution—they were hooked to the rails and then spiked to the sleepers—and they soon became the standard form of attachment on North American railroads. Over the following half-century, Dilworth, Porter made more than 300 million of them.

Not long after he took the helm of Dilworth, Porter & Company, Joseph Jr. married Annie Wood, Dewees Wood's second daughter. The match linked two families made wealthy by the railroad—locomotives sheathed in Dewees Wood's planished iron would have rolled over tracks nailed down with Dilworth, Porter spikes. The couple had two children, both sons. The first was born in 1889, and was named Dewees after his grandfather. The second son, born nine years later, was christened with the maiden name of his Dilworth grandmother, Louisa Mendenhall Richardson.

CHAPTER TWO

A Gilded Youth
Begins in Gloom
Black smoke, white beaches

Richardson Dilworth was born in Pittsburgh on August 29, 1898. His family
lived near the center of town on fashionable Bidwell Street. Their red-brick
Victorian house had a wide porch running around three sides. It should have been
a comfortable existence for a kid. What stuck in Dilworth's mind years later, however, was the awful atmosphere. "When the mills were going, you could hardly see
your hand in front of your face," he recalled. "Pittsburgh was as sooty as any city
you'll ever see."

Pittsburgh was sooty because it was busy. The city's economy was rocketing
ahead thanks in part to a discovery 39 years earlier in the tiny village of Titusville,
about 90 miles to the north. That was where Edwin L. Drake transformed worldwide methods of illumination—and later transportation—by boring a well and
pumping oil from it. On his first full day of operation in August 1859, Drake
pumped 25 barrels of oil. It was America's first oil well, and the rush that followed
Drake's discovery saw wildcatters extending the oil fields for 50 miles along the
Allegheny River toward Pittsburgh. Almost overnight, the city became a center
for oil refineries and banking.

DR. TRACHTENBERG

As investigative reporter Ida M. Tarbell wrote in her history of the Standard Oil Company, northwestern Pennsylvania had long been shunned by many pioneers as "too rugged and unfriendly for settlement." But the discovery of oil transformed the region, she said, "into a bustling trade center where towns elbowed each other for place, into which three great trunk railroads had built branches and every foot of whose soil was fought over by capitalists."

Nine years after Drake's discovery, when historian James Parton wrote a profile of Pittsburgh for the *Atlantic* magazine in 1868, he was awed by the energy and activity of the city. He counted some 500 "manufactories and works," including 50 glass works, 31 rolling mills, 33 machinery manufacturers, 46 foundries, and 53 oil refineries. When Parton climbed one of the hills that surround Pittsburgh for an evening view of the city, he was met with "a spectacle as striking as Niagara.... The entire space lying between the hills was filled with blackest smoke," he wrote, and "hidden chimneys sent forth tongues of flame, while from the depths of the abyss came the noise of hundreds of steam hammers." At times, Parton noted, "the whole black expanse would be dimly lighted by dull wreaths of fire." It was, he said, like "looking over into hell—with the lid taken off."

Yet Parton was impressed, and Pittsburghers took pride in their smoky city. Smoke and soot symbolized the industrial might on which the city's first families—the Carnegies, the Fricks, and the Mellons—built the immense fortunes that enabled them to dominate Pittsburgh society and wield vast power nationally. The Dilworths, too, earned their wealth through heavy industry. They ranked a notch or two below the robber barons, but like the super-rich, they were very conservative Republicans.

Richardson Dilworth remembered his father as a "prominent citizen in Pittsburgh, an easygoing fellow who very much enjoyed a good time—a very good time." Biographer Joe Alex Morris described the elder Dilworth as "an attractive man with deep-set eyes and a large mustache—a dashing figure in a stiff-brimmed boater"[4] who liked to drive his two-wheeled cart behind a spirited horse on summer outings.

It was Dilworth's mother, Annie, however, who was "the undisputed arbiter of family affairs," wrote Morris. Her son put it this way: "Mother was a terribly hard-driving woman, very attractive but very domineering. And she could never be still."

Dilworth spent kindergarten and the first two grades of elementary school at Shady Side Academy. Founded by wealthy Presbyterians in 1883, Shady Side was the school where the Carnegies and Fricks sent their boys.

---

[4] Journalist Joe Alex Morris was paid by Dilworth to write his campaign biography when he ran for governor in 1962.

When Dilworth was five or six years old, his father fell seriously ill. Family members now say he likely contracted syphilis. Dilworth said that by 1906, his father "had become a complete invalid. He couldn't walk any longer." At that point, Annie decided to move the family to Manhattan. "We moved to New York because in those days it was believed you could only get good medical attention there," Dilworth recalled. His father would live on until 1928, but with the move to New York it was his mother, more than ever, who ran all aspects of their lives.

Mrs. Dilworth decided that if they were going to live in New York, they had better "conform to what looked like New York standards." In Pittsburgh, the Dilworths had been Presbyterians, but when Annie discovered that upper-class Manhattanites belonged to the Episcopal Church, she switched denominations. Her son remained an Episcopalian all his life.

With the move to New York, Mrs. Dilworth enrolled eight-year-old Dick in the Browning School, a day school then on West 55th Street. John A. Browning, a Columbia College graduate, founded the school in 1888 with four students in a private home. His teaching ability drew the attention of John D. Rockefeller, who helped Browning relocate to the building on West 55th Street. Rockefeller's son, John D. Jr., attended the school from 1889 to 1893 and became one of Browning's greatest admirers. The Browning School moved to its present location at 52 East 52nd Street, between Madison and Park Avenues, in 1922. It remains a boys' day school, and its annual tuition exceeds $40,000.

As Annie Dilworth began to make connections in New York, she struck up a friendship with August Belmont Jr., a financier and a breeder of thoroughbreds who built Belmont Park racetrack. He was also a ranking member of the city's social set. Belmont recommended that Annie send her sons to the elite St. Mark's School, which had been founded in Southborough, Massachusetts, in 1865 as a boarding school for the sons of upper-class Episcopalians. Dilworth claimed that Belmont, who was Jewish, had gotten his own sons into St. Mark's by making a "tremendous contribution" to the school. (The St. Mark's football field is named for Belmont.) According to Dilworth, Belmont "told Mother that this was the best school there was," and he smoothed the way for Dick, his brother Dewees, and several of his cousins to be admitted to St. Mark's.

Dilworth entered St. Mark's in the fall of 1911. Tuition was $1,000 a year, and most of the boys came from families in the upper reaches of society in Boston and New York: Sears, Pell, Lowell, Whitney, Grew, Morgan, Van Rensselaer. The school's literary magazine ran Brooks Brothers' advertisements offering liveries suitable for "stable, garage or club" and for "manservants." Such was the environment that Dilworth's mother sought for her son.

Under the Reverend William Greenough Thayer, St. Mark's headmaster since 1894, the school was tightly run "in conformity with the principles and spirit of the Episcopal Church." Daily prayers were said. The school catalogue informed parents that "important letters and telegrams should be addressed to the Headmaster," adding that "boxes and packages of all kinds are forbidden without the express permission of the Headmaster." Leaves of absence would not be granted "except under extraordinary circumstances." Some of the boys referred to St. Mark's as "the monastery." The school's emphasis on rules may have irked Dilworth, but he performed well academically, athletically, and socially.

Dilworth's first year at St. Mark's was the school's 50th anniversary, and a report marking the occasion noted that "some of the graduates were disturbed because St. Mark's was becoming more and more a rich man's school." It recommended "competitive scholarships, or something of that sort." In dismissing the finding, a school committee wrote that the headmaster's influence was "so wisely exerted that the boys at St. Mark's were in little danger of becoming snobbish, or of laying undue stress on the mere matter of wealth." To Dr. Thayer, "distinction of brain and physique, opportunity and personality" were what made "this world worth living in."

In a 1972 interview, Dilworth noted that when he was young, "a lot of the well-to-do families followed the English custom" of sending their sons off to boarding school at the age of six. He considered it "brutal" to separate boys from their parents at such a tender age. Dilworth himself started at St. Mark's at the age of 13 and spent six years there. He played varsity baseball and football and studied such English authors as Macaulay, Defoe, Pope, Swift, Scott, Milton, Tennyson, Dickens and, of course, Shakespeare. The boy would remain an avid reader all his life. Family members say Kipling was one of his favorites.

In his senior year at St. Mark's, Dilworth captained the baseball team as a slugging center fielder with two triples, two home runs, and a .391 batting average. He played right end on the football team. "I wasn't by nature a particularly good athlete," Dilworth recalled, "but I worked hard at it." Either way, he shone. A Boston sports writer who covered St. Mark's losing football game against Groton in 1916 reported that Dilworth, tall and slender with an easy smile and a fierce competitive spirit, was the best tackler he'd seen all season. According to the school paper, Dilworth, then 18 years old, was five feet 11 inches tall and weighed 161 pounds. He was the second tallest on a team whose right halfback stood just five feet four. His weight was the team average; not a single player weighed as much as 180 pounds.

Dilworth recalled doing "reasonably well in studies" at St. Mark's, ranking sixth or seventh in his senior (or sixth form) class of 23. He was vice president of the class and a leading member of the debating team. And evidently a good dancer. For the Sixth Form Dance in January 1917, the St. Mark's seniors brought in dates from New York, Philadelphia, Boston, and elsewhere. The school paper reported that there were 17 dances before supper and two more after supper, followed by the cotillion, an elaborate formal dance. "Owing to the skill of Dilworth and Miss Lee of New York," said the paper, "the cotillion was most gracefully conducted. The figures chosen proved to be most attractive, and the favors left nothing to be desired."

Although the youthful Dilworth lived in a rarefied atmosphere of wealth and privilege, he was not unaware of life's less fortunate. In an essay published by the school paper, he deftly described his long train ride home to New York for vacation. Awaiting him at his parents' luxury apartment in Manhattan was a butler to take his bag, a rich oyster dinner, and a large, soft bed. But his essay dealt with sights outside the train window.

"Darkness has fallen by the time the fringes of the city are approached," he wrote, "and you press your face against the window in order to see the fleeting shapes.... The express is now running on the elevated track, and you can see into most of the tenements. Most of the rooms are bare, with gloomy green walls." While you could occasionally glimpse a "more prosperous room with electricity and an imitation mahogany table in the middle," he wrote, "the majority of rooms seem to be small, bare alcoves with sputtering gas jets. The only ornaments, as a rule, are the bed and the washstand. Somehow or other you cannot help feeling dejected after looking upon such poverty, and even the joy of homecoming is marred for the moment." Many decades later, Mayor Dilworth would witness such deprivation in Philadelphia, and the dejection he had felt as a youth was reflected in his later determination to improve conditions for the underprivileged.

The Dilworth family spent their summers in Southampton, the beach town of the wealthy at the extreme eastern end of Long Island. It was there, as a teenager, that Dilworth met Joe Clark, who was nearly three years younger. Although they never became close friends, the relationship struck up on Southampton baseball fields would later blossom into a remarkable political alliance. It was in Southampton, too, that Dilworth got into the habit of drinking, sometimes to excess. "I did a good deal of drinking in those days," he remembered, "and got into a good deal of trouble through it." He told of attending the "coming out" party for Ailsa Mellon, a Pittsburgh debutante. Her father, Andrew, one of the nation's best known—and most feared—financiers, served as Secretary of the Treasury through the 1920s and then as U.S. Ambassador to the United Kingdom.

"Old Andrew came down to Southampton in the summer with Ailsa," Dilworth remembered. "I think Ailsa was just a year younger than I was. I went to her coming out party and I was dancing with her and was terribly drunk. I lost my lunch all over Miss Mellon and her dress." The next day, said Dilworth, "even Father gave me a working over and what Mother did was incredible. She didn't trust me, so she marched me around to the Mellon household. Old man Mellon was the coldest man I ever saw and I don't believe he had ever been drunk. So I was ushered in by Mother and had to apologize to the old man, and it was like talking to the statues on a stone mountain. He just sat there absolutely frozen, and he said, 'Well, I'll overlook it because of your mother.' "

In spite of episodes like this one—or perhaps because of them, since Dilworth always relished a good story—the summers he spent at the seaside in Southampton remained bright in his memory. In a 1968 letter to a friend from that era, Mrs. R.S. Humphrey, Dilworth reminisced about learning to play bridge at her house and getting into "such rows as a result." And then he wrote, "I know of no more pleasant years than those summers in Southampton, prior to our entry into W.W. I."

CHAPTER THREE

Over There

The maximum of action in the minimum of time

" I am writing to tell you good bye," 19-year-old Private Dick Dilworth, of the U.S. Marine Corps, informed his parents in April 1918, "for my next letter won't be mailed till we reach the other side." Dilworth had left Yale in the middle of his freshman year to enlist, and three months later his unit had received its sailing orders. They would be joining the Allied Forces in France just as Germany was undertaking a series of offensives that threatened to tip the scales in the long-stalemated Great War. "I am doing just what I want to do," Dilworth's letter home continued, "and I wouldn't change places with President Wilson. It is a pleasure and a delight for me and it is hard only on you...but I am sure I will come back, and [I will] act as a decent gentleman and soldier ought to while I am over there."

The United States had entered the war a year earlier, on April 6, 1917, as Dilworth was completing his senior year at St. Mark's School. Woodrow Wilson, who had kept the U.S. out of the fight during the first years of the war, changed course after German submarines sank seven American merchant ships. Before the war ended in November 1918, it would cost the lives of more than eight million soldiers and many millions of civilians. But to Richardson Dilworth and other idealistic young recruits of all nationalities, the war looked not like a meat grinder but a glorious opportunity for action and heroism. At the start of the war, one German soldier wrote that "it seemed a wonderful dream to be permitted to fight for our country's greatness."

The bloodbath had begun in August 1914, sparked not by an invasion or other dramatic act of national aggression, but by the assassination in Sarajevo of Archduke Franz Ferdinand, heir to the throne of Austria. The assassin, 19-year-old Gavrilo Princip, caught at the scene, was one of many Slavic Austrians who wanted an independent Balkan state. Within days of the shooting, it was discovered that Princip and his four compatriots had been armed by a shadowy nationalist group from neighboring Serbia. Austria presented the Serbian government with a list of demands and threatened war if they weren't met. At first, the Serbs seemed ready to capitulate. But when word arrived that Russia's Tsar Nicholas II supported them, their mood turned defiant. Over the next several weeks, the seemingly isolated dispute between Austria and Serbia triggered provisions in a network of alliances and assurances between the major powers, and Europe was at war.

As the British historian A.J.P. Taylor has written, "All imagined that it would be an affair of great marches and great battles, quickly decided." Instead, it was an unspeakable slaughter in slow motion, a four-year deadlock in which the same ground was won and lost repeatedly. It was a war waged from rat-infested trenches across muddy, shell-pocked terrain littered with splintered trees and rotting corpses. The millions of soldiers sent "over the top" of their trenches to attack enemy positions often fought their way through bales of barbed wire, clouds of poison gas, and sprays of shrapnel only to be cut apart by machine gun fire.

Every war is worse than expected, Paul Fussell pointed out in his book, *The Great War and Modern Memory*. But this war, he wrote, "was a hideous embarrassment to the prevailing meliorist myth which had dominated the public consciousness for a century. It reversed the Idea of Progress." In four years of war, the Central Powers—Germany, Austria-Hungary, the Ottoman Empire, and Bulgaria—would have three and a half million of their fighting men killed. The Allies—18 countries including Britain, France, Russia, and the United States— would have more than five million killed and nearly 13 million wounded. The French alone, from their total mobilized force of 8.4 million soldiers, would suffer 5.6 million casualties—a horrifying 67 percent casualty rate.

Before the fighting began, Britain had not known a major war for a century. Peace had prevailed between France and Germany for nearly 50 years. Few European men in the prime of life knew what all-out war was like. "Never such innocence again," wrote the poet Philip Larkin. Fussell, paraphrasing Larkin, described the combatants on both sides of the senseless struggle as "those sweet, generous people who pressed forward and all but solicited their own destruction."

Fussell and others have noted that, at least in its early stages, the Great War was often described in the terms of sport rather than combat. The Allies' principal propagandist, Lord Northcliffe, publisher of *The Times* in London, praised English tank crews for going to battle "in a sporting spirit with the same cheery enthusiasm they would show for football." The Germans, by contrast, were thought to have, in Fussell's phrase, "an inadequate concept of playing the game."

As patriotic fervor swept the United States following its declaration of war, 18-year-old Dick Dilworth was caught up in it. He was desperate to join the fight. But he needed parental permission to enlist, and there he encountered an immovable object. "Father was willing but Mother was dead set against it," he recalled. She was determined that he enter Yale in the fall, and her son really had no choice. As consolation, his parents gave him a new Ford automobile to drive around New Haven.

Before starting his freshman year, however, Dilworth spent eight weeks during the summer of 1917 at a training camp in New Jersey run by Regular Army officers. There were a dozen such camps around the country offering military basics to young men not yet in uniform. The first of these camps, at Plattsburg, New York, was founded in 1915 by the Preparedness Movement, a group of military and political leaders, including former President Theodore Roosevelt, who saw America's involvement in the Great War as inevitable and sought to increase the country's readiness for the conflict.

When Dilworth arrived at Yale that fall, sport was the only outlet he had for his desire for combat, and he played on the freshman football team. His thoughts, however, were on the fighting in France. One of his classmates, W. Sheffield Cowles Jr., was similarly preoccupied. Cowles was a nephew of Theodore Roosevelt, and his uncle, who had led troops in the Spanish-American War, wanted to know why Cowles wasn't in uniform. Roosevelts had been in every U.S. war—why was his nephew not in this one? Teddy recommended that Cowles and his friends join the Marines. It was, he said, "the logical thing to do."

On the one hand, it didn't seem logical. The Marine Corps, founded during the Revolutionary War, was a small branch of the Department of the Navy, and the Navy's participation in World War I, principally a land war, was bound to be limited. Small numbers of Marines had been sent to Mexico, Haiti, and Santo Domingo in 1914 and 1915 to prevent Germany and the Central Powers from meddling there. But the corps' total complement in 1914 barely exceeded 10,000 men.

On the other hand, the Marine Corps commandant, Major General George Barnett, was determined to secure an overseas assignment for his troops. And when America's entry into the war was followed by legislation authorizing the drafting of half a million young men, the Marine Corps was transformed into a force that would have more than 70,000 under arms by the end of 1918. Moreover, the Marine Corps, which only accepted volunteers, had always made up in spirit what it lacked in sheer numbers. With strong backing from Navy Secretary Josephus Daniels and Daniels' assistant, Franklin D. Roosevelt, Barnett persuaded Secretary of War Newton Baker to accept two regiments of Marines for a combat role under Army command. "We had used the slogan 'First to Fight' on our posters," General Barnett later explained, "and I did not want that slogan made ridiculous."

American troops were urgently needed to bolster the British and French armies as they confronted strengthened German forces on the Western Front, which ran on a southeasterly slant from Belgium down through France. The abdication of Tsar Nicholas II, whose troops supported the Allies, had weakened Russia's military position. And even before the Bolshevik government sued for peace in December, the Germans had begun shifting forces from the Russian engagement on the Eastern Front to the Western Front, where the Central Powers had been fighting the Allies to a bloody draw for so long.

In a strategy meeting in November 1917, the German high command, calculating the time it would take for America to muster, equip, train, and transport a major fighting force, decided to gamble everything on a series of spring offensives along the Western Front. The strikes were designed to win the war before the Americans could arrive in numbers large enough to affect the outcome.

The first contingent of the American Expeditionary Force (AEF), which included some Marines, stepped ashore in France in July 1917. In a war involving tens of millions of soldiers, it was a token force of some 14,000 troops. General John J. Pershing, commander of the AEF, insisted on proper preparation for his men, and although the number of American troops in France would eventually exceed one million, they would not arrive in the hundreds of thousands until the spring of 1918, a year after America declared war.

Throughout his freshman fall of 1917, Dick Dilworth had continued pestering his parents for permission to enlist, and by January 1918, his efforts had paid off: "I finally persuaded Mother that if she didn't agree, I'd go down and enlist and give a false age somehow." Letters he wrote at the time are charged with his excitement at the prospect.

In mid-January, Dilworth got an invitation that he hated to refuse. Katherine Van Ingen, a student at the Westover School in Middlebury, Connecticut, and a girl he'd known from summers at Southampton, asked him to join her for a performance at the Metropolitan Opera House in New York.

"Of course, there is nothing I'd rather do than go to the Met with such a charming, winsome, feminine beauty as you," he wrote, "but as I have just received permission to enlist in the Marines, I will have to pass up this marvelous opportunity." Dilworth wrote that he expected to enlist on February 9. "I'm scared to death that something will keep me from going at the last minute, for it seems too good to be true."

Then he laid it on thick: "I really can't tell you how deeply it touches me not to be able to go to the Met with Kate, the famous red-haired vampire and charmer. But be that as it may, I'm afraid, my own true love, that I won't be able to have that pleasure, but do hope that if I do go [into the Marines], you will cheer my lonesome hours by an epistle or a sock or something." He signed the letter "Yours affectionately, Dick."

The letter was postmarked January 22. On February 9, Dilworth and five other Yale freshmen—Sheffield Cowles, D.C. Dines, Robert Warren, Harvey Bradley, and Stephen Hord—joined Dilworth's close friend Wells Cumings, a Princeton freshman, at the Marine Corps recruiting station at 24 East 23rd Street in Manhattan. Word that Teddy Roosevelt's nephew was abandoning campus life for the fighting in France had gotten out—TR had written a congratulatory telegram—and newspaper reporters covered the collegians. *The New York Herald* ran the story on February 10 under a headline that had to be shoehorned into a narrow space and would win no journalism awards:

> Yale Freshmen, War Appetites
> Whetted, Join Marine Corps

Noting that the seven enlistees were under the draft age of 21, the *Herald* quoted Sheffield Cowles, who wore a coonskin coat and a derby hat for his induction, as saying that they wanted "the maximum of action in the minimum of time." Cowles pointed out that he and his classmates "could have joined the Reserve Officers Training Corps at Yale, but that was too slow for us."

When the college boys in their fancy clothes arrived for basic training at the Marine Corps base at Parris Island, South Carolina, they were greeted with hooting and heckling. Working-class recruits taunted the newcomers. Insults were exchanged and fistfights broke out. After D.C. Dines punched one of the hecklers in the jaw, loosening a couple of teeth, things quieted down. But the antagonism persisted. One day, when Dilworth, on latrine duty, was mopping the toilet floor, a Marine with muddy boots tramped in and made a mess of the place.

"Look," Dilworth protested, "I've just got this head ready for inspection. Why don't you get the hell out of here so I can clean up your tracks?"

"Why don't you get your valet to do it?" the Marine shot back.

Dilworth swung his mop, striking the Marine's face and smearing his clean shirt. Then he struck him in the head with the mop handle, driving him outside. After this incident, the heckling subsided, and Dick and his friends got along better with their comrades in the United States Marines.

Dick's parents sent him two food parcels, which were "all gone about 10 minutes after they got here," he wrote. He advised them not to send any more for some time, however, because the first packages "caused quite a mess in the bunk-house and if that happens too often, I'll get walked all over."

Dilworth wrote home that the Marines were planning training camps for officers, but said he wanted no part of them. "I would much rather stick to my company as a plain private," he told his parents. He might have been expressing solidarity with the rank-and-file Marine, but most of all he felt an urgent need to get overseas as fast as possible. Further training would mean further delay and Dilworth, as innocent as the soldiers Paul Fussell described, didn't want the fighting and killing to end before he got there. If he went directly, the prospects were favorable, he thought. "The Germans certainly seem to be raising the devil over there, and it looks as though the war [will be] good for some time longer," he wrote.

Dilworth's observation that the Germans were raising the devil was accurate. After a quiet winter in the West, the German armies under General Erich Ludendorff had launched the first of their spring offensives. The Germans' overall plan was to attack the British Army—the strength of the Allied Forces—crippling it and forcing the French to surrender as well. The majority of British forces were in northern France and Belgium, and the Germans decided to strike directly into them with the first two offensives. The third offensive was to be launched farther south, into French troops. It would be a thrust toward Paris.

The first offensive struck in the area of the River Somme in March 1918, and quickly plunged 40 miles into the British rear. It was a stunning victory. British casualties reached 300,000 in seven days. On April 12, Field Marshal Douglas Haig issued an order indicating the insecurity of the British salient: "Every position must be held to the last man. There must be no retirement. With our backs to the wall and believing in the justice of our cause, each one must fight on to the end."

The Americans, enlisting and training soldiers as fast as possible, felt the pressure to move quickly to counter the German advances. Dilworth's unit was ordered overseas in April, even before its 12 weeks of basic training had been completed. From Parris Island, the new soldiers traveled by train to Quantico, Virginia, for equipment before shipping out. Dilworth's mother, who was a friend of Marine Corps commandant Barnett's wife, got wind of the move.

According to Joe Alex Morris, Dilworth and his fellow trainees, stripped to undershirts and pants, were lined up waiting to draw their combat gear at Quantico when "a sleek black limousine slid to a halt nearby. Mrs. Dilworth descended majestically and rushed to throw her arms around her son. The line of Marines gaped at her, eyes bulging.

" 'Mother—for God's sake, Mother,' Dilworth whispered hoarsely. 'You can't do this to me.'

"Mrs. Dilworth, however, could. She pulled him out of line and to the limousine where Mrs. Barnett waited, all smiles. Sweating with embarrassment, Dick got into the automobile while his battalion joined in giving him the raspberry."

After a trip to Washington with the two women, Dilworth caught up with his outfit in Philadelphia as they prepared to ship out. But there was more humiliation ahead. According to Morris, Mrs. Dilworth and Mrs. Barnett were at the pier as the troops boarded their ship and, for Dilworth, "the previous day's agony was repeated amid the jeers of the entire battalion."[5]

Except for Sheffield Cowles, all of Dilworth's college friends had remained together. (Cowles, who had expressed their common hope for "the maximum of action in the minimum of time," attended officer candidate school and joined a battalion that saw no action at all.) Now the friends boarded the Navy transport *Henderson,* which would make 17 trans-Atlantic trips with men and materiel during the war. Dilworth found the crossing uneventful. He wrote his parents that there were "no alarms or disturbances and good weather."

The account of a fellow Marine on the ship, Carl Andrew Brannen, was less sanguine. Brannen's brief memoir of the war, *Over There,* written years later, describes a path that closely paralleled Dilworth's for the first six months of their enlistments. Brannen, a Texan, remembered marching toward the *Henderson* to the strains of "Over There," the popular George M. Cohan song inspired by America's entry into the war. Once on the ship, which had space for 1,500 men and 24 mules, the soldiers were "stuffed in like sardines. I got seasick the first day by the time we were out of sight down Delaware Bay, and remained sick and miserable the entire 13 days crossing."

"The ship was kept in complete darkness at night," Brannen wrote, "as a light would have betrayed us to any submarine nearby. Each fellow wore a life preserver at all times," and sleeping in one was quite uncomfortable, he remembered. When the ship "entered the real submarine zone near Europe, orders went out that if anyone fell overboard, the ship would not stop to pick them up."

Dilworth's vivid and informative letters from France, which his parents kept and passed on to later generations, began with the welcome his unit received as it was docking at the French seaport of Brest on May 7, 1918. "An old lady hoisted an American flag in her window, which produced tremendous cheers from us," he wrote, "and she was so moved, she wept." But the dark side of war was soon brought home to the freshly arrived soldiers. "Just as we landed," his letter continued, "about 20 wounded men filed by us.... Some of them were pretty badly hashed up."

After a couple days of rest, the soldiers traveled by rail to the Vosges Mountains of eastern France. They rode for two days and nights in the notorious Gallic boxcars meant to carry 40 men or eight horses. Dilworth reported that the train ride was "a tight squeeze when you get in there with your packs and rifles and rations. Once you sit down, you have to stay till the rest feel like getting up....

---

[5] Dilworth himself never mentioned these implausible events in long interviews with the author, but Morris' reporting was always creditable. One can only wonder what General Barnett thought of his wife's breach of military security, surely a court martial offense if committed by anyone in uniform.

Night time is the worst on the cars, for it is absolutely pitch dark, and everyone crawls over everyone else, and every time you doze off, someone either sticks a foot or a fist in your face. By morning the confusion and jumble is so bad that it seems as tho you never would get a hold of any of your stuff again."

At several stops, Dilworth recalled, the Marines were given coffee, cocoa, and chocolates issued by the Red Cross, "and it was certainly a relief." In a later letter, however, he indicated that it wasn't just hot drinks that the men in the boxcars were enjoying. "I can't tell you how terrible the trip was," he wrote, "for our entire car got drunk as lords, and when 40 men are in a boxcar with about 30 drunks, why things begin to hum."

Carl Brannen's account explained where the drinks came from. He said that when the troop train halted near a flat car carrying a barrel of wine, some of the Marines forced open the barrel. "There was a mad scramble out of the cattle cars, all with cups and cans ready. Soon the wine was ankle deep on the ground so that some of the men began getting it there." He added that those too drunk to return to the rail cars were court-martialed. While the enlisted men fought for space in the cattle cars, the officers "rode comfortably and uncrowded in the better cars."

The troops then moved to a mountain encampment near the Swiss border not far from Dijon for two and a half weeks of training. On May 31, Dilworth wrote home about being billeted in a small village, a "very quaint little place with its stucco buildings and red-tiled roofs. The country around here is very hilly and our parade ground is on a hill about two miles out and it is a wonderful sight to look down on this little place in the valley, surrounded by cultivated fields." Having studied French in school, Dilworth found that he could "get on pretty well, and I have struck up quite an acquaintance with an old woman 78 years old. She lives in one of the little houses by the café and she tends her cows, chickens, field and house all by herself as her husband is dead and her sons at the front. It is almost criminal the way those old ladies work."

Of the training, he wrote, "we drill pretty hard but it is all very interesting. We have about four hours drill in the morning, which is divided up into close-order drill, bayonet drill, bomb throwing, gas practice, and games. You have to do everything on the jump and whenever you get a bit dead, they give you some game to snap you up." There was no ammunition to spare, and so they had no rifle practice. Much of their time was spent hiking while wearing gas masks, which were very cumbersome. Still, Dilworth wrote home, "I have enjoyed the whole thing greatly and only hope we will get in training for real fighting and not be shoved off for guard duty."

His wish was soon granted. On the night of June 4, the brigade marched 30 miles to the railroad and boarded freight cars for the front. They passed close to Paris, and Dilworth reported seeing the Eiffel Tower. Up to that point, the six collegians had stuck together. Then their tiny band was broken up. Dilworth, Wells

Cumings, and Harvey Bradley were assigned to the Sixth Marine Regiment. Robert Warren, D.C. Dines, and Stephen Hord went with the Fifth Regiment. For Warren and Hines, the parting from Dilworth was permanent. He would never see them again.

*   *   *

The battle Dilworth and his brigade were headed toward would prove one of the most pivotal of the war. It centered on a small, dark forest near Chateau-Thierry, a killing ground that will forever be remembered as Belleau Wood. In ferocious fighting lasting most of the month of June, U.S. Army and Marine units struggled with the Germans for control of the forest. The confrontation took place at the spearhead of the Germans' third major spring offensive, the thrust aimed straight for Paris.

The offensive had been launched on May 27, and made astonishing advances. On the first day, the Germans penetrated 12 miles, and in five days they had pushed as far as 40 miles in one sector. Over the course of the first week of the offensive, as the Americans were rushing to the site of the fighting, the Germans took 55,000 French prisoners.

The importance of this, the Americans' first fight, was not simply a matter of strategy or territory but of morale. An order issued by the German 28th Division commander on June 8, 1918, read in part: "Should the Americans at our front even temporarily gain the upper hand, it would have a most unfavorable effect for us as regards the morale of the Allies and the duration of the war." The most vital outcome of the fighting ahead, the memo continued, "would not be a question of the occupation...of this or that unimportant wood," but of "whether Anglo-American propaganda, that the American Army is equal to or even superior to the Germans, shall be successful."

When German units reached the banks of the Marne 50 miles from the French capital on May 31, their scouts found the Americans dug in along a defensive line just north of the village of Lucy-le-Biocage. Belleau Wood was a no man's land between the two armies. On the evening of June 2-3, the Germans entered the mile-square forest and on June 4, they attacked the American line. Allied artillery and machine-gun elements arrived just in time to turn them back.

At dusk on June 5, Dilworth's unit, the 80th Company, 2nd Battalion of the Sixth Marine Regiment, was brought up from the rear to join the fight. "We came up to the front on trucks and went right up there that night into the woods," he told his parents. "A flare went up and they spotted us and gave us a terrible shelling."

Incoming shells, he wrote, sounded like "a wagon going down a rocky road," while machine-gun fire sounded like riveting. New soldiers quickly learned to identify the various types of artillery. "Whiz-bangs" were high-explosive shells from what Dilworth considered "the best field gun in the war." When a whiz-bang struck, he recalled in 1972, "You didn't hear a thing until a sudden *whiz-bang*, so it was quite a nerve-wracking weapon." Mixed in with the explosive shells were shells carrying poisonous gas. "You could tell a gas shell," he said. "The explosion was very hollow. It was a flat explosion—and then you got into your gas mask." He noted that the masks offered protection, but at a price. "Those World War I gas masks were murder. They covered your whole face. You couldn't breathe. You couldn't see."

Decades later, Dilworth remembered the disillusionment of his first night at the front. As his unit moved up from a reserve position to the front lines, German artillery was pounding away, and "French troops were just *streaming* through us, going to the rear in no form of order. They were just streaming back, obviously having broken ranks. Some of them actually running...and as they went through us, they were yelling, 'Finis la guerre! Finis la guerre!' So it was a very depressing start to combat service."

On June 6, the French corps commander ordered the Marines to drive the Germans out of Belleau Wood. French intelligence indicated that the enemy held only a corner of the wood; in fact, a complete regiment of heavily armed Germans occupied the entire forest. The attack began at dawn and went badly. American troops were outmanned and outgunned. Crossing a wheat field while exposed to enemy machine guns, Sergeant Dan Daly rallied his men with a legendary cry: "Come on, you sons of bitches, do you want to live forever?" Hundreds of Marines were cut down in the abortive advance.

That day was one of the deadliest in Marine Corps history, with 1,087 men killed or wounded. Although Dilworth didn't describe the fighting of June 6, he was certainly near the action for his company was at the front on that day. And when Carl Andrew Brannen was assigned there two days later, he found only about 80 men from the original complement of 250.

Because of the Marines' exposure at the front, Dilworth wrote, the Germans could shoot at them from three sides. Heavy shelling at night made movement dangerous. "Everything is pitch dark and you have to hang on to the man ahead of you, and you can't see where you're running, and then all of a sudden a star shell pops up and you might think you were on Broadway."

Dilworth was first armed with a French light machine gun called a Chauchat, which had a 20-round clip and was mounted on a tripod. Each 12-man unit was issued one Chauchat. The gun had a punishing recoil, and according to Dick, who was a crack shot with a rifle, the Chauchat "bounced up and down and was heavy as lead. You couldn't hit anything more than 25 yards away." It also jammed constantly and was, he said, "the worst weapon I think I ever saw." The American military, locked into a contract with an exploitative French manufacturer, had bought 40,000 Chauchats. The gun was described by F.W.A. Hobart in his *Pictorial History of the Machine Gun* as "one of the crudest, most unreliable and cheaply made guns ever to come into service." American troops joked that they were made out of sardine cans. Dilworth and many other Marines quietly discarded their Chauchats for conventional Army rifles.

In one letter home, Dilworth described life on the front line in Belleau Wood. There were no trenches, nothing but shallow dugouts for two or three men, he wrote, "and you can't so much as stick your head up during the day without being sniped at." He said they got one meal at night that had to last for 24 hours. One night the chow cans were smashed by artillery and the troops went 48 hours without food.

"They bring the cans down and stick them in a little clump of bushes behind the dugouts, and you crawl up one at a time and get your chow. There are no communications trenches whatsoever and [the Germans] always seem to spot you when you go back for a detail, and let fly with a few shells." What was most perilous, he said, was moving in and out of the dugouts. "There is always a mixup of some kind or other, and we wander around the woods in a sort of aimless manner before we finally get there."

Going into reserve was no bargain, either, "for you have to keep under cover all the time, and they keep shelling you with shrapnel and gas. Every time we left reserve to go up to the front, we got into a gas attack. Believe me, when you hear them shout 'Gas!' it makes you hop. There were an awful lot of gas attacks, and those were very frightening to me."

Fierce fighting continued in Belleau Wood throughout the month of June. The combat was chaotic. "It was pretty constant fighting in there," Dilworth said in 1972, "but, no, we never saw any actual hand-to-hand fighting. In fact, the woods were so thick you very rarely saw Germans. Every once in a while you'd see them moving around. And of course you never had any idea where you were or what you were doing, really."

In his letters home, Private Dilworth described the monotony of combat. At one point, he got "as sick as a dog" with nothing to eat but a little bully beef and bread. "All day long you had to lay in your hole and then dig at night."

After several days on the front, his battalion moved to the rear for four or five days. Then at one o'clock in the morning, he and the others fell in with combat packs and hiked "at a furious rate" to a village where they drew extra ammunition and then "struck out across a big field" to advanced positions. "We were spotted going in," he wrote, "and they laid a regular barrage down on us. I went by one fellow who had the whole back of his head blown off."

After two days of shelling and gas attacks, his company went to the rear for a week and then returned to the front. "We stayed a week this time and that was the hottest place we were in," he wrote. The Germans knew the exact coordinates and pummeled the position. "The trouble was that the place had been captured the afternoon before…so the Germans were shelling all the communication paths and dugouts…. I had all the canteens blown off my side one night when I was on a water detail."

Dilworth's accounts didn't spare the sensibilities of his parents in their luxury apartment in Manhattan, and the military censors did little editing. "The smell in those woods is something awful from the dead and powder," he wrote. "The first dead man I saw was an infantry-man with his brains running out, and right beside him was a man with his whole chest caved in."

It was on June 24 that the tide finally turned in Belleau Wood. Following a 14-hour bombardment of the German positions by French artillery, U.S. Army and Marine machine gunners led the assault to clear the area. German counterattacks early on June 26 were beaten off and by the end of the day the Allies could at last claim control of Belleau Wood. Two hundred ambulances were needed to evacuate the Allied wounded.

Over the course of that month's fighting, of the 8,000 Marines that fought at Belleau Wood, some 5,200 were killed or wounded. One of the men wounded on the 26th was Dilworth's close friend, Wells Cumings. Dilworth wrote that their company had taken up a position at the foot of a hill near the village of Bouresches when his Princeton friend was struck by a chunk of high-explosive shell that entered his back and exited through his stomach a little below the heart. Dilworth and Harvey Bradley saw him fall. They carried him two miles back to a dressing station where a doctor who examined the wound said that he thought Cumings would pull through. Dilworth, who praised Cumings for never having so much as let out a groan and having the "constitution of an ox," was hopeful. But the doctor was wrong. Cumings died three days later. "I feel like a lost soul without Wells," Dilworth wrote. "We used to be together all the time and he was as good a friend as anyone ever had."

The Germans never again got so close to Paris. Even so, some historians have argued that the Battle of Belleau Wood, so costly in lives, should never have been fought, that American generals should never have agreed to unite the Allied command under the French marshal, Ferdinand Foch, and that they should have resisted French orders to mount the attack.

There was also inter-service controversy among the Americans. The final assault had been a joint effort of the Army and Marine Corps. Through a communications mistake, however, the Marines alone got credit for the victory. Such headlines as "U.S. Marines Smash Huns" appeared in American newspapers. Historian Robert Moskin said the press reports caused "smoldering resentments" on the part of the Army units whose crucial efforts went unrecognized.

Though the Battle of Belleau Wood was later seen as a tipping point, it was hardly the end of the slaughter. The Marines remained in the Belleau Wood sector until the middle of July. Then Marshal Foch gathered his forces—Americans, Scots, Moroccans, French—for a counteroffensive against the German salient. "There were battalions of [French] Foreign Legion, regular French infantry and a whole mass of French cavalry with their breast plates," Dilworth recalled in 1972. "I think it was the last time the French cavalry appeared anywhere."

The Americans boarded French trucks at about one o'clock in the morning of July 16 and rode for 12 hours until the traffic "got so thick we had to walk." The road, he wrote, was filled "with artillery, tanks, trucks, ambulances, carts, cavalry, armored cars, and other contraptions. You have never seen such a mob." Walking might have been better than riding in the French trucks, which Dilworth remembered as "miserable…big open trucks with hard rubber tires…and they jammed us in there."

A violent thunderstorm erupted, and the soldiers "hiked all night in fairly heavy rain but under the cover of woods." Dilworth said his company now consisted mostly of new officers and men who replaced those killed or wounded at Belleau Wood. The newcomers had not been taught how to deploy in combat formations, so they had "kind of a hard time."

The Marines' Fifth Infantry Regiment began a counterattack near Soissons early on the morning of July 18. Dilworth's Sixth Regiment was in support and advanced about 12 miles before halting for an hour's sleep and their first food in more than 40 hours. They passed "a lot of dead Germans, French and Americans, German field guns, machine guns, and all sorts of booty," he told his parents.

That night they found shelter in a rock quarry near the town of Vierzy. Next to the rock quarry were wheat fields stretching out to the north and east. At sunrise on the 19th, Dilworth's regiment passed through the Fifth Regiment of Marines and pressed the attack. His Yale classmate, Harvey Bradley, was with him. They came under heavy artillery fire from German guns half a mile away. Tanks led the advance, and their slow pace restricted the speed of the men on foot. According to Carl Andrew Brannen, "in order to stop the charge, the Germans turned loose everything they had. It seemed to rain shells."

"We had advanced about 200 yards," Dilworth wrote, "when I got walloped." Shrapnel from a high-explosive German shell tore into his left arm near the shoulder, knocking him to the ground. "For a minute," he wrote, "I thought the arm was off, for it was knocked way out of shape." Somehow, he made his way back nearly a mile to a first aid station where his wound was dressed. All the trucks transporting badly wounded soldiers to hospitals were packed, but Dilworth managed to climb onto the fender of one. He rode it back to a field hospital.

At one point in the trip, he said, his truck pulled over to the side of the road to make way for an amazing sight: a Scottish brigade in kilts marching to the front in formation, bagpipes blaring. "I'd never seen anything like it," Dilworth recalled. "Each battalion had its own bagpipe band and here they were getting near to where they would be under shellfire, marching in formation, swinging along, and singing those Scottish songs. It was the most amazing thing to me." After the Scottish brigade passed by, Dilworth's truck resumed its trip.

While he was bumping toward the field hospital, his friend Harvey Bradley was lying helpless on the battlefield. After Dilworth was hit, Bradley had continued advancing and had gotten "almost clear across the field" when one enemy bullet knocked off his gas mask and a second one nicked his spine, causing paralysis.

Bradley was one of many soldiers who lay wounded in the wheat field, unobserved and unattended to. Carl Brannen, who made it across the field before being pinned down under fire all day in a ditch, reports that "In 30 or 40 minutes, our regiment had been almost annihilated. The field which had been recently crossed was strewn with dead and dying. Their cries for water and help got weaker as the hot July day wore on."

For 12 hours, Bradley lay immobilized in the wheat field as American and German tanks attacked one another. "He'd see these tanks coming and wondered whether he was going to get run over or not run over," Dilworth recalled. "Finally, they carried him off." Even those wounded who did make it off the battlefield were then confronted with a near-total breakdown of medical support. The French had ordered ambulances off the roads to make way for ammunition and supply trucks, so any medical evacuations had to be made by truck. The Sixth Marine's regimental aid station, set up in a large cave, treated 2,000 casualties from the fighting on July 19. A battalion surgeon wrote that, with the closest ambulance pool 15 kilometers away, the station "was forced to carry on its work without dressings, water, food, litters, morphine, or any other form of medical supplies."

All told, there would be some 12,000 U.S. casualties at Soissons. The battle, however, was a critical element of the French and American attack on the Marne salient, a campaign often referred to afterward as the "turn of the tide." The Germans never launched another offensive, and the Allies mounted a series of additional offensives throughout the fall that led to the German surrender on November 11, 1918.

Dilworth had been lucky to get out of the line of fire on the wheat field and onto a truck. After the dressing on his wound was changed at the field hospital, he was put on a train for Paris, arriving the next morning. With all the hospitals in the French capital crowded, newly arrived soldiers faced long delays. Dilworth waited for some hours at the American Red Cross Hospital and then passed out. A nurse looked at his arm and called a doctor. Attached to his hospital gown was a note written in pencil:

D-3
Dilworth, Richardson
Gunshot Wound left arm
Operation—Urgent

The doctors who operated on Dilworth found that part of the bone in his left arm was not just shattered but blown away, and the wound was badly infected. "If I hadn't gotten to an American Red Cross hospital," he said in 1972, "I wouldn't have an arm today. There's no question about it. After four years of war, the French Army surgeons were real butchers. They just stood there with these great big butcher knives, and if a fellow came in with a really shattered fracture, they'd just hack it right off. The amount of one-armed and one-legged French veterans of the First World War was tremendous."

The Red Cross Hospital's staff was headed by Colonel Joseph Blake, a prominent New York surgeon whom Dilworth termed "wonderful." He was bed-ridden for two months and underwent half a dozen operations. Doctors rigged up a leather harness to keep the arm in a rigid position during the long healing period.

A military attaché at the American Embassy in Paris visited Dick in the hospital. "He is a lucky youngster to have escaped with his life," the attaché informed Mrs. Dilworth by letter. "He was wounded on Sunday morning at seven o'clock just south of Soissons after his regiment had been in the attack at Chateau-Thierry and had been sent to reinforce another. As he told me, it was too bad to get it just as the fun was beginning." And in a letter from the hospital, he wrote his parents: "My only regret is that I got hit so early in the drive. I would like to have been able to go through with it." Dilworth spent his 20th birthday—August 29—in the hospital and was discharged just after the Armistice on November 11, 1918.

*   *   *

Of the seven collegians who enlisted together, three—Wells Cumings, D.C. Dines, and Robert Warren—were killed and three others—Dilworth, Harvey Bradley, and Stephen Hord—were wounded. Bradley's paralysis on the battlefield turned out to be temporary. He regained the use of his legs, though he never again walked without a limp. Only Theodore Roosevelt's nephew, Sheffield Cowles, who saw no combat, got through the war unscathed.

How did Dilworth's war experience affect his later life? When asked that question in 1972, he said that before becoming a Marine, he had led "a very sheltered life in boarding school, summers at Southampton and [with] Mother keeping a terribly watchful eye on me."

"And so the war did liberate me," he added. Liberation indeed. As a soldier in combat three thousand miles from home, Dilworth expressed himself in ways that he may never have dared to do in his mother's presence. The letters to his parents contain diatribes against people and institutions, prefiguring his often blistering style decades later as a politician. The fighting, tough-talking young Marine would morph into a fighting, tough-talking politician, sometimes wrong but never in doubt.

Dilworth's dogmatic opinions from France might have lacked subtlety, but they made crystal clear where he stood on the issues. In one instance, he declared flatly that "the Red Cross is a fine organization, but the YMCA is a big bluff." His gripe was that YMCA staffers rarely made it to the front. He said that "all the French people believed that money grew on trees in America," and "the trades-people stick you good if they get a chance."

Dilworth was convinced of the superiority of the Marine Corps. "I never realized how good the Marines were till I saw them along the side of the Army, militia and draft men here," he wrote. "We outclass them in absolutely every way." This was probably true. Small in numbers and with tight, centralized control, the Marine Corps did a better job of preparing front-line soldiers than did the Army. In some instances, Army infantrymen were sent into combat without firearms training. Replacements rushed to the front often lacked rudimentary military skills.

Dilworth complained that it was the infantry alone that saw the horrors of war. "They do all the dirty work and fighting, and I don't want any artillery-man or aviator to try and tell me anything about war," he wrote. He denounced a friend who opted not to serve, calling him a "no-good slacker," and added: "I think that everyone should get into this war and if they aren't old enough for commissions, let them enlist as privates. All these summer camps don't do any good. The only way you can learn is [to get] right in and mix it up."

There was a more nuanced and thoughtful side to the young man, however. In a letter to his parents from his hospital bed in Paris, Dilworth demonstrated maturity beyond his 19 years. "I have learned in the service more than ever that a smile when you feel like weeping is the only way to get on. There are times when it rains for a week and you have no covering but a blanket, and mud to sleep on, and you are ringing wet all day and all night with mighty little to eat, and machine guns and shells cutting loose at you all the time, when you just feel like getting out of your hole and letting some shell fill you full [of] holes, but if you can just squeeze out a smile somehow or other, why you decide it is nice to be alive after all."

CHAPTER FOUR

Over Here

Pulchritude, Prohibition, and the innocent little sphere

With his injured arm in a harness, Private Dilworth sailed home on an aged freighter in December 1918. After the trauma of combat and long months in the hospital, he was looking forward to spending time in Manhattan, enjoying himself for a while before returning to Yale. But his mother had other ideas.

By his own account, Dilworth had led "a very insulated life" through his teens. "Mother kept a terribly watchful eye on me," he recalled. His only sibling, brother Dewees, nine years older, had gotten married when Dick was 14, leaving him alone in his domineering mother's care. If Dilworth thought her grip would loosen now that he was a war veteran, he was mistaken. His discharge came on February 11, 1919. When he arrived home and his mother heard of his plan to have a vacation before returning to school, she sprang into action. "You've got to get educated," she declared, "and if you just hang around New York, you'll get into a lot of trouble." She was determined to impose her will, and as Dilworth remembered, "Mother was taking no chances—she rode the train up there with me." As for his dreamed-of relaxation in New York, "I think I had four days— which seemed an outrage to me—before she hustled me back [to Yale]." Despite his grumbling, Dick remained in most respects the dutiful son through his college years. But he began to assert his independence of thought.

In Dilworth's day, Yale's student body, like those at other private colleges and universities throughout the northeastern United States, was all-white, all-male, and virtually all-Protestant. Its faculty also reflected America's dominant Wasp culture. As late as 1946, there was not a single Jewish tenured professor at Yale. Most of Yale's students came from families with long traditions of Republicanism, as Dilworth did. He described his parents as "very staunch" in their support of the GOP. "Father was a reasonable man in most things," he remarked, "but in Pittsburgh everybody thought if you didn't have 100 percent protection for every product, you'd go broke. The thought of Democrats and free trade absolutely panicked Pittsburgh." It wasn't just Democrats whom the Dilworths and other conservatives reviled. They also hated Theodore Roosevelt, the Republican president from 1901 to 1909, whose trust-busting administration filed suits against more than 40 corporations. Dilworth said his father viewed TR as a "dangerous radical."

Of course, it was Teddy Roosevelt who had urged Dilworth and his friends to enlist in the Marines. Dilworth never lost his respect for the former President, and shortly after his return to Yale, he parted company with his parents politically. He attributed his conversion to his wartime experience and to the leadership of President Woodrow Wilson. Wilson sought vainly to get the United States to join the League of Nations, which was intended to establish cooperation between countries and prevent another catastrophic war.

Dilworth majored in history, and one of his history professors, Charles Seymour, had been an advisor to Wilson during the planning of the League of Nations. Seymour, who later became Yale's president, greatly admired Wilson, and his thinking deeply influenced Dilworth, who became very active in the Yale Union for the League of Nations. "I became a Democrat right after I came back from the war," he recalled. "I thought Wilson was absolutely marvelous. And he was right. How could we just turn our backs on the world? It seemed to me that the League of Nations really made sense."

Years later, Dilworth remembered that at his initiation dinner for Scroll and Key, one of Yale's exclusive social clubs, the main speaker gloated about the defeat of the League of Nations. But an eloquent supporter of the League stood up and answered back on every point, receiving rousing applause. "I believe that night decided it for me," Dilworth told biographer Joe Alex Morris. "I greatly admired Wilson and thought he was a man of vast courage. I decided I was a Democrat, and in '20 I voted for James M. Cox and Franklin D. Roosevelt." Dick's embrace of the Democrats "completely infuriated" his mother, and after that they were never able to talk politics.

Dilworth's drinking was another wedge between him and his mother, and produced just the sort of trouble she had tried to avert by sending him straight back to Yale after the war. As he was returning to New Haven in the spring of 1919, the

18th Amendment to the U.S. Constitution was enacted, prohibiting the manufacture and sale of alcoholic beverages. One consequence of Prohibition, according to Dilworth, was that alcohol actually became easier to obtain on campus. "In the old days there was no liquor in the rooms at Yale," he noted. "Prohibition brought liquor into the rooms. Fellows came around every week with your supply." He described himself as a "weekend drinker," but added, "those weekends got very wild, unfortunately."

On one such weekend during his last years of college, he was in New York with some old friends and got "terribly drunk." He recalled returning to his parents' house very late, dressed in a coonskin coat and escorted by a somewhat less-inebriated friend. When his friend pushed him through the door, "there waiting was Mother" with an umbrella in her hand. "The next thing I knew, she was beating me over the head with the umbrella."

His friend carefully kept out of the way, but later reported that he overheard Dick say, "Mother, Mother, for Christ's sake, you should know enough not to antagonize a JAG!"[6] Which infuriated her further and led to a redoubled pounding with the umbrella. Dilworth remembered that the next morning, he was "wakened by the maid very early and summoned to Mother's room for sharp talking. She would say, 'It's no use my sending you in to your father, because he won't do anything about it.' "

No doubt, Dilworth's escapades with alcohol were embarrassing. But the severity of his mother's reaction to his wild behavior may have had a second source. He described his father as something of a man-about-town, and it was when alluding to the condition that left his father a paraplegic that Dilworth said with a wink that his father "enjoyed a good time—a *very* good time." If this was code for carousing that led to a case of syphilis, as some in the family suggest, it is not hard to imagine Dick's mother reacting strongly to seeing too much of the father in her son.

By Dilworth's account, his mother could be cruel about his father's condition. He recalled that when he was 10, the family took a motoring trip in Europe. They were being driven one day in a large touring car in Italy. The roads were very rough, and when the car hit a huge bump, his father, who had virtually no use of his legs by this time, "went about three feet up in the air" and came down on the floor of the car "with the most terrible crash." At this, Dilworth's mother, whom he described as normally impervious to almost any sort of humor, "got absolutely hysterical with laughter. It took her half an hour to stop." His father, meanwhile, got furious. It was "one of the few times in my life I ever saw Father really mad."

---

[6] A reference to the Judge Advocate General corps, the legal arm of the U.S. Navy and Marines.

Sometime during his first few months back from the war, Dilworth made a trip to Philadelphia that would alter the course of his life. His close friend and classmate, Wells Cumings, who was killed at Belleau Wood, had left behind a fiancée in Philadelphia. Her name was Elizabeth "Bobbie" Brockie, and she was the stepdaughter of William G. Warden, one of the wealthiest men in Philadelphia. Dilworth went to extend his condolences and speak of his friend's last months. By late spring, his expression of sympathy had blossomed into something more, and he invited Bobbie Brockie to his prom in New Haven.

Through the rest of his time at Yale, Dick would see Bobbie often, and soon the two were talking of marriage. Neither got much encouragement from their families. Dilworth's mother thought both of them were too young to marry. They should wait, she believed, "until he had completed his education and had established himself in his profession," according to Joe Alex Morris. "My family thought very little of my bride-to-be," Dilworth recalled, "and my bride-to-be's family thought even less of me—because I did some real drinking in those days and got into a great deal of trouble through it."

Dilworth's friends and fellow Marines, Harvey Bradley and Stephen Hord, also returned to Yale—though they were able to enjoy themselves for a while before getting back to campus—and the three wounded veterans roomed together. The fact that they had seen combat and were wounded in action would have been great marks of distinction on campus, where the war effort was esteemed as one of heroism.

The school had been transformed during the war. As former Secretary of War (and Yale alumnus) Henry L. Stimson said in a 1920 address at the dedication of a memorial on campus for Yale men who died in World War I, "Practically the entire momentum of this great institution was thrown into the scales of war." Yale gradually became "both a military training camp and a completely militarized university...her faculties and laboratories turned their resources entirely over to the arts of war." There was officer training for the Navy and the Signal Corps on campus, as well as "one of the foremost artillery schools in America." Doctors and assistants were trained for service in Army hospitals, and the university's "chemists conducted research for the Chemical Warfare Service."

Some 8,000 Yale alumni and students "went to the colors," Stimson said as he eulogized "the 227 of these men to whom it was granted to seal their effort with their lives." And he reserved special praise for the "more than 80" among them who were "chosen for that highest gift—death in action."

The three wounded roommates—Dilworth, Bradley, and Hord—had all been advised by their doctors that exercise would help them recover from their injuries, and all three engaged in challenging sports. Dick was so eager to make Yale's varsity football team that he reported early for practice at the start of his junior year. He still had not regained full strength in his left arm, but his doctors rigged up some protection for it. The protection didn't help. On the first day, he took a hit that reinjured the arm. Bone chips became infected, and he was forced to give up football that fall.

Dilworth subsequently underwent three operations, but he built up his arm by working out with Yale's swimming team under its noted coach, Robert Kiphuth. By his senior year, his arm had gotten much stronger. Although he would lack full arm strength for the rest of his life, he managed to play end on Yale's varsity football team in the fall of 1920.

In those days, with no competition for coverage from professional football—the National Football League was just being formed in September 1920—college football commanded the sports pages. The state universities whose juggernauts dominate the bowls and headlines today were little heard from. Instead, it was the Ivy League, and especially its Big Three—Harvard, Princeton, and Yale—that received the most extensive national coverage.

Yale had actually been central to the genesis of the game of football. A Yale alumnus, the sportswriter Walter Camp (class of 1880), known as the Father of American Football, had helped transform rugby into football in the late 19th century. Camp invented many of the new game's rules (its system of downs and its scoring), plays (its snap from center), and formations (seven linemen and four backs). The game caught on so well that by 1914, Yale had seen fit to erect the Yale Bowl, which at the time was reportedly the largest stadium built since the Roman Coliseum. In Dilworth's day, the crowds were enormous and interest was intense. As newspaper coverage swelled, so did the grandiloquence of the reporting. Sportswriters adopted the "Gee Whiz" style that would characterize the '20s, a blend of the florid and the faux-heroic.

On November 13, 1920, Yale played Princeton before a record crowd of 52,000 at Princeton's Palmer Stadium. A *New York Times* sportswriter described "Tigertown" as the "football metropolis of the nation" and referred to the ball itself both as the "leather ovoid" and the "innocent little sphere." Pointing out that "Princeton took the measure, the scalp and the goal of Yale," the writer reported that the game "failed utterly to uphold the tradition of the fixture." Princeton embarrassed Yale, 20-0. Describing the betting on the game, the *Times* reporter wrote, "Princeton took unto herself divers clusters of coin of the realm brought to the New Jersey plains by optimistic supporters of the Blue, and wagered by them upon the fortunes of their game but outclassed team."

Despite the lopsided loss, Dilworth and his teammates received a heroes' welcome on their return to New Haven. More than 1,000 undergraduates marched to the train station in steady rain. On the trip back to campus, the players rode in cars up front and the crowd, led by a brass band, followed on foot, singing football songs and cheering the team.

The contest against Harvard that fall attracted nearly 80,000 spectators to the Yale Bowl, and the *Times* said it was the "largest crowd ever to see a football game in this country." Special trains carried fans from New York and Boston, and the *Times* estimated that 12,000 cars were parked outside. "Were there ever so many automobiles parked anywhere as there are outside the Bowl today?" wrote one wide-eyed reporter.

Another reporter focused on the crowd in the stands. "Intercollegiate football contests always bring together great arrays of feminine beauty and starkly color effects," he rhapsodized, "but this particular event surpasses all others. It is a riot of pulchritude, animation and color.... Surely it is the greatest beauty show in the world and of all time." It is very likely that one of the young women in attendance that afternoon was Miss Elizabeth Brockie of Philadelphia.

At the opening kickoff, Dilworth, who had been "circled several times" by running backs in the Princeton game, was on the bench. But he was soon sent in, and he played most of the game, which Harvard won with three field goals, 9-0. *New York Times* reporters could not agree on his performance. The principal story found Yale "magnificent on defense" and added: "The line was expected to be powerful and invincible, and it was all of this. But the ends, around which Princeton's fleet halfbacks had dashed with ease and impunity, excelled even the fondest expectations of [Yale coach] Tad Jones. Harvard soon found that to circle the flash of the Blue line was a task of difficulty." That would seem to have been a tip of the hat to Yale end Dick Dilworth.

In a separate story, however, another reporter gave a totally different account. "The Yale ends were not up to the usual Blue standard," he observed, "and Harvard was able to gain considerable ground around either wing." Years later, Dilworth told biographer Joe Alex Morris that he had been unable to stop the Harvard running backs on their end sweeps. And that after the game, in a mock ceremony at the Harvard Club of New York, he was awarded a Crimson sweater with the letter "H" on the front. According to Dilworth, Percy Haughton, Harvard's legendary coach, jested that he was "the best end Harvard ever had."

In a 1972 interview, the old footballer tended to agree. "I played very bad end on one of Yale's worst teams," he said. Although his team won six games against three losses, the stinging shutouts by Harvard and Princeton did make it a desolate season. But as to his evaluation of his own performance, one must take into account that light-hearted self-deprecation was characteristic of the man. In any event, what seems most noteworthy is that he managed to play varsity football at all with only one good arm.

At the urging of his surgeon, Dick went out for crew in the spring of 1921. "He advised me to row because the arm was terrible," Dilworth recalled. "There was a certain adhesion of nerves and muscles to the bone, and he said rowing would loosen things up—and it did. Thank God I did row." He rowed with the varsity until an attack of boils set him back to the second string. Things did not go well there. "I rowed behind a fellow who was a little quick on the strokes, and I was a little slow, so I'd always catch him in the back.... He'd turn around and say, 'You son of a bitch, if you hit me in the back again, I'm gonna hit you over the head with the oar.'"

Harvey Bradley and Stephen Hord also rowed for Yale. Bradley, who had lain paralyzed on the battlefield at Soissons and returned to Yale with a pronounced limp, was named captain of the university's lightweight crew. Hord, who suffered a hand injury that left him with virtually no feeling in two fingers, captained the varsity crew. Both would be lifelong friends of Dick's and would become prominent businessmen.

Aside from athletics, Dilworth was active in the Political Union and in the Yale Union as a debater.He graduated in the upper third of his college class, despite having "a terrible time with mathematics." He would have ranked "pretty damn well up in my class," he said, "if it hadn't been for mathematics."

Dilworth, Bradley, and Hord were all "tapped" for Skull and Bones, the most prestigious of Yale's secret societies. But Dick turned down Skull and Bones for the lesser-known Scroll and Key. "I thought it was more congenial," he explained. "Bones was heavy, heavy."

Tap Day, the ceremony for selection of the new members of the secret societies, dates to the 19th century and is one of Yale's most mysterious traditions. "The whole junior class was virtually made to go out and stand under this great tree on the Old Campus for over an hour," Dilworth remembered. "There were three senior societies then and 15 men in each, so these 45 men would go around doing the tapping. If you accepted the tap, you went to your room. There was a little mumbo-jumbo and you were told what day you were to report for your initiation." Dilworth's class numbered about 250, so fewer than 20 percent would have been selected. Referring to the social pressures and anxieties Tap Day created, he noted that "It really was a brutal ceremony."

Although Dilworth enjoyed his time at Yale, he chafed under the social strictures there and frequently left campus to socialize in Manhattan. He never felt quite comfortable in the exclusive world of the secret societies, and, he recalled, "In those days you had to go to chapel every day including Sunday, which I found oppressive. So I got away as much as I could." Many of his weekends were doubtless spent in the company of Bobbie Brockie.

In June 1921, Richardson Dilworth graduated from Yale College with two goals. He wanted to attend law school and he wanted to marry Bobbie Brockie. His father said he would "finance one or the other" but not both. Dilworth next approached Bobbie's parents about it and got essentially the same response: if you want to get married, get a job. "We sparred around a while," he recalled, "and finally both families agreed that if I would go to work and would stop drinking for a year," they would support the marriage.

So Dilworth went to work in the summer of 1921 for the M.K. Kellogg Company, a steel fabricating firm based in Jersey City. Its owner, Morris Kellogg, a friend of Dick's parents, ran an innovative training program for promising college graduates. Kellogg's idea, which would later be widely adopted by industry, was to prepare trainees for administrative positions in his company by exposing them to its various lines of work. Dilworth was enrolled in Kellogg's program and—given his family's manufacturing background—might have been expected to excel. He didn't. Recalling the experience many years later, he said that he found "the whole thing inexplicable," and described himself as a hopelessly inept trainee at Kellogg's foundry, rolling mill, and machine shop.

Dilworth struggled at work but kept his eye on the goal: marrying Bobbie. On January 11, 1922, their engagement was announced in the Philadelphia newspapers. "Miss Brockie has held a high place in the young set of Philadelphia since her debut during the winter of 1919 and 1920," *The Philadelphia Inquirer* reported.

The wedding, on May 20, 1922, was held at St. Luke's Episcopal Church in the Germantown section of Philadelphia and was termed "one of the most important weddings of the season." *The Bulletin* published a photograph of the 21-year-old bride with her six attendants on the lawn at Red Gate, her stepfather's estate at School House Lane and Wissahickon Avenue in Germantown, and called the wedding "most notable."

The Reverend William Greenough Thayer, the headmaster of St. Mark's School, officiated at the service, which attracted a "fashionable assemblage" of guests from New York, Pittsburgh, and Baltimore. The bride was given in marriage by her stepfather. The 23-year-old groom's best man was his brother, Dewees. Among the ushers were young men prominent in New York and Pittsburgh social circles—Thomas Hitchcock, Joseph Harriman, Charles Havemeyer, and Thomas Carnegie.

After the marriage, Dilworth took on a different assignment with M.K. Kellogg, traveling with his bride to Ponca City, Oklahoma, where the company was erecting high-pressure oil stills. He worked there with a structural steel construction gang for three months and then was assigned to Kellogg's sales department in Pittsburgh. This move put him in the same town and the same business as so many of the men on both sides of his family who had excelled at producing and selling iron and steel. "I was there a little over six months," Dilworth remembered, "and I set a record—never made a sale." It was while he and his wife were in Pittsburgh, however, that their first child, Patricia, was born on March 24, 1923.

Dilworth quit Kellogg and returned to New York, hoping for permission to attend law school. Again his father said no. Instead, he took a job with a real estate firm, which sent him to Palm Beach, Florida. Bobbie's parents, who had a house in Palm Beach and were prominent on the social scene there, invited the young family to stay with them. But the luxury accommodations didn't make Dilworth's new career any smoother than the previous one. His assignment was to sell apartments in a proposed new apartment house in Palm Beach. But there had never been an apartment house in the fashionable town and property owners, he realized, were "determined that no apartment was ever going to go up." His position made him "very unpopular" with the residents. "We were very nearly ostracized in addition to making no sales."

He stuck it out for eight fruitless months and then returned to New York. "I said to Father, 'I think it's going to be cheaper in the long run to send me to law school.' " This time his argument proved persuasive, and in the spring of 1924, Dilworth entered Yale Law School. He plunged into the work with the energy, intelligence, and enthusiasm that would mark his later life. Remaining in school year round, he became an editor of the *Yale Law Review* and was named to the prestigious Order of the Coif, graduating cum laude in 1926.

During his last semester of law school, Dick and Bobbie had a second daughter, Anne. And after graduation the young couple and their little girls moved to Bobbie's hometown, where Dilworth began his career in the law.

CHAPTER FIVE

The Two
William Wardens

*Some good men flatter us,
but it's only for our money*

The job that Dilworth found in Philadelphia after graduating from law school was most likely offered to him as a favor to his father-in-law. His own family was certainly very well off, living comfortably on Fifth Avenue in Manhattan despite the fact that Dilworth's father had retired in his early forties due to his disability. But the family he married into was one of even greater wealth and influence, and his father-in-law would loom large in his life, first as something of a mentor and later as something of a menace.

Bobbie Brockie's father died when she was eight or nine. Four years later, her mother, Agnes Morgan Brockie, married industrialist and Standard Oil heir William Gray Warden. Warden adopted Bobbie and her sister and raised them at Red Gate, his Germantown estate, and in Palm Beach, where he built what *The Bulletin* described as "one of the most beautiful houses on Ocean Boulevard." Warden, known as The Duke to his children and grandchildren, had been acquainted with Agnes Morgan since she was a girl, and had wanted to marry her years earlier. But Agnes had married William Brockie instead.

Brockie was a native of Scotland whose family immigrated to Philadelphia in 1865 when he was one. His father, also William Brockie, quickly succeeded in business in the city, becoming a prominent grain exporter and president of the Philadelphia Maritime Exchange. The younger Brockie, who graduated from the University of Pennsylvania in 1885, followed his father into the shipping business, taking over William Brockie & Son when the elder man died in 1890.

It was sometime in the mid-1890s that Agnes Morgan disappointed William Warden by marrying William Brockie. Brockie might have caught her eye on the pitch at the Germantown Cricket Club, where he was captain of the club's successful cricket team. He was also a member of the Gentlemen of Philadelphia cricket team, which traveled abroad for matches and hosted international teams at various Philadelphia clubs. *Wisden Cricketers' Almanack*, the authoritative annual English guide to all things related to cricket, wrote in 1910 that William Brockie was "at one time one of the foremost American cricketers...a sound and stylish batsman with good hitting powers, and one of the most brilliant fieldsmen ever identified with the game in America."

Brockie's cricketing days seem to have ended in 1899, when he took a job as vice president of the Johnson & Higgins insurance company in New York City. He rose to become president of the company, and he and Agnes were living in New York with their two young daughters when he died of appendicitis in 1909 at age 45.

In 1913, Agnes Morgan Brockie married William Warden. Her new husband's late father, also named William G. Warden, had been one of the richest—and in some quarters most reviled—men in America. He had founded two large Philadelphia firms, the Atlantic Refining Company and the United Gas Improvement Company. Atlantic Refining, which Warden started in 1865, was the first oil refinery in Philadelphia, and it remained by far the city's largest, even against the stiff competition that later developed. Atlantic Refining was very profitable, but wealth on a different order came to Warden as a consequence of his close association with John D. Rockefeller and Standard Oil.

Allan Nevins, in his biography of Rockefeller, placed the elder Warden in the "distinguished group" of executives, "perhaps the ablest in the history of American business," who, as trustees of Rockefeller's monopolistic Standard Oil Trust, were responsible for "a great part of Rockefeller's success." With their help, he amassed what has been described as the largest personal fortune in world history.

Just as the computer transformed American business and industry in the 20th century, so did petroleum in the 19th century. "The speed with which the market for oil expanded astonished everybody," Nevins wrote. "A commodity that had been a curiosity when Lincoln was nominated had become...the staple of a vast commerce before he was murdered." The speed with which John D. Rockefeller moved to dominate the market was equally astonishing. He was just 24 when he established his first refinery in Cleveland in 1863. When he founded the Standard Oil Company in 1870, he was barely 30, yet he controlled 10 percent of the nation's refining capacity. And he was just getting started.

In 1874, Rockefeller invited William Warden to a secret meeting at a hotel in Saratoga Springs, New York. At the meeting, he outlined a plan for a clandestine alliance. Rockefeller would buy Atlantic Refining with shares of Standard Oil stock, but the sale would not be made public. Warden would remain in charge of Atlantic, and would help Standard buy up other refineries in his region. These deals, too, would remain secret, and all the allied companies would carry on as though they were still competitors. The secret consolidation, Rockefeller maintained, would give the alliance tremendous leverage in setting oil prices and in negotiating rates with the railroads that transported their oil.

Warden agreed to the arrangement, and Rockefeller quickly cut similar deals with key refinery operators in Pittsburgh and New York. All of these negotiations were conducted covertly. "Within a single week," wrote Nevins, "Standard had taken possession of the inner citadels of refining in Pittsburgh and Philadelphia and had added a powerful strategic unit to its New York stronghold, and nobody outside the group immediately concerned knew what had happened."

Warden and the other refiners who had sold to Rockefeller were "more than ready," Nevins noted, "to join in a gigantic effort to coax in or buy out the remaining independents." In 1875, Warden was named to Standard's board of directors. He began 1876 by absorbing the Franklin Oil Works in Philadelphia, and before the year was out, three other refineries had "made arrangements" with him.

To pave the way for their plans, Standard and other oil companies routinely bought the influence of politicians. At one point, Warden wrote to Rockefeller "in some perplexity" over what to do about Matthew Quay, Pennsylvania's venal Republican leader. Warden told Rockefeller that Quay "needed" $15,000. Warden had "lent" him $5,000 and said he "didn't know whether to do more or not.... I feel that Mr. Quay might be of great use to us in the state...but he is fearfully expensive."

Allan Nevins described William Warden as a "big, genial but earnest man" who was popular in Philadelphia and "active in numerous enterprises." Nevins wrote of him: "His acquaintanceship, his skill in conference, his persistence and force of personality, always brought results that were acceptable and sometimes won notable success." Warden was so devoted to his work that he "never took any recreation." And Rockefeller once observed of Warden, "He was effusive. He would sit up till two in the morning writing me a letter."

As the consolidation continued, Standard rolled up a larger and larger share of the market. The true nature of the cartel inevitably surfaced, and independent refiners bitterly attacked the concentration of power in the hands of so few.

Rockefeller, Warden, and their associates were slow to perceive "the depth of the passions they had aroused," as Nevins put it. Standard was denounced as "the Monster" and "the Octopus," and its officers were branded "robbers." An outraged newspaper, the *Oil City Derrick*, published a "black list" and warned that any producer doing business with Rockefeller, Warden, or the others "risked his property or even his skin."

Nevins, scrupulously fair in his history of Standard Oil, found some of the practices of Rockefeller, Warden, and the others "utterly indefensible," running counter, he said, "to the essential spirit of fair play and democracy in American enterprise." In 1879, a grand jury in western Pennsylvania indicted Rockefeller, Warden, and seven other Standard Oil officials for seeking to control the market prices of crude and refined oil through "fraudulent devices." Warden was one of four Pennsylvanians who were arrested and released on bail. The indictments were dropped one year later, and Standard Oil promised to reform its practices.

In 1882, in response to new laws intended to break up his business, Rockefeller established a new holding company, the Standard Oil Trust, which had responsibility for all of the properties owned or controlled by Standard Oil. Warden was one of nine trustees named to run the remarkable new entity. "Never before in history had such an imposing array of industrial units been banded together in a single organization," Nevins observed. "Never before had any really great industry come under so nearly complete control, for in the early 1880s, the trust comprised about 80 percent of the refining capacity of the nation, and about 90 percent of the pipelines."

Denunciation of the oil barons continued, and Warden was shaken by the criticism. "It's many a day since I have troubled you with a letter," he wrote to Rockefeller on May 24, 1887, "and I would not do so now could I justify myself in being silent. It is very much impressed upon me that we as a company approach one of those times…when we are being placed in balance to be weighed."

Warden noted that Standard Oil had met "with a success unparalleled in commercial history," and its name was known "all over the world." And yet, he added, "We are quoted as the representative of all that is evil, hard-hearted, oppressive, cruel…we are pointed at with contempt, and while some good men flatter us, it's only for our money…. This is not pleasant to write, for I have longed for an honored position in commercial life. None of us would choose such a reputation; we all desire a place in the good will, honor and affection of honorable men."

Whatever misgivings he might have felt, William Warden continued to enjoy the fruits of his partnership in the Standard Oil Trust. When Rockefeller moved his headquarters from Cleveland to New York, Warden commuted to meetings there in a private railroad car from his home in Philadelphia. And in 1887, while lawmakers were targeting Standard Oil with the Interstate Commerce Act, Warden built an enormous, crenellated Moorish Revival mansion in St. Augustine, Florida, that quickly became known as Warden Castle.[7]

Warden also funded a school for blacks in St. Augustine, though any local goodwill he might have gained by that gesture was doubtless vastly overshadowed in 1890 when Congress passed the Sherman Anti-Trust Act, another piece of legislation aimed squarely at Rockefeller, Warden, and the other trustees of the Standard Oil Trust.

William Warden died in 1895, leaving an estate of $25 million, which ranked him among the 100 wealthiest men in America. John D. Rockefeller retired from daily participation in the business two years later, but the attacks on Standard Oil only grew. In 1902, muckraking journalist Ida M. Tarbell published her *History of the Standard Oil Company,* which introduced Rockefeller's practices to a wider audience. And with Theodore Roosevelt in the White House, the criticism grew even more clamorous. In a special message to Congress in 1908, Roosevelt called for a "moral rejuvenation of business" to prevent "a repetition of the successful effort by the Standard Oil people to crush out every competitor." Three years later, in 1911, Standard Oil was ordered to divest itself of all its subsidiaries and separated into 35 different entities, each with its own officers and directors. One of these was William Warden's Atlantic Refining Company.[8]

While Warden was taking part in the great commercial battle of his age, he and his wife, Sarah, found time to raise 10 children. Such prominent Philadelphia families as Strawbridge, Bodine, and McLean married into the prolific Warden clan. One of the most successful of the couple's children was William G. Warden's namesake.

While the older William Warden had been close to John D. Rockefeller, the younger one was close to Andrew Mellon, the Pittsburgh industrialist, financier, and longtime U.S. Secretary of the Treasury whom Dick Dilworth, as a bibulous teenager, had encountered on Long Island.

Andrew Mellon was a Cabinet secretary in the administration of President Calvin Coolidge in 1924 when he and his brother, Richard, acquired 25 percent of the stock of the Pittsburgh Coal Company. With control of the business in their hands, the brothers installed their friend William G. Warden as chairman of its board of directors. Founded in 1899, Pittsburgh Coal was the world's largest

---

[7] The house was sold after Warden's widow died in 1941, and was turned into a hotel. Some years later, it was sold again, this time to *Ripley's Believe It or Not,* and it still serves, largely unchanged on the exterior, as one of that company's museums.

[8] Atlantic Refining remained independent and successful through the following four decades. In 1966, it merged with Richfield Oil to create Atlantic Richfield, also known as ARCO. Two years later, ARCO struck oil at Prudhoe Bay, Alaska, which turned out to be the largest oil field in North America. ARCO was absorbed by BP in 2000.

bituminous coal producer with 17,000 workers at more than 100 mines in Pennsylvania, Ohio, and Kentucky. Coal mining was a dangerous business then as it remains today. In December 1907, an explosion and fire had killed 239 Pittsburgh Coal miners near Van Meter in Westmoreland County. It was the worst mine disaster in Pennsylvania's history.

When the Mellon brothers took over, Pittsburgh Coal's miners were represented by the United Mine Workers union, which had recently negotiated pay of $7.50 per day for its members. Typical pay at the time for non-unionized mineworkers, mostly in the South, was $5.00 a day. In August 1925, the Mellons broke the labor agreement they had inherited. At the Mellons' bidding, Warden had notices posted to the effect that miners' pay would be cut from $7.50 a day to $6.00, and all of its mines would be non-union.

The announcement caused a furor. The workers went on strike, and the company locked them out. Warden, testifying before a U.S. Senate committee, was asked why Pittsburgh Coal had locked out its workers. "We were losing money," he responded. Pittsburgh Coal, he told the committee, had lost money consistently since the end of World War I.

Pittsburgh Coal may have languished, but William Warden did not. Following in his father's footsteps, Warden built himself a palatial winter home in Florida. He was a social arbiter as well as an uncompromising executive, and he chose to build in Palm Beach, which by the 1920s had become a vacation enclave of the wealthy and socially prominent. He hired Addison Mizner, one of the country's most fashionable residential architects. Mizner designed a handsome, sprawling, Mediterranean-style palazzo for the Wardens with colonnades, cloisters, and a terra-cotta tiled roof.

The house went up in 1922, just as Bobbie Brockie was marrying Richardson Dilworth, and it was the setting for scores of luncheons and gatherings of the social elite through the 1920s and '30s.[9] But even this capacious house could not accommodate the scope of the Wardens' socializing. In 1924, William Warden and his wife hosted a luncheon for 150 guests at the Gulf Stream Golf Club, a party that was described by *The Bulletin* as "the first important social event of the season" in Palm Beach. Warden was president of the club, which had been organized the previous year with membership limited to 200.

Dick Dilworth's father died in 1928, and the estate's executors sold Dilworth, Porter to a larger company. "The old spike and tie-plate mill," he noted, had "at one time been a really prosperous thing, but had gone down, down, down." After Dilworth's father had been forced to retire, the firm was run by his partner's sons, "who just milked it," in his opinion. Still, he inherited $150,000 in cash from the

---

[9] Converted to condominiums in the 1980s, The Warden House is now listed on the National Register of Historic Places.

sale, and he turned to his father-in-law for financial counsel. "We were very friendly in those days," Dilworth recalled, "and he told me he thought one of the really good buys was Pittsburgh Coal." Taking Warden's advice, Dilworth spent a chunk of the inheritance on Pittsburgh Coal stock.

Dilworth bought the stock on margin, a common practice in the 1920s when the market was rocketing ahead. Buyers on margin put up only a fraction of a stock's sale price with the balance in an interest-bearing loan from the broker. As long as the stock's price rises, the buyer is safe. In the first half of 1929, Pittsburgh Coal's shares rose sharply with the rest of the market—at one point, Dilworth's shares had nearly tripled in value. But when the stock market crashed in October 1929, he received a "margin call," requiring him to pay the full cost of his Pittsburgh Coal stock or face the loss of his shares.

Dilworth couldn't meet the call and spoke to his father-in-law. "I'm about to have this stock sold out from under me," he told Warden. "What do you want me to do?" And Warden replied, "I'll take it over because I really can't afford with my position to have all this stock floating around." Dilworth signed a promissory note to Warden for the original purchase price of the stock, which Warden needed for tax purposes.

Pittsburgh Coal spent three years and millions of dollars fighting the union, and William Warden led the fight, which "broke the power of the United Mine Workers in the Pittsburgh field," according to an obituary following Warden's death in 1941. He had resigned as Pittsburgh Coal's board chairman in 1930, but continued to be a major stockholder. Another account pointed out that "the destruction of the union by Pittsburgh Coal did not bring economic prosperity" to the company. For 20 years afterward, Pittsburgh Coal failed to pay dividends to its stockholders.

CHAPTER SIX

Philadelphia Lawyers
Men of learning, ability, and eloquence

W hen Richardson Dilworth moved to his wife's hometown to begin his law practice in 1926, he found himself in a city long known for the quality of its lawyers. Since Andrew Hamilton's landmark triumph for press freedom in his successful defense of printer Peter Zenger in 1735,[10] Philadelphia had been served by a succession of lawyers "learned in the law, resourceful in practice, and of commanding influence in the community." That is how former Senator George Wharton Pepper put it in his autobiography in 1944.

Historian Edgar P. Richardson emphasized the "great responsibility" of lawyers in the formation of the national government. Philadelphia lawyers, he said, "set a tone of dignity, learning, and urbanity." Nicholas B. Wainwright found them in a later period full of "learning, ability, and eloquence." He said they were "men of high professional honor and moral worth." Such was their influence that

---

[10] Zenger, publisher of the *New York Weekly Journal*, had been charged with sedition and libel for printing articles attacking William Cosby, the colonial governor of New Jersey. Hamilton argued in his defense that criticism of public officials was proper. The jury acquitted Zenger, and the case set a precedent that has persisted to the present day.

the admiring expression "smart as a Philadelphia lawyer" had entered the language. The city's attorneys led the nation in founding a trade group, the Philadelphia Bar Association, to represent them in 1802. A daily newspaper, *The Legal Intelligencer*, started reporting on their activities in 1843. It is still being published five days a week and is the lone survivor among such papers dating back to the 19th century.

Following the Civil War and the rise of industrialism, the profession was transformed. The changes were described by Dilworth himself in a column in the *Philadelphia Daily News* in 1972. He wrote that after the war, large law "factories" headed by "very conservative men" came to dominate the field in the major cities. This "concentration of power" resulted in "reactionary" policies by the large firms. He quoted Woodrow Wilson as charging that "able lawyers have, to a large extent, allowed themselves to become adjuncts of great corporations.... We hear much of the corporation lawyer, but far too little of the people's lawyer."

Philadelphia's stratified social milieu also affected its law firms. The city's legal traditions were strong, but so were its often-restrictive customs. Other cities had their "Establishments," but Philadelphia was unusual for its conservatism and exclusivity. Mark Twain memorably made the point that while in Boston they asked, "How much does he know?" and in New York, "How much is he worth?" in Philadelphia the question was: "Who were his parents?" Although the primary target of Twain's criticism was Wasp hegemony over the city's banks, insurance companies, and other businesses, the legal profession might also have been in his crosshairs.

In the *Daily News* column, Dilworth noted that when he began his career, the hiring practices of law firms were "very restrictive" in the major cities. "No women, no blacks, no Jews, and very few Catholics were found in the big law firms in any eastern city," he wrote. "The result was a very sterile bar."

The same restrictions applied at Evans, Bayard & Frick, the 12-lawyer firm that hired Dilworth in the fall of 1926. It is likely that Dilworth got his position there on the recommendation of his father-in-law, William Warden, who was one of the firm's major clients. Although the firm had eight partners, it was led by Ralph Evans, a prominent litigator whom Dilworth termed "one of the most wonderful people I've ever known."

Evans had been the protégé of John G. Johnson, a towering figure in the law who is more often remembered today as the self-taught art connoisseur who left his great group of Flemish and early Italian masterworks to the Philadelphia Museum of Art, where it remains one of the cornerstones of that internationally renowned collection. Johnson amassed more than 1,200 paintings, so many that, hung floor to ceiling, they covered every inch of wall space in his mansion on South Broad Street and forced him to hang some on the foot of his bed. George

Pepper, a noted lawyer in his own right, said of Johnson, "He was, all things considered, the most prodigious man I have ever known."

The son of a blacksmith, John Johnson was born in 1841, and in a career that spanned 56 years, he is reported to have handled some 10,000 court cases, 2,000 of them before the Pennsylvania Supreme Court. Before the U.S. Supreme Court, where 10 cases for a lawyer's career is a high number, Johnson argued a total of 168. When he died, in 1917, *The New York Times* called Johnson, "in the opinion of some well-qualified judges, the greatest lawyer in the English-speaking world."

Johnson won his cases not with flights of oratory, but with powerful concision. The *Times* obituary quoted one colleague as saying of him, "He gets hold of the real point at issue and will not be turned from it. He fuses it into a thunderbolt in the heat of argument." Johnson represented many of the country's most powerful corporations and is said to have collected a single fee of half a million dollars. Yet he was never known to turn away a small case, regardless of how little money it promised. "It was not unusual," one account related, "to see J.P. Morgan in Mr. Johnson's waiting room, sitting beside a local merchant with a $100 claim."

Although John Johnson never had a partner, he mentored a number of younger lawyers, and they divided up his huge practice after his death. The brightest of his followers, Ralph Evans, developed into one of the nation's foremost trial lawyers. Just as Evans was a protégé of John G. Johnson, so was Dilworth mentored by Evans. As his assistant and chief investigator, Dilworth tackled trial and appellate work, quickly earning a reputation as a tough courtroom lawyer.

Dilworth had been practicing only two years when the Philadelphia Bar Association asked him to help investigate an accident ring run by a handful of corrupt lawyers. He was paid $1,500 to work with Henry S. Drinker, chairman of the bar association's board of censors. They discovered that unscrupulous attorneys had paid police, ambulance drivers, and emergency room workers in exchange for tips about car crashes. Then they arranged for generous awards for victims from a malleable judge. As a result of the investigation, the ring was broken up.

When a large anthracite coal company sued some 100 independent coal miners for working abandoned deposits in upstate Pennsylvania without paying rent, the miners had difficulty finding a lawyer. That was because the coal company enjoyed backing from powerful Republican politicians in the region. Dilworth welcomed the challenge and agreed to defend the miners. Their defense was difficult. The miners kept no books, were prone to exaggeration, and drank heavily on the Saturday nights when Dilworth met with them.

Then came a break in the case. The GOP boss of Northumberland County, testifying under oath against the "bootleg" miners, perjured himself. Dilworth knew the witness had lied and, on cross-examination, got him to repeat it. That turned the trial around. Injunction proceedings against the miners were dropped. "The result won Dilworth many friends among the independent coal miners,"

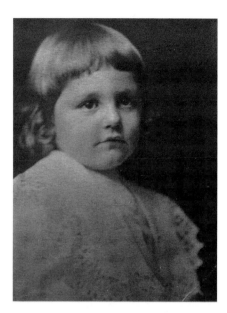

Richardson Dilworth at
age three or four in 1902.
Photo: Dilworth family

Dilworth several years later with his only sibling, older brother Dewees.
The family lived in Pittsburgh until Dick was eight, when his father fell ill
and they moved to New York City. Photo: Dilworth family

Dilworth's maternal grandfather, W. Dewees Wood, was "the best known and best liked man" in McKeesport, near Pittsburgh, where his steel mill employed some 1,000 workers. Revered by his employees and rewarded with solid profits, Dewees Wood managed his mill from the 1850s until his death in 1899.
Photo: Dilworth family

Annie Wood Dilworth was "a terribly hard-driving woman— very attractive but very domineering," according to her younger son, Richardson.
Photo: Dilworth family

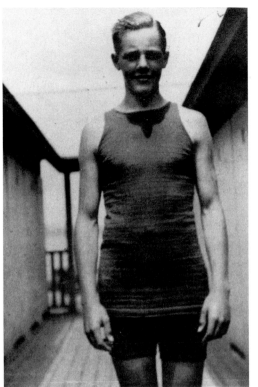

Dilworth in Southampton, New York, in 1914, the summer he turned 16. A beach town at the eastern tip of Long Island, Southampton was (and remains) a summer resort for the wealthy. Dick met his future running mate Joe Clark on the playing fields there at about this time.

Photo: Dilworth family

In June 1917, the month of his graduation from St. Mark's, Dilworth (*center, left*) and some friends strike a rakish pose on a visit to Revere Beach, Massachusetts. Photo: Dilworth family

When Dilworth and six friends—five fellow freshmen from Yale and one from Princeton—enlisted together in the Marines in February 1918, they entered the purview of Sergeant Michael Fitzgerald at the 23rd Street recruiting station in Manhattan. Photo: Dilworth family

Within two months of enlisting, Dilworth (*far right*) was on his way to join the fighting in France. Photo: Dilworth family

Elizabeth Brockie, known as Bobbie, was the girlfriend of Dilworth's close friend Wells Cumings, who was killed in action at Belleau Wood. After the war, Dilworth paid a condolence visit to Brockie, and several years later the two married. Photo: Dilworth family

Dilworth had eight children all told—four with Bobbie Brockie, his first wife; two with Ann Kaufman, his second wife; and two stepchildren from Ann's first marriage to Crawford Hill, Jr. Here, in 1936 or '37, Dilworth holds baby Deborah and is surrounded by (*clockwise from right*) Marie, Pat, Anne, Warden, Louis Hill, and Brockie. Deborah's brother, Dickie, was not yet born. Photo: Dilworth family

Within a few months of the Japanese attack on Pearl Harbor, Dilworth obtained a commission as a captain in the Marines and shipped out to the South Pacific. His unit saw intense fighting against the Japanese on Guadalcanal, one of the Solomon Islands northeast of Australia.

A tiger in the courtroom as well as on the campaign trail, Dilworth took his own defense at a 1948 libel trial stemming from accusations he made against Philadelphia's deeply entrenched and deeply corrupt Republican political machine.

Photo: Special Collections Research Center, Temple University Libraries, Philadelphia, PA. Used with permission of *Philadelphia Inquirer* ©2014.

In the summer of 1949, Dilworth debated Philadelphia County sheriff Austin Meehan (*left*), a wealthy paving contractor and a powerful force in the GOP. He resumed his attacks on Republican corruption, accusing Meehan of racketeering and bribing the police.

Photo: Special Collections Research Center, Temple University Libraries, Philadelphia, PA. Used with permission of *Philadelphia Inquirer* ©2014.

Dilworth introduced Minnesota senator Hubert Humphrey (*left*) as guest speaker at a meeting of the Philadelphia chapter of Americans for Democratic Action in 1950. Dilworth and Joseph Clark were among the founders of the Philadelphia ADA, and the organization helped propel them to power.

wrote Joe Alex Morris, "and later was to be of importance to him politically in that area."

In another case in northeastern Pennsylvania, Dilworth defended the *Wilkes-Barre Sunday Independent* against a $100,000 libel suit filed by the mayor of Nanticoke, Anthony B. Dreier. The newspaper had run an ad in which opponents of the mayor accused him of profiting from his position. Pointing out that he had bought a new car and a house soon after taking office, the ad concluded with the jibe, "Not bad, Mr. Mayor."

When the case came to trial, Dilworth confronted Mayor Dreier with a litany of transgressions. He put a policeman on the stand who testified to paying Dreier $50 to get his job on the force. Dreier's secretary testified that the mayor had urged her to falsify receipts and to lie before a grand jury that was investigating rackets. There were many other allegations, including the accusation that the mayor had, in collusion with Nanticoke's police chief, conducted mock trials of inebriates picked up on Saturday nights, pocketing $10 per drunk.

Fearing the mayor's wrath, many of the citizens with first-hand knowledge of his crimes refused to testify at the trial. However, Dilworth made sure they were in the courtroom when the mayor took the stand. Joe Alex Morris gave this account of Dilworth's interrogation:

> "Did you use city labor to do work on your private home?"
>
> "I did not," the mayor replied firmly.
>
> Dilworth motioned to several laborers sitting at the front of the courtroom. They stood up.
>
> All of them had worked on the mayor's home while being paid by the city.... The mayor blanched but stuck to his denial. The workers sat down.
>
> "Did you have law books bought by the city removed to your home?" Dilworth asked.
>
> When the witness denied it, Dilworth motioned to the mayor's former secretary, who stood up.
>
> "Do you recall conducting mock trials of drunks and splitting the money with the police chief?" Dilworth asked.
>
> "I do not and did not," the mayor answered.
>
> "You are going to stick to your story then?" Dilworth began. But the mayor had already seen his former police chief starting to stand up in the front row. His bravado vanished and he gave up, withdrawing his suit.

In the months that followed, the local district attorney launched an investigation into the testimony from the libel trial, and a grand jury indicted Anthony Dreier on seven counts. Dreier was eventually found guilty of bribery and was forced to resign as mayor.

Dilworth loved litigation and was a master at it. In the years before he pursued elective office, he probably tried more libel suits than any other Pennsylvania lawyer. His exposure to wrongdoing in Nanticoke and other precincts provided insights for his later attacks on corruption in Philadelphia.

Dilworth's versatility as a lawyer was demonstrated in his defense of Connie Mack, owner-manager of the Philadelphia Athletics, against a group of angry baseball fans in 1935. Born Cornelius McGillicuddy, Connie Mack was a legendary figure in baseball. A canny manager and a shrewd judge of baseball talent, Mack skippered the A's for 50 seasons before retiring at age 87 in 1950. His teams won nine American League pennants and five World Series titles. But success on the field never seemed to translate to black ink on the balance sheet. Three times Mack assembled great teams, and three times the A's had to sell off their best players to make ends meet.

Shibe Park, the A's stadium in North Philadelphia, was built in 1909 with a seating capacity of 23,000 fans. As the crowds grew, the A's added upper decks and left-field bleachers that provided 10,500 additional seats. Bleachers couldn't be built in right field, because 20th Street ran right along that side of the stadium. Yet if a player hit a mighty home run over the right-field wall in Shibe Park, the ball had a chance to land in an unorthodox set of bleachers.

Just across 20th Street was a row of two-story houses, and from the rooftops of these one had a fine view—over Shibe Park's 12-foot-high right-field fence—of the A's in action. Ever since the stadium opened, fans had found their way up there. But at some point, enterprising homeowners on 20th Street had erected bleachers that stretched across 20 houses and accommodated over 1,000 fans. They charged admission, keeping prices lower than tickets for the park itself. This was the case when Jimmie Foxx, Mickey Cochrane, and Lefty Grove carried the A's to World Series titles in both 1929 and 1930, and went on to capture a third American League pennant in 1931.

The 20th Street bleachers had been a source of irritation to the A's ownership for years. But when the club sold off its great team following the 1931 season and ticket sales plummeted, the A's decided to address the situation. In 1933, they sued the 20th Street homeowners. When their suit failed, the A's ownership ordered workers to raise the right-field fence by 22 feet, blocking the view from the unauthorized seats. Furious fans accused the A's of erecting a "spite fence" and took them to court. The club responded by hiring Dilworth, who won the case. The fence would stand, and within a few years the unused bleachers were torn down. The A's victory in court was unmatched on the diamond. They never won another pennant in Philadelphia.

CHAPTER SEVEN

Corrupt and Discontented

Grafters, gamblers, and goons

Philadelphia was entirely controlled by Republicans when Richardson Dilworth, a Wilsonian Democrat, came to town in 1926. The GOP had been running the city since shortly after the Civil War, and showed no signs of yielding power. Republican W. Freeland Kendrick had been elected mayor in 1923 with 89 percent of the vote—286,000 votes to his opponent's 37,000. A year after Dilworth's arrival, when there was a three-way race for mayor between a Democrat and two Republicans (one of whom, having lost in the Republican primary, ran under the banner of the Citizen's Party), the Democrat received 10,000 votes and the two Republicans combined for 426,000—98 percent of the vote.

If the GOP's hegemony was near total, so was its corruption. Populated with "grafters, gamblers, and goons," as one observer put it, the Republican machine was Philadelphia's longer-lived (if less-noted) version of New York's Tammany Hall. In the rogues' gallery of Republicans who ran the city, Boies Penrose stood out. Born in 1860 into one of Philadelphia's richest and most distinguished colonial families, Penrose graduated from Harvard Law School and quickly moved into politics, winning a seat in the Pennsylvania House of Representatives at age

24. There he soon became the protégé of the charming and unscrupulous Matthew Quay, the unchallenged boss of Pennsylvania.

Historians Nathaniel Burt and Wallace E. Davies wrote that Penrose, following Quay's perfidious example, became "the most corrupt and devious of bosses." Standing a bulky six feet four, Penrose was, according to Burt and Davies, "a gargantuan eater, a cynical lecher, like Quay a master of intrigue. He played politics the way others played chess: not for personal profit, since he was a man of inherited wealth, but for the pleasure of winning."

After two years in the Pennsylvania State House, Penrose spent 12 years in the Pennsylvania State Senate before being elected to the U.S. Senate in 1897, where he served for 24 years. After Matthew Quay died in 1904, Penrose succeeded him as the political kingpin in Pennsylvania, and throughout his life, he retained a vise-grip on Philadelphia politics.

One office that Boies Penrose coveted but didn't win was the mayoralty of his native Philadelphia. He made a bid for mayor in 1895, but was forced to withdraw when enemies of his mentor Quay threatened to release a photograph of Penrose leaving a well-known brothel. According to Penrose biographer Walter Davenport, such an excursion would not have been an isolated event. Penrose, Davenport wrote, never married and "never kept a mistress. When he wanted a woman, he rented one—a professional. He scorned amateurism in everything." *Time* magazine, in a review of the biography, described Penrose as a man "with big appetites, a cold heart, a shrewd head," who "took to lowlife like a hippopotamus to water."

Penrose set an impressive example, but his successor as city boss may have outdone him. When Penrose died in 1921, William Scott Vare took the reins. With his brothers Edwin and George, Bill Vare held power through control of ward politics, especially in the slums of Center City and the rowhouse precincts in South Philadelphia. The Vares were contractors as well as politicians, and the benefits of their political influence flowed directly into the coffers of their company, Vare Brothers. Tens of millions of dollars in city contracts went to the Vares, and that money in turn helped finance their political operations. According to historian Paul Beers, when the Philadelphia Museum of Art was being built, the Vares not only received the enormous excavation contract, but managed to sell back to the city all the stone they extracted from the site. To sweeten the deal further, the Vares had their trucks loop around and repeatedly pass the checkpoint so that the same load of stone was counted again and again. Gifford Pinchot, twice Republican governor of Pennsylvania, said of the Vares, "They're gangsters first and Republicans as a matter of convenience."

Soon after Dilworth started working at Evans, Bayard & Frick, he received a first-hand lesson in machine politics. The Vares' tentacles, he discovered, reached into obscure corners; corruption was everywhere. "As a young lawyer," he recalled, "I had to do a good deal of City Hall work. In the Prothonotary's office, no writ or pleading was accepted unless accompanied by at least 50 cents. The sheriff's office gave no service…unless properly rewarded. The fire marshal's office, which issued permits for oil burners, refused to act on an application unless paid 10 cents for each gallon of capacity of the oil-storage tank. Commercial and industrial water installations were not metered. The amount paid the city by industrial and commercial users was negotiated after a suitable amount of cash was passed under the table."

The GOP organization controlled the city's cops by placing police stations immediately adjacent to Republican clubs in every ward. "No district police captain dared make a move," Dilworth noted, "without the approval of the Republican ward leader. There was then no government welfare, relief, unemployment insurance or Social Security. Consequently, when hard times hit, the many families affected had no place to go except to the police station, where the ward leader would preside in handing out buckets of coal, loaves of bread, and simple foodstuffs."

"Never before," Burt and Davies wrote of Bill Vare, "were all the Republican leaders of the city's wards so firmly united behind the will of one man." Dilworth, writing in the *Philadelphia Daily News* in 1972, went even further. He called Bill Vare and his brothers "the most powerful political bosses any big city has ever had." They "even organized the public schools. No teacher could get a job or a promotion without paying the Vare organization. And the Vares assessed everyone in the school system two percent of his or her salary."

During 1926, Philadelphia witnessed an amazing political tableau. Although Bill Vare controlled virtually everything in the city, his authority was challenged statewide by Joseph R. Grundy of nearby Bucks County and by the Mellons in Pittsburgh. To gain outright leadership of the Pennsylvania GOP, Vare decided to run for a seat in the U.S. Senate. In the Republican primary his two opponents were the incumbent, George Wharton Pepper, and sitting Pennsylvania governor Gifford Pinchot. Despite his rivals' prominence, Vare barely campaigned; he gave no speeches and, in fact, never left Philadelphia. It turned out that he didn't need to. Although he was outpolled in all but two of Pennsylvania's 67 counties, Vare won the nomination by rolling up a 228,000-vote margin in Philadelphia.

In the general election, Bill Vare ran against Democrat William B. Wilson, a former coal miner and union leader who rose to become Secretary of Labor under Woodrow Wilson. Vare's tactics were the same as in the primary, and so were the results, with Vare victorious. But William Wilson struck back, petitioning the Senate to declare the election fraudulent. Charging "corruption and voting irregularities," Wilson called the election a "grotesque and fantastic travesty." Accusations of corrupt fundraising centered on contributions to the Vare campaign by the city's contractors. Critics also questioned how Philadelphia sheriff Thomas Cunningham, with an annual salary of $8,000, could contribute $50,000 to the city's GOP boss. Governor Pinchot, having finished a distant third in the Republican primary, refused to certify the results of the general election, contending in a letter to the Senate that Vare's victory was "partly bought and partly stolen."

Following a three-year investigation, the U.S. Senate voted 58 to 22, on December 6, 1929, to deny Bill Vare the seat. It marked the first time in American history that the Senate had taken such action. Although Vare was accused of excessive spending, Pepper, who was backed by the Mellons, had actually spent more than twice as much in losing the primary—some $1.8 million compared to Penrose's $780,000. And although it's clear that Vare was thoroughly corrupt—one single-family house in his stronghold of Philadelphia was listed as the dwelling for 122 registered voters—there was evidently fraudulent activity on all sides. J.T. Salter, a political writer at the time, concluded that Vare was thrown out of the Senate not so much because of corruption but because "he was a ward politician without social background." Vare himself considered the investigation "the most merciless...ever conducted by any committee of the United States Senate." Despite losing his Senate seat, Vare retained control in Philadelphia until shortly before his death in 1934.

Against this sordid backdrop, Dilworth and a few other reform-minded young Philadelphians—many of them lawyers—began working to awaken the dormant Democrats. In 1927, they founded a small group called the Warriors, which they intended as the nucleus for a reinvigorated party. They started slowly, conducting registration drives, canvassing Democratic voters and placing watchers at the polls. Their ability to influence local races was minimal at first, Dilworth later explained, because the machine was so powerful that "the Democratic candidates were all nominated by the Republicans." But the Warriors helped to turn out huge crowds in Philadelphia for Alfred E. Smith, the Democratic candidate for President in 1928. Although Smith, the first Roman Catholic to be nominated for the presidency, lost the election to Herbert C. Hoover, he received 40 percent of the vote in GOP-controlled Philadelphia, and the Warriors were heartened. Four years later, Franklin D. Roosevelt would capture 45 percent of the city as he defeated Hoover for the presidency.

One of the Warriors was a young lawyer from Chestnut Hill named Joseph Clark, who shared political ambitions with Dilworth. Both came from wealthy Republican families and both were Ivy League graduates. While Dilworth's schooling was at St. Mark's and Yale, Clark had attended Middlesex and Harvard. They had played on opposing baseball teams at prep school. And as teenagers, they had vacationed at the same lush summer resort. "We learned the American way of life together on the beaches of Southampton, Long Island, about as plutocratic an institution as one could find," said Clark, recalling a summer when he was 14 and Dilworth was 17. He added that Dilworth was "always a very glamorous figure. I admired him very much." Despite profound personality differences that would emerge later, the two patricians built an alliance that would change Philadelphia's politics.

Joe Clark was the first of the pair to run for political office. In 1933, after the death in office of Bill Roper, a Philadelphia city councilman from Germantown (who also happened to be Princeton's outstanding football coach), a special election was held to replace him. Clark ran for the seat with Dilworth as his campaign manager. Although Clark lost, he made a decent showing. Elsewhere, the Democrats gained significant inroads, winning the elections for city controller and city treasurer.

With Roosevelt in the White House, Philadelphia's Democrats naturally gained strength, and they contributed significantly to the victory in 1934 of Governor George H. Earle 3d, who became the first Democrat to hold the office since 1894. Earle's election also buoyed Dilworth's personal fortunes. His father-in-law, William Warden, although a staunch Republican, had contributed to Earle's campaign, "hedging his bets," in Dilworth's assessment, with an eye toward protecting his extensive real estate holdings. After the victory, Warden used his influence to get his son-in-law assigned a post as a deputy attorney general, and Dilworth was put in charge of the Philadelphia closed bank division.

The Warriors played a part in the Democratic resurgence, but more significant was the role of a handful of men prominent in business who were emerging as leaders of the Democratic Party in Philadelphia. In a clear break with the past, these men were not beholden to the opposition party. They included builders Matthew McCloskey and John B. Kelly, real estate entrepreneur Albert M. Greenfield, and publisher David Stern, whose *Philadelphia Record* became the party's organ. Their combined energy and influence gave the city's Democratic Party a powerful jolt.

Kelly and McCloskey were especially active in the revitalized party organization, and they would wield decisive influence in Dilworth's career for decades to come. Looking back, Dilworth said that he and Joe Clark "would have been very happy to work with the organization if they had been willing to work with us, but we got such a kicking around from them." Kelly and McCloskey, both Irish Catholics and self-made men in a city dominated by white Protestants with old money, "had an intense dislike for Wasps," Dilworth contended. "I learned that very early in the game. They made it very clear by their actions, the way they'd double-cross you, the contempt they'd show for you."

"I always liked Jack Kelly and I liked McCloskey," Dilworth admitted. "But it was clear they never really liked us or trusted us. There was this very chip-on-the-shoulder attitude toward us." The Wasps "had excluded them from the social life, the club life, even the residential life of Philadelphia, so they had to make their own way—and they made it and made it damn successfully." Kelly and

McCloskey "knew they needed a few [Wasps]. But if the Wasps really gave them any trouble, they'd kick them out. Any chance they had to give it to you, they did."

Relations did not get off to a good start. In 1934, McCloskey approached Dilworth and suggested that he run for the state Senate seat in the wealthy Chestnut Hill section. If he ran, he would be up against the incumbent, Republican George Woodward, an eccentric figure who was a medical doctor and a real estate developer as well as a state senator. Woodward was a reformer and a rare Republican who had never been under the sway of the GOP machine. He also happened to be Dilworth's landlord. Along with his wife and their young children—who now numbered four, three girls and a boy—Dilworth had rented one of the hundreds of solidly built Woodward Houses that dotted the area.

George Woodward, a teetotaler who always wore knickerbockers and putted around Chestnut Hill in a little electric car while checking on his properties, reportedly wrote into every lease a provision that permitted him to inspect the premises at any time, with or without notice. Dilworth was reminded of this peculiarity early one Sunday morning after a "really gay Saturday night." Describing the incident years later, he recalled waking up "with the most dreadful hangover and this terrible thirst." Emerging naked from his bedroom, Dilworth "came staggering down the stairs" and "suddenly realized that Dr. Woodward was standing at the bottom...he took one look at me and said, 'Young man, you've been drinking.' I said, 'Doctor, you don't know the half of it.' He just turned around and left the house." Dilworth was afraid he'd be evicted, but he never heard anything more about the episode.

Despite the discomfort of running against Woodward, Dilworth decided to accept the challenge, and Joe Clark agreed to be his campaign manager. Some days later, however, McCloskey called Dilworth in and said he would have to put up $2,500 for the campaign fund if he wanted to run. "I didn't have $2,500 in those days, so they slated Izzy Finkelstein," a little-known accident lawyer. Dilworth was incensed, and he decided to "buck the Party" and run in the Democratic primary against Finkelstein.

To finance his race, Dilworth scraped together about $1,200. Then along with Clark he visited all the ward leaders to drum up support. "They were all the biggest whores," he recalled years later. "They'd take one look at us and decide we were real patsies.... There was very little money they could get out of us, but what they could they did and just pocketed it." One of them was Herb McGlinchey, Democratic leader of the 42nd Ward. Dilworth said that he turned over more than a third of his money to McGlinchey before the election, only to get fewer votes in the 42nd Ward than in any other ward in the district. "I spoke a little crossly to Herb about this," Dilworth wrote years later in a column in the *Philadelphia Daily News*. "He simply replied: 'That's your first political lesson; never trust a ward leader.' It was excellent advice, but expensively come by."

Unlike Joe Clark, who was starchily dismissive of political leaders in the city's working-class wards, Dilworth found them fascinating, if rarely admirable. "In a way it is a shame to see the old-time ward politicians vanishing," he wrote. "They were a colorful lot, and Herb was one of the most colorful. They were all amoral. They had an amazing instinct for politics and self-preservation. None contributed much to the well-being of their communities beyond the fact they had a certain sense of order." Dilworth said of McGlinchey, a ward leader for more than 40 years: "Herb does plenty for himself, but very little for the residents of his ward. He has managed to remain in power by his extraordinary talent for keeping his opponents off balance, confused and separated."

In 1972, it was rumored that McGlinchey, who had just lost his seat in the state Senate, would be named to the post of Senate Librarian. Dilworth thought that was hilarious. "The last time Herb was in a library," he wrote, "was when he ran in there to escape the truant officer, and that was close to 60 years ago." Alas, Herb McGlinchey never became the Senate Librarian.

If McGlinchey's 42nd Ward performed badly in the 1934 primary, the other wards were not much better. Recalling the campaign with a chuckle years later, Dilworth said that he and Clark "worked very hard but very ineffectively." The district, which he described as "virtually entirely white Protestant," voted overwhelmingly for Izzy Finkelstein, who got 11,000 votes to Dilworth's 1,000. But Finkelstein was crushed in the general election by Dilworth's landlord, George Woodward.

Although Woodward's easy victory was yet more evidence of continued Republican dominance at the polls, Philadelphia Democrats were heartened by George Earle's success in capturing the governor's seat. One year later, in 1935, they aimed squarely at the mayor's office with John B. "Jack" Kelly as their candidate.

Kelly, the son of working-class Irish immigrants, was a three-time Olympic gold medalist in sculling who made a fortune in brick contracting. (His daughter, Grace Kelly, would grow up to be a Hollywood star and the royal spouse of Prince Rainier of Monaco.) Jack Kelly had learned to row on the Schuylkill River and became one of the most celebrated single-scull oarsmen in the sport's history, at one stage winning 126 consecutive races. His accomplishments in the sport of gentlemen brought him worldwide notice, but couldn't separate him entirely from his origins. In 1926, at age 37, having already won six U.S. National Championship titles, Kelly applied to compete in the prestigious Diamond Sculls at the Henley Royal Regatta in England. Considering his record in the sport, the application ought to have been a formality. But just before he was scheduled to set sail for England, word came that his application had been denied. He'd been deemed ineligible when it was discovered that he had worked as a bricklayer, violating the regatta's prohibition against anyone who had worked "for wages [as] a mechanic, artisan or labourer."

Dilworth experienced some class strife himself during Kelly's run for mayor in 1935. He worked in the campaign and on election day, when a dispute arose between Democratic and Republican workers at a polling place in one of the wards along the Delaware River, he was dispatched from Democratic headquarters to intervene. The river wards were notoriously tough, blue-collar districts, still very much in the Republican camp. The ward Dilworth was sent to had "a great many Polish longshoremen," as he recalled. When the Ivy League Democrat arrived at the storefront polling place on that bitterly cold day, he was wearing a symbol of wealth and privilege—a coonskin coat. "I barged in," Dilworth remembered, "and got in an argument. They pointed out that I had no business in the polling place, particularly not in a coonskin coat. The next thing I knew, I was literally heaved right through a plate glass window. I beat a hasty retreat back up to Democratic headquarters."

In the previous mayoral election, in 1931, the Democrats had endured another in a seemingly endless string of drubbings, winning just eight percent of the vote—31,000 out of 393,000 votes cast. But this time the Democrats were hopeful. In Jack Kelly they had a candidate with money, influence, drive, and a measure of fame.

Kelly did run a strong campaign, but he lost to Republican S. Davis Wilson. But in doing so, he put a severe scare into the Republicans—and a charge into the Democrats—winning 47 percent of the vote to Wilson's 53 percent in an election that doubled the voter turnout from four years earlier. Kelly charged that he was cheated out of the election through the manipulation of voting machines, and Dilworth said in later years that he believed it was true.

Through the rest of the 1930s, Joe Clark and Richardson Dilworth continued to be politically active, but with little effect. Dilworth's observation captured the times: "We were always on the outside looking in."

CHAPTER EIGHT

Unholy Moses—
Old Man Annenberg

*An attractive and amusing fellow
with an absolutely vicious temper*

The biggest break in Richardson Dilworth's law career occurred in the summer of 1936 when Moses L. Annenberg arrived in Philadelphia. Annenberg, an immigrant who had grown up on the streets of Chicago and made the beginnings of his fortune battling in the sometimes bloody circulation wars between newspapers there, had just purchased *The Philadelphia Inquirer*, the city's oldest daily paper, which relished its reputation as "the Bible of Pennsylvania Republicans."

Annenberg bought the paper on July 31. Some weeks later, he was holding a reception for prominent Philadelphians in *The Inquirer's* 18-story Beaux Arts–style building on North Broad Street when a handsomely attired but uninvited guest approached him. The man served Annenberg with a subpoena. The lawsuit was the first volley in what would become a fierce battle between *The Inquirer* and J. David Stern's liberal *Philadelphia Record*. "A fine welcome to Philadelphia," Annenberg reportedly quipped. "When I get off the train, Dave Stern has me arrested."

The suit sought an injunction to prevent Annenberg from breaking *The Inquirer*'s joint distribution agreement with the *Record*. He needed a Philadelphia lawyer, and quickly, to block Stern's move. Looking for the best possible trial attorney, he first contacted the widely admired Ralph Evans, Dilworth's mentor at Evans, Bayard & Frick. But Evans was away in Eagles Mere, a vacation spot in the mountains of northeastern Pennsylvania, and was too ill to travel. As it happened, Evans was in the first throes of a struggle with heart disease that would end his life three months later. Annenberg next sought the representation of former senator George Wharton Pepper. But Pepper was on vacation in Maine. "And being Pepper," Dilworth observed, "he refused to come down." Moses Annenberg's representatives reportedly offered Pepper "a tremendous sum if he'd come back," but the senator "wouldn't even talk to them." Annenberg then tried to persuade another prominent attorney, Henry Drinker (with whom Dilworth had investigated crooked lawyers in 1928), to represent him. But Drinker, an avid sailor and fisherman, was vacationing at the New Jersey shore, and he also declined. Annenberg tried two or three other attorneys, but they, too, were on vacation and couldn't be recalled to the city.

As Annenberg was discovering, August was the prime vacation month for Philadelphia's lawyers. But something else was afoot as well. As soon as Stern heard who had purchased *The Inquirer,* a cascade of fiercely negative stories about Annenberg began appearing in *The Record.* The day the paper was sold, a front-page story in *The Record* cast Annenberg's career in the most alarming light, linking him to gangland Chicago and suggesting that he was a stalking horse for William Randolph Hearst. No doubt all the lawyers Annenberg contacted relished their vacations, but as Dilworth saw it, "they had no desire to come back because the publicity *The Record* had given old man Annenberg was murderous." Dilworth had no such qualms himself. When Annenberg asked him to take on the case, he leapt at the opportunity. Win or lose, he was taking an enormous risk by aligning himself with a man whose very presence in the tradition-bound city instantly elicited animosity on all sides. And soon after accepting it, he saw that the case would be very difficult—if not impossible—to win.

Dilworth's new client, Moses Louis Annenberg, was born on February 11, 1878, in a tiny East Prussian hamlet near the Russian border. His father immigrated to Chicago in 1882, and three years later the rest of the family, including seven-year-old Moses, joined him. Annenberg's father ran a junk shop on the ground floor of a three-story building on State Street. The family lived on the floor above. Moses worked with his father for a time, but his first paying job was as a Western Union messenger boy. He also sold newspapers and swept out livery stables.

In 1899, at 21, Moses married 19-year-old Sadie Friedman, who would be the mother of his son and seven daughters. One year later, publisher William Randolph

Hearst, fresh from a bitter newspaper battle with Joseph Pulitzer in New York, started a new daily in Chicago. Hearst's paper, *The Chicago American*, gave the city a Democratic voice to compete against Colonel Robert McCormick's conservative *Chicago Tribune*. Moses' older brother Max quit his job in *The Tribune*'s circulation department to work for Hearst. Max soon became *The American*'s circulation manager and hired Moses. When Hearst opened a morning paper, *The Chicago Examiner*, he named Moses Annenberg as its circulation manager.

Through the years, Max and Moses Annenberg have been accused of starting the bloodiest circulation war in the history of journalism. They were certainly involved, but were not necessarily the instigators. Eight daily papers fought for circulation on the street corners of Chicago. Hearst was a latecomer, and most of the best street corners were occupied when his newsboys started selling *The American*. As biographer Gaeton Fonzi explained, the "only way Hearst could gain a foothold was to use muscle," and a "rough business became rougher." There were daily fistfights, broken bones, and wrecked newsstands. In an unpublished account of his early years, Moses Annenberg acknowledged handing out baseball bats to the boys who worked under him. "I was threatened every day with extermination," he wrote, "and I would leave home, as a result, with a revolver in each of my coat pockets, ready for action."

One confrontation between Moses' crew and a wagon full of tough boys hired by the rival *Chicago Daily News* ended with the rival group's leader, an African American named Clark, shot dead. Describing the incident in his memoir, Annenberg wrote that after Clark reached for a gun, "quick as a flash, one of our members struck him in the face, and another fired a bullet into his head." One of Annenberg's boys, Lawrence Finn, was charged with murder, but Hearst hired Clarence Darrow to defend Finn, and he was acquitted.

Moses left Chicago for Milwaukee in 1901—following a quarrel with his brother—and after his departure, Chicago's brutal circulation wars turned even bloodier. Half a dozen men and boys were killed, and many of those who survived the experience would later help give Chicago its reputation as the cradle of organized crime.

In Milwaukee, Moses went into business for himself, representing big-city dailies in distribution of their newspapers in outlying areas. He ultimately controlled the distribution of all the Chicago papers in 30 surrounding towns. In 1917, Annenberg became publisher of a Milwaukee paper owned by Arthur Brisbane, who had been William Randolph Hearst's star columnist and editor. When the paper expanded, Brisbane sold it to Hearst, who kept Moses as publisher. Hearst watched the paper's circulation climb, and in 1920, he decided to bring Moses Annenberg to New York and put him in charge of circulation for all Hearst newspapers and magazines. Before accepting the job, Annenberg told Hearst that he wanted to continue running his own businesses while working for him. Hearst acquiesced to the unusual arrangement, and Annenberg operated his Milwaukee distribution agencies and monitored his real estate holdings from New York. Although Hearst paid him a princely salary—$50,000—as circulation director, Annenberg managed to make five times as much through his other interests. To find the time to do both jobs at once, he reportedly slept only four hours per night.

In 1922, while still working for Hearst, Annenberg looked for yet another moneymaking venture. He found it in *The Daily Racing Form*, a Chicago-based horseracing publication packed with statistics. Horse racing was proving increasingly popular in the Roaring Twenties, and so was off-track betting in illegal bookie joints. *The Racing Form,* published six days a week, listed all the horses running on tracks each day, along with their histories and past performances. Annenberg brought in two partners and bought *The Racing Form* for $400,000, which he paid for in cash. Moses quickly expanded the tip sheet, setting up printing plants in seven cities and distributing the paper all over the U.S. and into Canada. Within the first year, on revenues of one million dollars, he cleared enough profit to cover the purchase price. Ten years later, he bought out his partners for $2.25 million and took total control of the money machine he'd built. In just the first year of sole ownership, Annenberg reaped $2.5 million in profits from *The Daily Racing Form*. The publication would continue generating enormous sums for the Annenberg family for another half a century.

Annenberg saw that while *The Racing Form* satisfied ordinary bettors at race tracks by providing fresh statistics on a daily basis, millions of bettors frequenting horse parlors, and especially professional gamblers and bookies at bookie joints, wanted information minute by minute, right up to post time. Since the late 19th century, such information had been delivered by telegraph, and "racing wire" services had become a lucrative—and dangerous—business.

There were an estimated 15,000 bookie joints across the country, all of them illegal and many of them controlled by racketeers, who made payoffs to police and politicians. In the 1920s, a mobster named Monte Tennes, who controlled 700 bookie joints, was the undisputed czar of gambling in Chicago. Tennes held his territory with bombs, gunfire, and arson when necessary. The Chicago Crime Survey reported in 1927 that he controlled "syndicate gambling as a phase of organized crime in Chicago." That same year, an aging Tennes, threatened by the appearance of 28-year-old Al Capone on the scene in Chicago, approached Annenberg with a business proposition. He would sell half his stake in his racing wire, the General News Bureau, for $650,000. Flush with the success of *The Daily Racing Form*, and having resigned from Hearst's employ a year earlier to concentrate on his own businesses, Moses decided to double down his investment in the horses.

Annenberg already had staffs of clockers, handicappers, and other equine experts at every racetrack in the country filing information on each race for *The Daily Racing Form*. Now he would increase those staffs and send the information out over the wire as well. And as he had with *The Racing Form*, he would create a near monopoly with his wire service, eventually known as *Nationwide News Service*. Annenberg's son, Walter, and others tried to dissuade him from entering a business so deeply tied into illegal betting and organized crime, but it was useless to argue with Moses when he had made up his mind. And it was impossible to argue with the profits: by the mid-1930s, *Nationwide News Service* would help make Annenberg one of the richest men in America, with an annual income that the FBI estimated at six million dollars.

When he moved east to work for Hearst in New York, Annenberg had bought an estate in King's Point, Long Island, from the Broadway songwriter and actor George M. Cohan (whose hundreds of songs included the popular "Over There"). The 32-room house—with a tennis court, two swimming pools, and a 16-stall stable—sat on 36 acres. Auto magnate Walter Chrysler lived next door, and the house F. Scott Fitzgerald used as the model for Jay Gatsby's mansion was nearby. With Hearst as one of his role models, Annenberg's ambitions outgrew even the great financial success he was having in New York. Though his businesses were thriving, he wanted more public clout and respectability. In particular, he wanted a newspaper, one that he could eventually hand on to Walter.

During the winters of the early 1930s, the Annenbergs had vacationed in Miami Beach, and in 1933, Moses purchased a villa there on Millionaire's Row. He was drawn south by the weather and the influx of money and powerful northerners, but he also had business interests to attend to. One of his *Daily Racing Form* printing plants was in Miami, and Miami's mayor and police chief had been campaigning to close bookie joints and to keep *Nationwide News Service* from doing business there.

Annenberg decided to start a newspaper to compete with *The Miami Herald* and *The Miami Daily News*, both of which had strong political connections. *The Daily News* was owned by James M. Cox, who had run for president in 1920 with Franklin D. Roosevelt as his running mate. Cox's enmity for Moses Annenberg, bred during the ensuing newspaper spat in Miami, would make Cox an influential adversary behind the scenes when Annenberg came to Roosevelt's attention several years later.

Annenberg built a $300,000 printing plant and started *The Miami Tribune*, which quickly made a name for itself by delving much more deeply into coverage of crime, mob killings, and local political malfeasance than either of its more cautious rivals. Exercising some of the influence his post as publisher gave him, Annenberg managed to help elect a slate of malleable Miami city commissioners, and they voted out the mayor. By aggressively investigating corruption, his paper pressured the police chief into resigning. But *The Tribune*, which Moses had started on something of a whim, was losing money. After his hard-charging editor, Paul Jeans, was killed in a head-on collision, Annenberg sold *The Tribune* to John S. Knight. Knight, who would go on to build one of the largest newspaper chains in the country, had recently purchased the rival *Miami Herald,* and he shut down *The Miami Tribune* the same day he took possession of it.

Annenberg's next stop was Philadelphia, and his next paper was *The Philadelphia Inquirer. The Inquirer,* which had shaped and reflected Republican control of Philadelphia for nearly a century, had fallen on hard times following the death in 1929 of its publisher, James Elverson Jr. His sister, a widow living in Paris, and her son, who owned a small newspaper there, inherited *The Inquirer* and were absentee owners for a time. Then they sold the paper to a Philadelphia group, only to take it back in 1934 when the purchasers failed to make payments. In July 1936, when Annenberg bought *The Inquirer,* published reports put the cash price at $15 million. Christopher Ogden, Annenberg's biographer, wrote that he actually paid a million dollars in cash, borrowed an additional three million, and assumed a debt of $6.8 million. But Annenberg, conscious of the power of money to intimidate, never denied the rumors about the higher figure or the stories that had him personally delivering the cash in suitcases.

Philadelphia's fusty upper-class Establishment was shocked that its "hallowed institution," in Ogden's phrase, had been taken over by a purveyor of racing information. John Cooney, author of *The Annenbergs: The Salvaging of a Tainted Dynasty*, wrote that while the Establishment knew little about the publisher, "what they did know they didn't like." Annenberg was a crony of the infamous William Randolph Hearst, and "he had made a fortune in the shady business of providing information to the nation's billion-dollar-a-year racetrack gambling industry. Now he had bought their paper...and they found that most upsetting."

In *The Inquirer*'s newsroom, however, tough-talking "Moe" Annenberg won instant popularity. Biographer Gaeton Fonzi quoted a veteran staffer: "Everybody who worked for the old man liked him. He was the kind of guy who made things hum, a man with a tremendous amount of energy for everything that interested him, from business to broads. He was always giving big parties and big bonuses."

Annenberg's lifestyle jarred staid Philadelphia. Soon after arriving, he installed a live-in girlfriend in his suite at the Warwick Hotel. She was listed as his secretary and was paid $150 a week, about four times the going rate, according to Christopher Ogden. She was described by Ogden as "a beautiful young woman with softly curled blonde hair" who first appeared on the payroll of Annenberg's *Daily Racing Form* in 1935, before he purchased *The Inquirer*. She was Annenberg's mistress, but also his personal secretary, and she traveled everywhere with him.

Annenberg's wife, Sadie, was so troubled by the relationship that she never moved to Philadelphia.

Dilworth spoke of Moses and Walter Annenberg with typical candor in a series of interviews with me in 1972. The picture he drew was of a crude, overbearing father and a submissive son who, in his father's presence, gave no hint of the brilliance he would later display as a billionaire entrepreneur. "I always liked him," Dilworth remarked about Moses Annenberg, "but he was vicious the way he treated Walter, and Walter adored him...the old man treated him just like dirt, but he always wanted him around...the old man never asked his opinion. If Walter spoke, he said, 'You don't know your ass from third base, shut up.' That kind of stuff."

Dilworth also recalled taking Moses Annenberg to a lightweight championship fight in the late 1930s and driving him back to the Warwick Hotel afterward: "In those days, the expensive cars had running boards—and ours was a very cheap car." At the end of the evening, when he stopped in front of the hotel, Annenberg opened his door, "stepped from the [car] and fell flat on his face." As he got up, Annenberg turned and snarled, "Are you so fucking cheap you can't even afford a car with a running board? I ought to charge you for a new pair of pants." And then came a torrent of profanity, Dilworth remembered with a laugh. "You never heard so many four-letter words."

Moses Annenberg's acquisition of a prominent and respected big-city newspaper was viewed with alarm even outside Philadelphia. "In the past," *The Nation* magazine observed, "Annenberg has often acted as the 'dummy' for Hearst in the acquisition of newspapers where Hearst influence was to be kept surreptitious." *Newsweek* wrote that Annenberg's name "once struck terror in the hearts of strong men." He and his brother Max were charged with "sowing seeds that make Chicago and gangland synonymous." *Time* magazine weighed in with an allegation that a "sinister aura...dogged them throughout their careers."

Without a doubt, the newspaperman most alarmed by Annenberg's arrival was *The Philadelphia Record*'s David Stern, the self-styled maverick publisher and staunch New Dealer. Stern had started as a cub reporter in 1908, and he bought his first paper four years later. In 1926, he purchased a Camden daily that became *The Courier-Post*. He wrote in his memoirs that he "went hunting for trouble" in 1928 and found *The Philadelphia Record*. The paper, Stern wrote, was then at "the bottom of the heap of six keenly competing dailies." Albert M. Greenfield, a Philadelphia real estate magnate who had been friendly with Stern, encouraged the publisher to make the purchase. Stern was at first reluctant, fearing that Greenfield, who wielded power in Democratic politics, might seek to influence the news coverage. Greenfield made the deal irresistible for Stern by investing $100,000 himself and arranging a $1.2 million loan from his holding company, Bankers

Securities Corporation. He thus put up more than half the purchase price of $2.5 million.

Thumbing its nose at proper Philadelphia and providing a liberal voice for readers, *The Record* saw its circulation soar. It rose from about 123,000 when David Stern bought the paper to 315,000 when Moses Annenberg bought *The Philadelphia Inquirer* eight years later. Over the same span, *The Inquirer's* weekday circulation stayed flat at about 290,000.

The first skirmish in the war between Annenberg and Stern was fought over the distribution of their rival papers in Wilmington, Delaware. There had been a longstanding agreement between *The Inquirer* and *The Record* for joint distribution in the suburbs. When *The Record's* circulation director warned Stern that Annenberg was assigning a man "from Chicago" to Wilmington, *The Record's* publisher interrupted. "If Annenberg gets control of the distributors," he predicted, "he can cut our circulation overnight, or force us to the terrible expense of a separate distribution system."

In recalling the episode, Dilworth said that Annenberg had reason to change the system. Despite the joint distribution agreement, Stern made sure that at the Wilmington newsstands, "*The Record* was always on top and *The Inquirer* was always down below." If there was one thing Annenberg understood, noted Dilworth, it was circulation, so "he just wiped out the whole system and started setting up his own."

In retaliation, David Stern ordered his staff to dig up all the dirt it could on Moses Annenberg's past and to portray him as a publishing menace and a disgrace to journalism. Then he directed his law firm to seek an injunction that would prevent *The Inquirer's* owner from breaking the distribution agreement, and they landed in court.

It may be that Dilworth really was Moses Annenberg's attorney of last resort. Or maybe not. For 10 years, the ex-Marine had been one of the city's busiest and most effective trial lawyers. He had proven himself a tenacious battler in the courtroom. And he was just the kind of lawyer that Moses L. Annenberg admired.

In a 1972 interview, Dilworth recalled that Judge James Gay Gordon heard the case without a jury for nearly two weeks. From the start, he was certain that Gordon would rule against him: "Although he was a good judge and fundamentally a fair-minded man, he was terribly prejudiced against Annenberg. He was a friend of Stern's and believed everything that he had told him. Stern had given him this caricature of Annenberg beating a crippled newsboy over the head with his own crutch." Dilworth said it was obvious that the judge "thought it was just a tragedy Annenberg had come into the city. He obviously wanted to drive him back to Chicago or Milwaukee." Because of the judge's clear disposition, Dilworth calculated that his best chance was to try the case with a view toward taking it to a higher court and winning on appeal. In stream-of-consciousness rhetoric punctuated with howls of laughter, he remembered his performance in Judge Gordon's court:

> "There were various questions I figured I had to get on the record and had to get answered, and he told me not to ask them. I told him I had to ask them, and he told me if I asked them, he'd fine me for contempt. Then old man Annenberg would say, 'How much?' It was a hundred dollars a whack. So the old man would pull a roll out of his pocket that would have choked a horse, and he would come up—and that really was embarrassing; thank God there wasn't a jury there. It would have been absolute murder—he would come up and plunk a hundred dollar bill on the bar of the court, and then we would go on. And it was pointed out that if the judge disqualified me that there would really be nobody to represent Annenberg because Kenworthey was sick. He was the only other trial lawyer in the firm, and they couldn't get any of these fancy lawyers. So we did complete the case. I think I was fined three times."

To Dilworth's surprise, Judge Gordon eventually denied Stern's petition for an injunction. Even so, according to Stern's memoirs, *The Inquirer* dropped its attempt to change agents in Wilmington and never again tried the ploy with other distributors.

Both publishers could claim a partial victory, but the undisputed winner was Richardson Dilworth, who, in the course of the raucous trial, won the client of a lifetime. David Stern conceded as much: "Moe was so impressed by Dick's truculent tactics that he followed him out of the courtroom to retain him as general counsel for *The Inquirer* at an annual fee of $50,000."

Stern wrote that he, too, recognized Dilworth's "unusual ability," and "offered to back him for any political post he wanted, if he would sever his connection with *The Inquirer*." Dilworth declined the offer, explaining: "I can't afford to give up that retainer."

Although David Stern, as publisher of *The Philadelphia Record*, was Moses Annenberg's immediate rival, a more potent adversary was lurking behind the scenes: Stern's backer, Albert Greenfield. Greenfield was, like Annenberg, an enormously ambitious, brilliant, cold-blooded millionaire, and Dilworth watched as these two men with such influence over his future—one his most important client, the other a kingmaker in Democratic politics—engaged in an epic personal battle that resulted in the bitterest, most vicious newspaper war in the city's history.

Like Annenberg, Greenfield was a Jewish immigrant who came to this country from Eastern Europe as a boy. Like Annenberg, he succeeded in business strictly on his own merits. Both of these remarkable entrepreneurs were disliked and distrusted in Philadelphia's Wasp society. Anti-Semitism was widespread in the 1930s, and Jews were excluded from executive positions in the city's best banks and businesses, and were ostracized from the upper echelons of society.

What divided Annenberg and Greenfield was their politics. Neither man was much of an ideologue, but both were extremely competitive and combative, and they found themselves on opposite sides of the political fight in Philadelphia. Annenberg started out as a strong supporter of Franklin Roosevelt. He voted for FDR in 1932 and sent an admiring telegram endorsing the New Deal. The editorial stance of *The Miami Tribune* favored the president, and the paper carried Eleanor Roosevelt's syndicated column.

When Moses took the helm of *The Philadelphia Inquirer* in the summer of 1936 and told his editors that he intended to write an editorial declaring the paper's independence and giving support to FDR, there were loud cries of complaint. *The Inquirer* had been firmly behind Alfred M. Landon all along, the editors said, and it would look foolish to switch sides at the eleventh hour. Annenberg conceded the point and the paper endorsed Alf Landon for president.

Still, Annenberg cast his own vote that year for Roosevelt, and after FDR's overwhelming re-election, he did write an editorial announcing that his paper would be politically independent. But as *The Inquirer*'s circulation battle with the fervidly pro-FDR *Record* raged on, Annenberg found himself criticizing the Roosevelt Administration and backing a series of Republican candidates. In an age when newspaper titans like his old boss William Randolph Hearst held enormous sway in politics, Moses Annenberg sought to cast himself in the same role—and perhaps the particular political orientation was of less weight to him than the clout itself. "In no time at all," wrote his biographer, Gaeton Fonzi, "he was being mentioned... as one of the triumvirate calling the shots in Pennsylvania Republican politics. And, as usual, when Annenberg got into a fight he never pulled his punches."

Like Annenberg, Albert Greenfield had also switched parties. He started as a staunch Republican. As vice-chairman of the GOP's national finance committee in 1928, he helped engineer Herbert Hoover's nomination for president. After Hoover's victory, film magnate William Fox referred to his friend Greenfield, in a letter to Hoover, as "that little bald-headed Hebrew Jew, who made it possible for you to become President of the United States." But Greenfield soon grew disillusioned with Hoover's economic policies and became a passionate New Dealer. Until their traumatic confrontation, Albert Greenfield and Moses Annenberg had never met. Annenberg's turf was Chicago and Greenfield's was Philadelphia.

Avrun Moishe Grunfeld was born on August 7, 1887, in a Ukrainian village near Kiev. His name was later anglicized to Albert Monroe Greenfield. He was nine years old when the family settled in Philadelphia. Greenfield quit school at the age of 15 to work as a clerk and errand boy for a real estate lawyer in Philadelphia. He was 17 when he opened his own real estate business in 1904.

Within seven years, he was making $60,000 a year. Before he was 30 years old, he was worth about $15 million. And Greenfield's company became the largest real estate business in Pennsylvania. He created a conglomerate that once employed 30,000 persons. It was a major holding company with interests in real estate, retailing, banking, hotels, and investments. In the 1950s, sociologist Digby Baltzell would refer to Greenfield as "perhaps the most powerful man in Philadelphia." He was nicknamed Mr. Philadelphia, and, as Baltzell wrote, "nothing of any significance" happened in Philadelphia without Greenfield's approval "and very little without profit to him."

Albert Greenfield's record as a businessman was not unblemished. His retail operation, City Stores, had outlets in many states and often failed in fierce competition with flashier retail businesses. Among the stores that he acquired and later closed were Hearn's, Franklin Simon, and Oppenheim Collins in New York; Landsburgh's in Washington, D.C.; R.H. White in Boston; and Snellenberg's in Philadelphia. In a scathing denunciation of the financier, writer Leon Harris charged that department store owners all across America characterized Greenfield as "a hyena, a snake, a vulture, the Bag-of-Bones man, the Angel of Death." As retailing businesses failed, he was everybody's favorite villain.

In his attack on Greenfield, Annenberg reached back to 1930. The Bankers Trust Company, which Greenfield had founded in the 1920s, was among the hundreds of banks that failed during the Great Depression. Other, bigger banks in Philadelphia could have come to its rescue, but failed to do so. Annenberg's *Inquirer* charged that Albert Greenfield had taken care of himself while hundreds of depositors lost their life savings in the collapse of Bankers Trust. An eight-column headline charged: "Greenfield's firm drew $300,000 from Bankers Trust, Lawyer Says." The story implied that Greenfield, knowing that Bankers Trust would fold, took out his money five days before it closed. What the story failed to disclose was that the transaction was a routine transfer of notes. Greenfield was still on the hook for the $300,000. Rather than declare bankruptcy and escape all liability, Bankers Trust paid a fraction of what it owed its depositors—a fraction but still better than nothing.

Moe Annenberg's attack outraged Greenfield. He paid for time on radio station WFIL and on September 21, 1938, he delivered a scathing counterattack. He likened Annenberg to Adolf Hitler and called him a "master of publicity and propaganda," who threatens "force and brutality against all who stand in his way." "We have in Philadelphia today," Greenfield declared, "a self-appointed evangelist of power. His greed for recognition and dictatorship is his ruling passion."

Greenfield spoke of the "American plan for Moe Hitler-Annenberg." He found it hard to believe "that thinking Americans will not realize there are lessons from Europe for us as well...stop and think before turning over Pennsylvania to a sinister character whose only desire is to destroy everything that stands in his way."

According to Greenfield, Annenberg had learned under Hearst "the racket of how to build a big newspaper circulation by means of the fist and the blackjack on the street and by means of poison and defamation on the printed page. Ready to his hand was the poor old *Philadelphia Inquirer*, battered by mismanagement.... Moe had the cash, and he had the wish. He saw in *The Inquirer* a chance to buy respectability." Annenberg returned fire. "Political skunks can wear themselves out directing their poison gas at me, but I shall continue to do my duty."

Then the Greenfield-Annenberg feud reached its peak. In the fall of 1938, when Pennsylvania's Democratic governor, Ralph Earle, ran for the Senate, he was strongly backed by *The Record* as well as by FDR. But he was hammered repeatedly in *Inquirer* editorials orchestrated by Annenberg. As Election Day approached, it looked possible that Earle would lose his race. At the same time, Annenberg's handpicked candidate to replace Earle as governor, Republican Arthur James, appeared headed for victory over Democrat Charles Alvin Jones. Annenberg continued attacking President Roosevelt's New Deal as well until finally FDR had had enough.

The president dispatched his loyal advisor, Secretary of the Interior Harold L. Ickes, to Philadelphia to excoriate Annenberg. The combative Ickes was an extremely effective orator, and *The Record* published every word of his speech. Ickes warned that "turning the public contracts of Pennsylvania and the whole law machinery of the state over to a man of the record of Moe Annenberg is the most alarming thing that has ever threatened my native state. For Moe comes from the world and from the law traditionally associated with Al Capone."

James won the race, but *The New York Times* noted that "much of the venom of the campaign" had been directed "not so much at the candidates as their backers." Although Annenberg and Greenfield sued each other for libel, their dispute gradually subsided, and in May 1939, both lawsuits were withdrawn with the signing of mutual public apologies. Annenberg's side conceded that his charge against Greenfield in the Bankers Trust closing was "based on the wrong interpretation of the information that was furnished."

Through it all, Dilworth somehow got along famously—and very profitably—with both sides. He represented Moses L. Annenberg for the rest of his life and would go on to represent Walter Annenberg for decades afterward. And Albert M. Greenfield would be a key figure in Dilworth's political future.

Despite the truce with Greenfield, Moe Annenberg's real troubles were just beginning. At the behest of FDR, the Internal Revenue Service had been checking his books for years. And on August 11, 1939, just three months after his peace treaty with Al Greenfield, Annenberg was indicted by a federal grand jury in Chicago. The IRS accused him of evading $3,258,809 in income taxes between 1932 and 1936. Interest and penalties raised the bill to some $10.7 million, then the largest tax case in U.S. history. His son Walter was also indicted, as were several of his employees.

The amount of damning evidence stacked up by the 35 Treasury agents, who worked on the case for two and a half years, was staggering. Even Dilworth, who was one of Moses Annenberg's two lawyers at the time of the indictment, said 30 years later that his client was guilty as charged. "They undoubtedly kept two sets of books," he said of Annenberg's organization.

It was also clear to Dilworth that the Roosevelt Administration had prosecuted Annenberg because of *The Philadelphia Inquirer*'s virulent opposition to the New Deal. "Oh, it was a vendetta," he said with certainty. "If he hadn't come to Philadelphia, I don't believe he'd have gone to jail. He didn't have any papers before [*The Inquirer*] where he could really attack Roosevelt."

Dilworth's view is abundantly supported by *The Secret Diary of Harold L. Ickes,* which documents the animosity that FDR and his men felt for Annenberg and details the tactics they used to bring him down. During the tax evasion trial, Treasury secretary Henry Morgenthau, who also kept a diary, met with Roosevelt and asked if there was anything special he could do. "Yes," the president replied. "I want Moe Annenberg for dinner." Morgenthau answered, "You're going to have him for breakfast—fried."

Presiding over the trial was Judge James Wilkerson, who had sentenced Al Capone to 11 years in prison for tax evasion in 1931. Dilworth was in the Chicago courtroom in April 1940 as Annenberg pleaded guilty to evading $1.2 million in taxes. Dilworth recalled that when the 70-year-old judge asked the defendant if he had anything to say, Moe looked at him and replied, "Yes, I'll live to piss on your grave." (For the record, Judge Wilkerson, who sentenced Annenberg to three years in prison, would outlive him by eight years.)

Despite his enormous income, Annenberg was strapped for cash as he faced the prospect of paying off nearly $12 million in taxes, fines, penalties, and fees. The government had gone after his assets, putting liens on most of his properties and businesses, and pressuring AT&T to stop providing service to his racing wire. Fearful that the wire operation exposed him to prosecution for ties to organized crime, Annenberg shut down *Nationwide News Service,* losing his largest source of revenue.

On top of the government bill, he had to pay his lawyers. According to Dilworth, as the trial was getting started and Annenberg was scrambling to justify his tax returns, his Chicago lawyer, Weymouth Kirkland, had asked Moe if he had any cash on hand and offered him a protective place to park it. "I'll simply put it in an attorney's account," Dilworth quoted Kirkland as saying, "and if anybody says anything to me, I can just say that this is on account of fees." Annenberg had two million dollars in cash and gave it to Kirkland. Dilworth, who described him as "a hell of a lawyer," also called him "the slickest fellow I've ever seen." When the trial was over and Annenberg asked for the money, Kirkland replied, "First we've got to make up a bill." And the bill, Dilworth recalled, "with a little exaggeration, but not too much, came to approximately one million, nine hundred fifty thousand dollars."

Annenberg had three weeks between his sentencing and the commencement of his prison term, and he tried to come up with the government's money in that time. His longtime Chicago bank, First National, which had lent him enormous sums over the years, "still had confidence in him," according to Dilworth, and agreed to lend him nine million dollars if he could secure three million from a bank in Philadelphia. First National referred Moe to Joseph Wayne, president of Philadelphia National Bank. Joe Wayne was, Dilworth claimed, "very different from all the other Philadelphia bankers at that time," and "would take a chance on a fellow like an Annenberg." But the bank's directors, who were "very stuffy," were far more skeptical. No Philadelphia bank had ever made a personal loan of that magnitude, according to Dilworth, and a special meeting of the directors was called on a Sunday afternoon to discuss the matter. Annenberg was required to be on hand to answer any questions that might arise.

Dilworth accompanied Moses and Walter Annenberg that day. As the session got under way, the three were asked to wait outside the boardroom. He remembered that Walter, who at just 32 would have to take the helm of *The Inquirer* when his father went to prison, was exceedingly nervous and began complaining about the situation in the paper's newsroom. One of Moe's girlfriends had recently been put on the payroll, ostensibly as a reporter. Dilworth quoted Walter as saying, "You've got to get her out of there, Father, because it's just as though you put a bitch in heat into a dog kennel…they're all fighting over her and it's causing the most terrible time." Moses then turned on his son, demanding to know "when did you get so goddamn moral? When I peddled papers outside a hotel in Chicago, for every buck I made selling papers, I made 10 dollars pimping for whores in the hotel."

"This was while we were waiting in the hall" just outside the boardroom, Dilworth recalled, "and I said to myself, 'Jesus, if they can hear this conversation, I know where the loan will go.' " But when the meeting broke up, Annenberg got the news that the loan was approved. And, Dilworth added, it was paid off "pretty damn fast."

One of the conditions of Moses Annenberg's guilty plea was that all of the charges against his son would be dropped. "And they should have been," said Dilworth. "Walter hadn't the remotest idea of what was going on." Walter Annenberg confirmed this account. In an interview with Christopher Ogden, he claimed that his father only pleaded guilty "so I wouldn't have to suffer."

The Roosevelt Administration's vindictiveness toward Moe Annenberg persisted long after the trial. As late as December 1941, Harold Ickes' diary finds him maneuvering to overturn a parole board decision that would have released a severely ailing Annenberg after two years in prison. Ickes quotes himself saying to

FDR in justification, "In his much smaller sphere, Annenberg has been as cruel, as ruthless, and as lawless as Hitler himself." Moses Annenberg died of a brain tumor on July 20, 1942, shortly after his release from prison.

David Stern's *Record* folded in 1947 after a battle with the newly formed American Newspaper Guild, and the Philadelphia *Bulletin* bought the paper's assets for $12 million. Without *The Record* pushing *The Inquirer* to the right, Walter Annenberg felt free to assail the Republican machine, and his paper published a series of articles detailing the graft and corruption in the administration of Republican mayor Bernard Samuel. And then in 1949, Walter wrote an editorial declaring *The Inquirer*'s political independence. After more than a century of endorsing only Republicans, the newspaper would be backing Democrats for some city offices (including Richardson Dilworth for treasurer). "No political party should be able to take any newspaper for granted," Walter wrote. "On October 14, 1939, my father, M.L. Annenberg, put on our logotype the slogan 'An Independent Newspaper for All the People.' He meant exactly what he said. I'm sure that if my father were alive today, and had the same opportunity, he would have done as I have done."

In subsequent years, *The Philadelphia Inquirer* under Walter Annenberg continued to have a distinctly Republican slant, but Richardson Dilworth the liberal Democrat retained his position as chief lawyer for the paper. He was also Walter's personal lawyer, and was chief lawyer for Walter's Triangle Publications. Spearheaded by the phenomenally successful *TV Guide* (which had 21 million subscribers at its height), Triangle made Walter Annenberg one of the nation's wealthiest men, and for decades afterward, he kept paying generous retainers to his lawyer. When Annenberg's longtime friend, the Australian press baron Rupert Murdoch, purchased Triangle for $3.2 billion in 1988, then the largest sum in the history of the communications business, Dilworth, Paxson & Kalish handled the sale.

Although Richardson Dilworth and Walter Annenberg differed on many issues over the years, their relationship remained strong. Dilworth wrote warm, gossipy letters to the publisher, and he and his wife visited Walter and Leonore Annenberg at Sunnylands, their palatial estate in Palm Springs, California. Moses Annenberg was never discussed on these occasions, but there could be no doubt of his son's enduring love for him. Walter kept a mahogany-and-bronze plaque by his desk with the fragment of an invocation that read: "Cause my works on Earth to reflect honor on my father's memory."

CHAPTER NINE

Pivot Point

A new wife, a new firm, a new life

It was through mutual friends in New York that Ann Hill, a tiny woman of strong will, met 36-year-old Dick Dilworth, the dashing Philadelphia lawyer with movie-star good looks and sparkling personality. She was smitten. So was he. To the astonishment of their families and friends, and to the lasting indignation of the Philadelphia Establishment, they left their spouses and their children—his four and her two—and went off together to vacation in Havana. They subsequently obtained divorces from their respective spouses and on August 12, 1935, were married in Reno, Nevada. Just as Moses Annenberg would transform Dilworth's professional life, so would Ann Hill transform his family life. In both cases, Dilworth's unconventional actions promised great rewards, but in the near term, they brought risk and turbulence that tested him severely.

Dick's new wife was born Ann Elizabeth Kaufman in Marquette, Michigan, in 1902. Like Bobbie Brockie, she came from money. Her maternal grandfather, financier Otto Young, helped build 19th-century Chicago. He owned land in the Loop where the Blackstone Hotel and the Carson, Pirie Scott department store were erected. Her father, Louis Graveraet Kaufman, started as a messenger in the small bank his father ran in rural Michigan and wound up creating the largest bank in New York City (now known as Chemical Bank). He pioneered national branch banking and was a key financier of the Empire State Building. He was also an early investor in General Motors and was on the company's board of directors for 22 years, beginning in 1910. When his bank failed in the Depression, Louis Kaufman was said to have sold one million shares of General Motors stock to make up the losses.

The family lived in Short Hills, New Jersey, in a house large enough to accommodate the eight Kaufman children plus French governesses for the girls. There was also a three-story apartment on Park Avenue in Manhattan, and frequent vacations in Newport, Rhode Island, and Palm Beach. For vacations back in Michigan, Louis Kaufman built a "camp" on Lake Superior in a spot where he had picnicked as a boy. The 26,000-square-foot log mansion, built between 1919 and 1923 by 300 Scandinavian craftsmen, was sited on a narrow point of land jutting out into the lake. It had 26 bedrooms, 30 stone fireplaces—each one unique— and 50 rooms overall. The Kaufmans' guests at the house included Bill Tilden, Fred Astaire, Cole Porter, and Mary Pickford. George Gershwin was a favorite visitor; he selected a piano for the house and played it for other guests after dinner. Called Granot Loma (a combination of the Kaufman children's names), the house is now on the National Register of Historic Places.[11]

When Dick met Ann Kaufman, she was the wife of Crawford Hill Jr., whom she had married in Paris in 1923. Hill, a graduate of Harvard, was descended from one of the most prominent families in Denver. His grandfather, N.P. Hill, was a U.S. senator and the owner of *The Denver Republican* newspaper. His grandmother wrote Denver's first "Social Register," and the Crawford Hill House was recognized as the city's "Social Capitol." Ann and Crawford Hill had two children: a son, Louis, and a daughter, Marie.

Richardson Dilworth's second marriage was very happy, as anyone who met the couple could quickly tell, and Ann Dilworth would play a pivotal role in her husband's political career. They would have a daughter, Deborah, and a son, Richardson, and the eight children in their extended ménage would later campaign for Dilworth when he ran for office. But the path was not an easy one. Perhaps Dilworth wouldn't have wanted it to be. He said that after their marriage, they were isolated socially. "We were both regarded as outsiders, so our first years together were really pretty rugged. We saw very few people." It was during this period that Dilworth became Moses Annenberg's lawyer. "I worked like hell and managed to really move ahead and do well in the law during that period, because we had very little social life."

---

[11] Built on an eight–square–mile property with three and a half miles of Lake Superior waterfront, Granot Loma stayed in the Kaufman family until the 1970s; it was purchased in 1987 by bond trader Tom Baldwin, who completely restored the building before putting it on the market in 2009 for $40 million.

Following the divorce, Bobbie Brockie moved with her children to Stockbridge, Massachusetts, where she was treated for alcoholism at the Austen Riggs Institute. She stayed in the area for several years, but eventually moved back to Philadelphia and remarried. If she felt resentment toward Dilworth, it never showed. Warden Dilworth, who was three years old when his parents divorced, divided his time between them while growing up. He said that he never heard his mother say a bad word about his father. And Warden's older sister, Anne, who was nine at the time of the divorce, said of her parents in an interview years later that "there was no animosity or any difficulty or disagreement…they could have written a thesis on how to be a divorced parent."

In the years after the divorce, Bobbie Brockie followed her ex-husband's career closely and never lost her respect for him. Her father was a less forgiving sort. The first hint of trouble was at the attorney general's office. Soon after the divorce, Dilworth discovered that he had been removed as a deputy AG. William Warden, who had arranged his son-in-law's appointment, quietly unarranged it.

Then, in November 1936, Dilworth's revered boss, Ralph Evans, died of heart disease at the age of 53 at his home in Haverford. He had been practicing law for 30 years and had founded Evans, Bayard & Frick 15 years earlier. "He really *was* the law firm," Dilworth recalled. "He was a terrific fellow. The nicest, finest man I ever knew—and a hell of a lawyer."

Evans' control over the firm had been unquestioned. "At the end of the year," Dilworth continued, "he'd bring in the balance sheet to show us how much the firm had made." Evans would then distribute the money to the partners. "He never asked whether you agreed to it or anything, but it was always so goddamn fair and generous that there was never any complaint."

Ralph Evans' death set off a three-way struggle for control of the firm. According to Dilworth, the three partners in question—Francis Sheets, Charles Kenworthey, and Dick himself—"really did nine-tenths of the law work in the office." And when Evans died, "We got into an immediate power struggle over who was going to be the top dog. All three of us wanted to be. For two years there was no conclusion to it."

Then William G. Warden stepped in. One day in the spring of 1938, three years after Dilworth had divorced Bobbie, Warden called on him at his law office. It had been nearly a decade since Warden had agreed to take care of the margin call on his son-in-law's Pittsburgh Coal stock. But now Warden handed him the promissory note he'd signed "for tax purposes" and demanded, Dilworth recalled, "something like $200,000."

"He said, 'You'll either pay me back or I'll bring suit against you and go to your partners.' I think he hoped that the marriage would break up right away and that would give him satisfaction, but the marriage was working out pretty well and we had two children. The law business was going well, so I guess the old man decided it was time to really give it to me."

And he did. Describing Dilworth as "a crook of the lowest order," Warden told Francis Sheets what had happened. That gave Sheets and Kenworthey the leverage to move against their partner. They came to see him one morning in the middle of July 1938, handed him the papers of Warden's lawsuit and advised him that as of the first of August, he "would cease to be a partner and had better find other employment."

"Weirdly enough," Dilworth recalled, the suit was settled without litigation when he borrowed $10,000 and paid it over to Warden in cash. But Warden had succeeded "in getting me kicked out of Evans, Bayard & Frick." What followed was a low point in Dilworth's legal career. "It was ghastly, it really was," he said in describing his search for a job. "I went to all the big law firms and they wanted no part of a fellow who would run off to Havana and had no foothold of any kind in the Establishment. I had no Philadelphia connections. My wife certainly didn't."

Dilworth's exile, though painful, was short-lived. By the end of the summer, after being rebuffed by all the Establishment firms, he landed at a firm with a mixed heritage but a lot of moxie. It had been started five years earlier by two lawyers who were themselves outsiders. One was Frank Murdoch, born to a working-class family in Camden in 1902. The other, six years younger, was Harry Kalish, the son of Jewish immigrants from Bialystok near the Russian-Polish border.

Murdoch's family had moved to West Philadelphia when he was a small boy. He studied hard in public school, winning a state scholarship to the University of Pennsylvania's Wharton School. He graduated in 1926, got married, and enrolled at Penn's law school. To pay his bills, he found a job grinding a movie camera in the old Stanley Theater near 16th and Market Streets. Murdoch spent long hours at the theater, turning the primitive camera by hand and earning the money to support his family and pay his tuition. He got his law degree in 1928.

The parents of Harry Kalish had joined the flood of Jews fleeing persecution in Russia at the turn of the previous century. They ran a grocery in the Northern Liberties section of Philadelphia and lived above the store. As a small boy, Harry would accompany his father to the city's principal market on Dock Street to buy fruit and vegetables for their grocery. Then father and son would push their cart loaded with produce back to the family store. "I'll have you know, that was a hell of a push," Kalish told the author of his law firm's history.

Harry Kalish attended Philadelphia's Central High School when it was recognized as one of the nation's finest public secondary schools. He went directly from Central to Dickinson Law School in south-central Pennsylvania, meeting expenses by working in an ice cream factory. Like Frank Murdoch, he graduated in 1928, with honors.

Under Philadelphia Bar Association rules at the time, law school graduates were required to serve six-month clerkships with judges or lawyers before being admitted to the bar. Both Murdoch and Kalish met this requirement in 1929 and started sharing space in an office at 1420 Walnut Street. Instead of forming a partnership, they functioned as single practitioners in the same office. They took whatever work they could find, mostly routine criminal cases. "When I had a client," Kalish said, "Murdoch would magically disappear. And when Murdoch had a client, I would do the same. Not that we had that many clients, though."

In the Wall Street crash, Murdoch and Kalish saw opportunities where others saw only disaster. Of Philadelphia's 3,400 building and loan associations, about 1,600 were wiped out or merged. *The Sunday Transcript*, a weekly business newspaper, reported on September 27, 1931, that "nowhere on earth has there been such a long and continued raid on real property as Philadelphia has endured."

Murdoch and Kalish knew that the city's banks were heavily invested in real estate through mortgages secured by Center City property. They also realized that there had been no effort to reappraise properties since the collapse in Philadelphia's property values. As a result, the banks' properties were overvalued—which meant that their taxes were excessive.

Murdoch and Kalish began representing banks before the Tax Review Board, and they convinced the board to reduce assessments on many properties held by their clients. In the process, they became experts on taxation. This work proved to be the firm's financial backbone in the Depression-wracked 1930s.

Meanwhile, a third lawyer had joined them. Although he was a Penn law school classmate of Murdoch's, Douglas Paxson had little in common with either Frank Murdoch or Harry Kalish. His family traced its lineage to the colonial era before the American Revolution. His grandfather had been Chief Justice of the Pennsylvania Supreme Court, and his father was an estates lawyer for many of Philadelphia's wealthiest families. After getting his law degree in 1928, Paxson entered his father's practice. Four years later, the elder Paxson died and his son was not comfortable practicing law by himself. When Murdoch and Kalish suggested that he become their partner, Paxson agreed.

"Truly, this was extraordinary," the firm's history recorded. "Paxson was on the top of the social heap. He had everything—money, a solid practice, total social legitimacy." Kalish and Murdoch did not move in his social circles, and he had nothing to gain financially by joining them. Moreover, prejudice was a virulent force in the 1930s. By partnering with two products of the working class—one of them Jewish—Paxson risked alienation in a real way. But he went ahead. The partnership was arranged on April 1, 1933, and the law firm of Murdoch, Paxson & Kalish opened in Paxson's old offices on the 21st floor of the Fidelity Building at Broad and Sansom Streets in Philadelphia.

The years from 1933 to 1938 were difficult for many law firms and businesses generally as the nation struggled economically. Largely because of Paxson's estates business and the work that Murdoch and Kalish were doing for the banks, the new firm of young lawyers survived. While other law firms were shrinking, theirs actually grew. Midway through 1934, Robert Green joined them. Like Paxson, he was listed in the region's Social Register, known as the "Blue Book." To mark his presence as an experienced corporate lawyer, the firm changed its name to "Murdoch, Paxson, Kalish & Green." Robert Green was followed by Joe First, who would later become Walter Annenberg's lawyer, and then, in 1935, recent law school graduate J. Pennington Straus was hired. "I was one of the few people in my class who got any job at all," Straus told the firm's historian. "People were not hiring lawyers. I knew Frank Murdoch, though, and he gave me a job for $1,500 a year."

Two years after its founding, the firm had grown from three lawyers to seven plus secretaries and a receptionist. It moved to larger offices on the Fidelity Building's 26th floor. The firm lacked major accounts, however, and its future was uncertain. Having broken with the "tradition of religious uniformity," said Kalish, it was "not encumbered with many paying clients." The firm's trajectory changed permanently on August 15, 1938, with the arrival of Richardson Dilworth.

The firm made a public announcement that day stating that Dilworth had "resigned" as a member of the firm of Evans, Bayard & Frick and joined Murdoch, Paxson, Kalish & Green. The Murdoch firm's official history tells the real story. It recounts that Dilworth had "become the focus of much distrust" because of his divorce. "The Establishment firms froze him out. His decision to join the Murdoch firm reflected this fact."

"By taking in Dilworth," the history continues, "Murdoch and his partners demonstrated their difference from Legal Philadelphia. They embraced a man—a divorced man no less—who brought the Annenbergs and other clients with him. And his irrepressible spirit would transform the firm's character and image forever."

According to Harry Kalish, Richardson Dilworth's arrival "did a great deal to steady our somewhat financially shaky status." Dilworth, he said, "gave us the injection we needed." His corporate accounts would include the Philadelphia Gas Works, the Philadelphia Electric Company, Otis Elevator, and SKF, the Swedish ball-bearing manufacturer. But the jewel in the crown was the Annenberg account, which Dilworth kept for decades. The firm's history noted that Moses Annenberg met with the partners to express his confidence in them. Kalish remembered the meeting. "Annenberg told us that he liked the idea of a Jewish-Gentile firm...he liked Dilworth because he was such a fighter, and he liked the firm. He thought it had merit—a lot of merit."

Six months after Dilworth joined Murdoch, Harold E. Kohn, the son of a Russian immigrant plumber, was hired at $1,800 a year to be his assistant. Kohn had graduated first in his class from the University of Pennsylvania's Wharton School and first in 1937 from Penn's law school. While subsequently serving a clerkship in Philadelphia's Common Pleas Court, Kohn checked out his prospects with major law offices in the city. He found that the most prominent ones were completely closed to Jews. It was a practice about which some of the firms, he said, were "quite frank." The Murdoch firm was one of the few that did not discriminate. Kohn joined it in January 1939 and for the next four years saw Dilworth nearly every day, assisting at trials, writing briefs, and doing what was necessary to prepare for litigation.

Just as John G. Johnson had taught Ralph Evans and Evans had taught Dilworth, so Dilworth taught Kohn. In a 1989 interview, Kohn, who by then had become one of the nation's top appellate lawyers, said of Dilworth: "He taught me to be a trial lawyer. As first in your class, Phi Beta Kappa, you tend to become ponderous, pompous. You look for the big words. He disabused me of all that. He gave me an opportunity to exercise responsibility that I could never have gotten in another office. We did a lot of libel work together. He taught me by example. He was a great one for picking up weaknesses of every group."

Harold Kohn would go on to become one of the city's most brilliant attorneys. And his mentor, while still practicing law, kept thinking about politics. In the first years after his divorce and remarriage, as he was changing firms and throwing himself into his work, Dilworth had little time to do much more than think about politics. But then in 1939, the Democrats reached out to him. They told him that he would be the party's candidate for district attorney in the fall.

After hearing the good news, Dilworth left with his family for a vacation at Ann's family's summer place on Lake Superior. When they'd been settled there for four or five days, he received a telegram from Jack Kelly, who had become chairman of the Philadelphia Democratic Party, asking him to return to Philadelphia at once. The ride home from the Upper Peninsula of Michigan was "a hell of a trek," he recalled, involving a night train to Chicago and then another night on the Broadway Limited to Philadelphia. Two days after receiving the telegram, Dilworth walked into Philadelphia Democratic headquarters. Kelly was not in the office, but his secretary said the plans had been changed. Without Dilworth's knowledge or consent, the party had decided to create a fusion ticket. Democrat Robert C. White would be the candidate for mayor, but a Republican, Lewis M. Stevens, would join him on the ticket, running for DA in Dilworth's place. It was a slap in the face, but there was nothing he could do about it. "So I simply put on my hat and went back to Michigan.... The next time I saw Jack Kelly, I said, 'What the hell happened?' and he said, 'Oh, we changed our mind.' That was all he said. And there was no use complaining, because it was going to get you absolutely nowhere."

Dilworth swallowed his pride and worked for the fusion ticket. The race was even closer than Kelly's had been four years before, with the result decided by 37,000 votes—four percent of the 760,000 cast. But the Republicans remained in power, electing Robert E. Lamberton as mayor. When Lamberton died on August 22, 1941, he was succeeded by Bernard Samuel, a genial ward leader who had worked his way to the presidency of City Council. And Barney, as he was known to one and all, would still be Philadelphia's chief executive in 1947, when Dilworth made his first run for mayor.

CHAPTER TEN

Back at War, Back at Home

On Guadalcanal—and off the wagon

Dick and Ann Dilworth were partying with friends in New York on Sunday, December 7, 1941, when Japanese warplanes attacked Pearl Harbor, the American naval base in Hawaii. Cutting their holiday short, the Dilworths went back to their hotel, packed up, and returned home. When the United States declared war one day later, Dick told his wife: "I can't stand to one side." Forty-three years old and the father of six children and two stepchildren, the busy lawyer was hardly a candidate for the draft. But he was physically fit and always itching for action. With letters, phone calls, and visits to Washington, he persuaded the Marines to take him back in. In April 1942, Dilworth received his commission as a captain in the U.S. Marine Corps and off he went, first to Quantico for training and then to intelligence school. In late summer, he was shipped to the South Pacific.

Dick's departure from Philadelphia did not go unnoticed. Without naming Dilworth, *The Inquirer* published a column concerning a "Marine Corps captain, well known in Philadelphia," who had dashed off to war with his wife's wardrobe rather than his own. "We can't give you dates and names and places for this story," the columnist wrote with tongue firmly in cheek, "because that might constitute information about troop movements—besides, we hope the captain will return safely."

Ann Dilworth took responsibility for the snafu. In a letter after the article ran, she reminded her husband that on the day of his departure, they celebrated with champagne to such an extent that "neither of us could see the bag, much less pack it." As a result, she said, "I found myself with two of your uniforms, ribbons and all, but couldn't find my mules. So I guess I must have put them in your bag as a reminder that you were still married and had six kiddies." (Not to mention the two children by her first marriage.)

Dilworth's undisclosed destination was Guadalcanal, a tiny, tropical island in the Coral Sea with nearly impenetrable jungle and mountains rising as high as 8,000 feet. Japanese troops had occupied the island shortly after their attack on Pearl Harbor, when their forces swept across much of the South Pacific. It was there, on August 7, 1942, that American troops began their first land offensive against the Japanese.

Guadalcanal proved to be one of the longest and most complicated campaigns of the war. "On its outcome," wrote historian David M. Kennedy, "came to depend not only the military balance in the Pacific but the war-morale of the American public. It was, as much as any single engagement could be, a decisive battle." There was a growing sense that, as Kennedy wrote, "in this remote and exotic corner of the South Pacific, men and machines were gathering for a historic showdown." President Roosevelt was gripped by it. He instructed the nation's military chiefs to "make sure that every possible weapon gets into that area to hold Guadalcanal." It would be the first amphibious landing of the war. After storming ashore and gaining a foothold, the Marines held on grimly against furious Japanese counterattacks.

As an intelligence officer assigned to fighter squadrons on Guadalcanal, Dilworth visited the front each week to consult with the ground troops. He wrote *Inquirer* columnist John M. Cummings that conditions for the fighting men were "frightful," and "the stink [was] beyond belief.... It makes the battlefields of the last war seem like sweet-scented violets." He described the typical Japanese soldier as a "rough, tough, tenacious, aggressive, wily fighter" who enters combat "with no holds barred."

"We see repeated examples of their fanaticism which are amazing," Dilworth wrote, "but it will also be their undoing for they can't stand being licked, and just charge in a frenzy." David Kennedy noted that the Americans, too, "learned much about the fiendish arts of jungle fighting" on Guadalcanal. He indicated that they did not always perform honorably: With their "military education came moral coarsening as well. Atrocities on both sides would grow in wretchedness as the war progressed."

Dilworth discovered at first hand the enemies' loyalty to the cause for which they fought. He accompanied the pilot of a seaplane whose orders were to pick up 18 Japanese airmen who had been captured on a nearby island by an Australian "coast watcher" after their planes had been shot down. Though unsung, the coast watchers played an important role in the defense of Australia. Their job was to watch for incoming enemy aircraft and alert the Allies by short-wave radio. Often they hid themselves on hostile islands. That was the case in the rescue mission that Dilworth took part in. The coast watcher radioed that he was holding the Japanese crewmen but that enemy troops were nearby and concealment was difficult. If the Americans didn't pick up the airmen, he said, he would have to kill them. Flying at night, the seaplane made rendezvous with the coast watcher in a small cove. Captain Dilworth, armed only with a pistol, oversaw the loading of the 18 airmen into the seaplane. Flying back to Guadalcanal, the pilot skimmed just above the waters of the Coral Sea to avoid detection.

The Americans hoped to obtain valuable intelligence from the prisoners. That didn't happen. Dilworth said that each of the 18 rose in turn, bowed politely, spoke in tribute of Emperor Hirohito, but refused to answer questions. Four hanged themselves. The others were shipped off to Australia where they were imprisoned for the balance of the war.

The fighting was fierce on Guadalcanal, with the U.S. suffering some 1,600 combat deaths and the Japanese nearly 15,000. And in the dripping equatorial jungle, bacterial diseases raged as well; everyone was affected by the conditions, and 9,000 Japanese died of disease. As the Marines' position on Guadalcanal improved, Dilworth's physical condition deteriorated. He lost weight and suffered from jungle rot on his arms and legs. He developed boils, prickly heat, and sciatica.

Dick wrote frequently to Ann and she to him. Her letters are full of concern for him, but are also laced with tweaking humor, news, and gossip. "It's god-awful not knowing where you are and how you are," Ann wrote in October 1942. "How is the leg? For heaven's sake, remember your six kiddies and don't forget they were your idea." In one letter, Ann sympathized: "Sorry to hear that sciatica is worse and that you have boils and prickly heat." But in another, she lectured him: "You had no business getting yourself out there anyhow."

"The big news around Philadelphia," she wrote not long after Dilworth left town, "is the marriage of Lira Harriman to Bill Elkins. . . . The old gal wastes no time apparently. She has a hunk of ice that is the envy of all and they have purchased the Baird House on Rittenhouse Square." In a letter from Palm Beach, Ann advised Dick that winter there "would not be complete without one row." She said the place was "buzzing with gossip that the Ladds have split up. Needless to say," she added, "they have been having fisticuffs for some time now and I have tried to keep at a distance as the pots and pans fly fast and hit hard. What with

Joan in a morose frame of mind and Bill flatulent as ever, it was bound to happen."

Also from Palm Beach, Ann informed Dick that Louis Hill, her son from her first marriage, "took a tumble for Patsy Pulitzer when down here." Ann said she was delighted, "as it's about time he thought of girls as something more than just crashing bores." She noted that Louis, who was then a heavyweight boxer at Harvard, planned to follow his stepfather into the Marine Corps. Hill, whose admiration for Dilworth never wavered, did in fact join the Marines. In another of her letters to Guadalcanal, Ann wrote Dilworth that Louis had said: "You know, Mommy, Dick is like George Washington, Hamilton and Jefferson. The kind of men that made America."

But Ann didn't just stay home writing letters. She did her part for the war effort by training as a welder in Florida. In November 1942, there were three other women in her welding class: "Hilda, a Swede and a grandmother of four or five; Bella, Irish and married to a truck driver; and Tillie, a big, fine-looking girl married to a sailor and grows her own corn."

"They call me 'Honey' and feel sorry for me because at the moment, as a welder, I stink," Ann confessed. However, she must have shown rapid improvement for on December 6, 1942, she wrote: "I have graduated the acetylene welding class. You will be amazed as I was to learn that I finished sooner by a month than anyone else who has taken the course." Ann said she might take up electric welding to qualify for shipyard work. The head of the welding school, she said, "wants me to go to an advanced class in Miami at which I will be paid $90 to $125 a month." But she had no car and public transportation was limited. Commuting from Palm Beach would be difficult. "There is no such thing as a seat left in any bus, so will have to think it over," she wrote. Her welding career ended soon thereafter, and in February 1943, Ann moved back to her parents' apartment at 420 Park Avenue in Manhattan.

Meanwhile, after six bloody months of battle on Guadalcanal, the Japanese were finally routed in February 1943, and the Americans could claim their first land victory. Dilworth, his jungle rot worsening, was ordered back to the United States. He underwent further training in radar tactics and techniques and was placed in command of an air warning squadron. There were to be 16 such squadrons using radar to assist ground troops assaulting enemy positions from the sea. But as the war wound down, the squadrons were disbanded.

Dilworth's age was catching up with him anyway. On August 28, 1944, he marked his 46th birthday. The following month, he left the service with a Silver Star, the nation's third-highest military award. He was cited for "gallantry and intrepidity in action." On October 6, 1944, Lieutenant General A.A. Vandegrift, the Marine Corps commandant, wrote a personal letter to Major Dilworth: "The Marine Corps will never forget how badly we needed you immediately after the attack on Pearl Harbor and how promptly and unselfishly you left the duties of civil life and offered us your services. Today the Corps is at its peak of combat efficiency, and to you goes a full share of the credit for making it so. Your patriotism and your fine devotion to duty have been an inspiration to the gallant young Marines of the present generation. Please accept my personal and official thanks for the part which you have played, and best wishes for your continued success in civil life."

After that marvelous sendoff from the nation's top Marine, Richardson Dilworth returned to the practice of law in Philadelphia. Just as Belleau Wood became part of the Marine Corps' storied history, so did Guadalcanal. Dilworth was one of the few Marines who took part in both epic battles.

Ironically, the end of the worldwide conflict in 1945 marked the start of perhaps the most troubled time in Dilworth's life. Recalling this period in a 1972 interview, he said that all the excitement of his military service had "vanished" with the conclusion of hostilities. "I started drinking really hard and really steadily." He referred to what he went through as "sort of a male change-of-life." In college and as a young lawyer, he had engaged in binge drinking at parties and on weekends, but had always sobered up in time for work. In this postwar despondency, he seemed headed for serious alcoholism. His youngest son, Dickie, said that Dilworth's drinking was "a terrible strain on the whole family. If he kept going the way he was, he would have drunk himself to death in a few years." Deborah Dilworth Bishop described her father's drinking as "the gorilla in the room. We didn't discuss it, but everybody knew he had a problem." Dickie, who said that his father came out of the war as "somebody who was really lost," believed that his "greatest achievement" lay in eventually overcoming his "tremendous drinking problem."

At his wife's urging in early 1946, Dilworth saw a neurologist, who told him he had gotten himself into bad shape and needed to "dry out" for 10 days at the University of Pennsylvania Hospital. On his release, he resumed drinking. The neurologist threw up his hands and told him to see someone he described as "the best in the city," Francis T. Chambers, who specialized in treating alcoholics at the Institute of Pennsylvania Hospital in West Philadelphia.

Dilworth found "Dutch" Chambers to be an "extraordinary fellow, one of the finest, nicest, most intelligent men I ever saw." Chambers had himself suffered from alcoholism; after recovering his health, he decided to devote his life to helping those with drinking problems. Dick, who went to "Dutch" for about six months, said that the doctor "really straightened me out."

After his time with Chambers, Dilworth did "postgraduate work" with a psychiatrist whom he saw three times a week for two months at the Institute of Pennsylvania Hospital. After that, he said, "I never got to the point where I had to go back." He acknowledged in 1972, however, that "every once in a while I'll go for two or three days on a fairly heavy drinking schedule."

Of course, these benders were of grave concern to his family. His daughter, Deborah, recalled that on the night in 1954 that she came out as a debutante at a ball in Philadelphia, her father got drunk and made a spectacle of himself. Although humiliated, she did not blame him: "It was an illness and I understood. He had this terrible demon that he fought. I just adored him." Dilworth himself said that he often felt the need to drink because of its "great releasing effect on me." And others spoke of his low tolerance for alcohol and his occasional binge drinking. There was never a hint, however, of alcohol compromising his performance at work or on the campaign trail.

Dickie Dilworth said that his father was encouraged by "Dutch" Chambers to get into politics, and, once involved, "he effectively stopped drinking." Harold E. Kohn, Dilworth's longtime law partner, made a point with which others agreed: "Politics and war took the place of drinking. They were the alcohol that made life interesting for him."

CHAPTER ELEVEN

The Machine Shivers
Graft, suicide, and the fat sultan

Both nationally and locally, prospects for the Democratic Party appeared bleak in 1947. Republicans had seized control of both houses of the U.S. Congress in 1946, and President Harry S Truman's chances of holding the White House in 1948 seemed slim. The little man from Missouri occupied the nation's highest office only because of the death of the much-admired Franklin D. Roosevelt in April 1945.

In Philadelphia, the GOP's iron grip on city government remained unchallenged. Over the previous six decades—stretching back to 1884—the Democrats had never gotten a mayor elected, while the Republicans took the office 16 times. And most of those races were almost comically lopsided. Aggregating all the votes cast for mayor from 1900 through 1944 shows the Republicans taking a staggering 68 percent. And a number of elections, exemplifying corrupt machine politics at the peak of hubris, ended with the Republican candidate receiving 90 percent of the vote.

As the 1947 mayoral election approached, the Democratic Party was in a shambles. When Congressman Michael J. Bradley became chairman of the Democratic City Committee in 1946, he discovered that the committee had just $186 in its treasury. The office rent of $1,000 was due within a week, and the committee's monthly payroll of $2,500 had to be met shortly thereafter. Bradley told Walter Phillips in an oral history interview that he and Bill Teefy, the committee's treasurer, bailed out the party using their personal funds, tiding it over until the Jefferson–Jackson Day dinner in May 1946 brought in enough money to pay them back and create a small cushion.

With their cash crisis eased, the Democrats needed someone to offer at least token opposition to Mayor Bernard Samuel, who was certain to be overwhelmingly favored for reelection. Bradley called a meeting of the party's policy committee on July 8, 1947, to choose a candidate. Interest was expressed by just two men, and both seemed to be nonentities. One was Joseph Sharfsin, a veteran party man. The other was Richardson Dilworth. He had enjoyed success as a trial lawyer, but he'd been soiled by his scandalous divorce and consequently spurned by much of the city's legal fraternity and social establishment. And his only previous run for office had been an embarrassment.

In the subsequent balloting, the policy committee's 14 ward leaders split down the middle—seven for Sharfsin and seven for Dilworth. Bradley then broke the tie, casting the deciding vote for Dilworth. "That was the best vote I ever cast in my life," he later told Phillips. The party's choice was unexpected. "Although Dilworth's name had been mentioned," wrote *The Inquirer*, "his final selection came as a surprise as it was generally reported he would not run." And some Democrats in the inner circle, Bradley noted, "were not kindly disposed toward Dick Dilworth." The conservative *Philadelphia Dispatch* pictured the nominee's task as thankless: "The truth of the matter is, none of those other Democrats would touch the nomination with a ten-foot pole."

In his folksy *Inquirer* column, John M. Cummings, who had corresponded with Dilworth when the Marine Corps officer was on Guadalcanal, joked about his apparently hopeless race: "Why in tarnation does Richardson Dilworth want to be mayor? Now here you have a fine lawyer in good standing at the bar angling for a job that could only bring headaches and heartaches and hot water for the feet if he should be lucky enough to win. But it takes more than luck for a Democrat to be elected mayor." Cummings noted that Guadalcanal had been a "tough spot, even for a tough Marine. But dislodging Barney Samuel from City Hall—well, Richardson, you ain't seen nothin' yet."

Actually, Philadelphia hadn't seen anything until Dilworth started campaigning. Instead of delivering set speeches in banquet halls, he went directly into the row-house neighborhoods to exchange views with working people of whatever political orientation. The idea came from Walter Phillips, who was a close friend of Joe Clark's. While bicycling around town, Phillips had observed that in this period before the advent of television, Philadelphians often sat on their front stoops and porches in the evening, chinning with their neighbors until dark. To Phillips they represented a great potential audience for a mayoral candidate. At lunch with Dilworth in July 1947, he suggested that the candidate reach out for that audience. And the candidate did just that.

At first, the crowds were small and the newspapers paid little attention. When the Hegeman String Band agreed to serenade Dilworth without pay seven nights a week, interest picked up and attendance grew. The rallies became family affairs. "All eight kids participated in the '47 campaign," Dilworth's youngest son, Dickie, recalled years later. He was 10 years old at the time and, unlike his father, did not much enjoy the street-corner scene. "Dad would speak from a sound truck," Dickie remembered. "We'd get a crowd with a little string band, which is why I hate string bands to this day. And the crowds were sometimes hostile…a lot of heckling…which I think Dad kind of enjoyed in a way, being a trial lawyer, a very aggressive trial lawyer."

Ann Dilworth, who was "totally enmeshed" in her husband's career, often joined him on the sound truck. "She didn't even enjoy politics," her son noted, "but she recognized after the war that if he didn't get into politics, the alternative was not going to be good. She saw it as the only career that he could really enjoy and make something out of." Small in stature but fiercely combative in defending her husband, Ann often handled the microphone for questions from the crowd. When the sound truck was parked outside a taproom one night, a heckler drew Dilworth's attention. "Please shut up," he shouted. "You've got all night to make a fool of yourself." With that, the heckler ran to the truck and started climbing a ladder to the platform where Dilworth and his wife were standing. Ann promptly slugged him with her loaded handbag, knocking him off the ladder and ending his assault. At another rally in a hostile ward, a man who didn't like Dilworth got his hands on the mike and refused to let go. Ann rammed the microphone into his teeth and sent him back on his heels. "She was marvelous with that mike," Dick told Joe Alex Morris. "A lot of people tried to louse us up, but none ever got the best of her."

With Joe Clark as his campaign manager, Dilworth ran on a pledge to clean up what he saw as rampant corruption in the city government. At his street-corner stops, he denounced graft in the police department and shakedowns in the water department. A bookmaker was blatantly taking horseracing bets in the corridors of City Hall, he charged, and in one ward, slot machines had been installed with permission of the mayor's son. According to Dilworth, business leaders knew of the corruption but were silenced by the GOP.

As the candidate hammered away, his crowds increased and the newspapers began to pay attention. One night, an estimated 12,000 people surged against police lines to hear him speak. The Republicans took notice and fought back. They persuaded 10 prominent business leaders to state publicly that Dilworth's charges could do "irreparable harm to the community as a whole." He angrily responded that eight of those business leaders lived in the suburbs "where they see to it that taxes are low and their government is good." He accused them of leaving the city to "get away from the gang they now urge Philadelphians to support."

Dilworth spent much of the campaign attacking the city's Republican bosses. Austin Meehan, a wealthy Irish Catholic paving contractor who had been elected county sheriff in 1943, was one of the most influential men in the GOP. The candidate accused him of controlling gambling activities in the northeast section of the city and making sure the police looked the other way. Meehan lashed back, but when Dilworth challenged him to a debate, Meehan's advisers, fearful that the sharp-tongued Democrat would embarrass their man, convinced him to decline.

Dilworth staged an empty-chair debate at the Academy of Music before an audience of 4,000 people on October 24. After reiterating his charges against Meehan, he accused the Samuel Administration of tapping his telephone line and having his wife shadowed. "This is the kind of thing that was done in Nazi Germany," he noted, by implication comparing Barney Samuel to Hitler. "This is the way our cowardly, corrupt Republican leaders react to criticism." Years later, he described Samuel as "a nice little guy." And then he added: "I don't mean he wouldn't cut your balls off. But he was always a nice, pleasant little guy."

In the final week of the campaign, Dilworth remained on the attack. He said the GOP, in an unprecedented move, was paying people eight dollars a day to visit the wards and drum up Republican votes. "These are the desperate tactics of a rotting machine that is falling apart."

That was his final salvo. Despite his nonstop assault on the entrenched Republicans and his call for an end to municipal malfeasance, the newspapers were unimpressed. *The Bulletin* conceded that Dilworth had conducted "a very lively campaign" and had succeeded in "stirring up the animals, some of which were torpid." But the paper's editors left open the question of whether his campaign was as "constructive as it might be...regarding the larger interest of Philadelphia." The implied answer seemed to be no.

Just before the election, *The Inquirer* reported that Democratic leaders were abandoning Dilworth. Some of those running for office pledged to back the rest of the Republican ticket if GOP leaders would support them, the paper claimed, adding that "the apparent collapse of the Democratic vote drive was heavily damaging to Dilworth."

When the ballots were counted in November 1947, Samuel had beaten Dilworth by more than 92,000 votes out of 734,000 cast, an edge of 56 to 44 percent. On election night, Samuel's victory margin left Dilworth and Clark terribly dejected. They feared that the reform movement was dead before it had truly begun. Then the two men went to the roof of the hotel where they had received the returns. And there the mood was electric. "We saw all these volunteers up there and they were jubilant," recalled Dilworth. The election was lost, but they were seeing the future. "Joe and I didn't know anything about analyzing returns but, by God, these kids did. They pointed out that they'd done a hell of a job in many city wards, and the fight was just beginning. And that's what caused us to really keep moving."

The Republican administration had withstood Dilworth's accusations during the campaign, but shortly after the election it became obvious that his charges of widespread corruption in the city government were not figments of his imagination. And, ironically, Mayor Samuel himself helped bring the wrongdoing to light.

During the campaign, Samuel had agreed to a pay raise for city workers. He knew the city had no money to fund the increase unless he raised taxes or cut services. But he couldn't do either. The mayor had made a campaign pledge not to raise taxes, and he wasn't going to take the political risk of cutting services in the election season. His solution was to agree to the pay raise while promising to appoint an advisory committee that would look through city finances and find a way to fund the increase. The committee was to go to work right after the election. Samuel assumed the committee would make the obvious recommendation: raise taxes. At that point, it would be politically safe to do so.

To limit the extent of the inquiry, the mayor gave the committee a small budget and just three months to complete its work. But he made the mistake of appointing to the committee, along with a handful of party hacks, some responsible citizens. The so-called Committee of Fifteen was composed of five councilmen and 10 persons representing various civic groups. Taking the job seriously, the committee hired a young Republican reformer from the Bureau for Municipal Research, Robert K. Sawyer, as its executive director. Then they started digging. At the end of three months, instead of rubber-stamping the pay raise and announcing that higher taxes were necessary to pay for it, as Samuel expected, the committee reported that there was plenty of fat that could be cut from the city budget. They had found so many inefficient and improper practices, they said, that without raising taxes or reducing services, they estimated the city could decrease its expenditures by two million dollars and increase revenues by five million. They asked for more time to conduct a fuller assessment.

Samuel would have liked to shut down the committee, but the response to their report from the newspapers and the public made that move untenable. He was compelled to give the committee eight more months to finish their work. Soon after resuming, they found evidence of graft in the Department of Supplies and Purchases. It came out that the department had not filed its required annual reports for the previous seven years and that $40 million in expenditures were left unaccounted for in that time span. The department's director, Charles H. Grakelow, a friend of the mayor, was arrested and charged with forgery, embezzlement, falsifying city records, and illegally obtaining city business for his florist shop. Grakelow was removed, but got off with a $1,500 fine. Sawyer and other committee members kept plugging away.

Their next target was the city's wage tax office, which was failing to collect about 20 percent of the wage taxes due each year. The mayor was informed that with 100 percent collection, he could increase the pay of city employees without raising other taxes. At this point, the committee wasn't making specific accusations of corruption in the office, but the heat was on. William C. Foss, chief of the amusement tax division, felt it. When the city controller asked to see his books, Foss suspected—wrongly, it turned out—that the Committee of Fifteen was on his trail. On May 22, 1948, Foss hanged himself in the basement of his home. He left a suicide note explicitly describing how the shortage of more than $200,000 in the amusement tax office had been siphoned off and divvied up over the years. Foss named seven city employees as his co-conspirators. In the end, only one went to prison—the courts held that Foss' note was hearsay.

Dilworth had lost the election but his message had gained traction, and he continued to be active in denouncing the corrupt Republican machine. As it happened, the summer of 1948 was the perfect season for a Philadelphian to receive national exposure. Philadelphia became the nation's political nerve center that year as the Republicans, the Democrats, and the Progressive Party all brought their conventions to town. It was the first time in American history that one city had hosted three major political conventions. Writers Rebecca West and Clare Booth Luce spent time in Philadelphia. So did broadcasters Lowell Thomas and Edward R. Murrow, and politicians such as Robert A. Taft and Arthur H. Vandenberg. And an army of television technicians provided the first TV coverage of political conventions.

Philadelphia spent $200,000 wooing the conventions and received favorable publicity. Paul Gallico, the noted columnist, hailed the host city's hospitality. "After five years of being snubbed, snarled at, abused or ignored by the frozenpusses embalmed behind New York hotel desks," Gallico wrote in *The New York Journal-American*, "one has a tendency to burst into tears the first time one is exposed to the kind and courteous treatment by the clerks in Philadelphia."

The Republican delegates arrived in Philadelphia in late June, fully expecting to nominate the next President of the United States. New York's governor, Thomas E. Dewey, had lost the 1944 election to Franklin D. Roosevelt, but he was expected to defeat FDR's unpopular successor. Dewey won the GOP nomination on the third ballot at Philadelphia's Convention Hall, and the Republicans departed after filling the city's hotels—the average rate for double-room occupancy was six dollars—and spending about five million dollars in all.

Two weeks later, the Democrats poured in to pick Harry Truman for a full term as president. In November, he would stun the nation with his surprising triumph over Dewey. But at the time of the nominating convention, he was out of favor and his party was split. Henry A. Wallace headed the Progressives, who offered a leftist alternative to the mainstream Democrats. Wallace had broken away to start a third party after Truman dismissed him as Secretary of Commerce for attacking U.S. foreign policy toward the Soviet Union and denouncing Great Britain as an agent of imperialism.

Meanwhile, a fight over a civil rights plank in the Democratic Party platform led to a walkout by Southern delegates, and Dilworth was in the thick of it. Not running for office himself in 1948, he served as floor leader for Minneapolis mayor Hubert H. Humphrey, who made an impassioned appeal for adoption of the civil rights measure. Joining in support of Humphrey's effort was the Philadelphia chapter of Americans for Democratic Action, an anti-Communist liberal group whose members ranged from labor leaders and ex-Socialists to intellectuals—and patricians such as Joe Clark and Dick Dilworth.

ADA's Philadelphia chapter had been formed in March 1947, two months after the national organization's founding in Washington. It evolved from a group known as the Philadelphia Citizens Political Action Committee, which had been organized in 1944, but split into pro-Communist and anti-Communist factions two years later.

The anti-Communists then formed Philadelphia's ADA chapter with a pledge not to support "adherents of any totalitarian philosophy of government." At the time of the Democratic convention, the chapter opened an around-the-clock headquarters near the site of the meeting. At two o'clock one morning when Humphrey was debating whether or not to address the convention, two of his aides went to the ADA's office. Emily Ehle, who was the chapter's executive director, gave this account of what happened next:

> "The Humphrey staff people indicated that his staff was almost equally divided on the issue with one side claiming that the speech would make him a national figure and the other side claiming that it would be national suicide if Truman were not elected. The two staff men, working on the assumption that ADA had the ability to influence Humphrey's decision, tried to persuade the ADA staff that they should suggest to Humphrey that he abandon the speech. ADA refused to intercede, the civil rights plank was won, and ADA achieved a cockiness that sustained it for years to come."

Humphrey's role in the 1948 Democratic convention in Philadelphia did, in fact, launch his career as a U.S. senator from Minnesota and, ultimately, as vice president. By contrast, Dilworth's participation as floor leader never got much attention. But his work with the local ADA, which he headed in 1948, linked him to Philadelphians of high social status, some of whom had previously rejected him because of his scandalous divorce. In *Hard-Core Liberals*, a sociological analysis of ADA's Philadelphia chapter, Harold Libros noted that the agency "played an unquestioned and vital role in enlisting aid for the successful campaigns of its two charismatic leaders," Dilworth and Clark.

To keep up the pressure on the embattled Samuel Administration, Dilworth went back on the campaign trail in 1949, running for city treasurer. His ally, Joseph Sill Clark, sought the office of city controller. At street-corner rallies, they slugged away at corruption in City Hall. Critics dismissed them as "Dilly and Silly," but their message that it was time for a change was getting through. William F. Meade, the tough, shrewd boss of Philadelphia's downtown district, who had been elected chairman of the Republican City Committee in 1948, responded by going on the offensive. Raising the hobgoblin of Bolshevism, he charged that "Communist Party-liners" were backing Dilworth and Clark. Americans for Democratic Action, Meade claimed, was "infiltrated with communists and loaded with socialists." In that tense time before Stalin's worst crimes were exposed, the Soviet Union did, in fact, have its supporters in the United States. However, Meade's allegations were wide of the mark. ADA's Philadelphia chapter had broken publicly with an earlier communist element. And Dick Dilworth did not take kindly to having his loyalty impugned. Without knocking, he stormed into Meade's private office, demanding that he name "one single communist or Red associated with the ADA."

"We will," responded Meade.

"When?" shouted Dilworth.

"At the proper time."

But Meade never did give a name. Instead, he denounced Dilworth as a "psychopathic madman." Dilworth replied equably that he was "invariably referred to as a madman" when his allegations against the Republicans could not be denied.

Both *The Bulletin* and *The Inquirer* had opposed Dilworth's run for mayor in 1947, but now they came to his defense. "To represent the Democratic candidate as tainted with Communism is the height of absurdity," wrote *The Bulletin*. "Such tactics are not likely to fool even an intelligent child." *The Inquirer* declared that "Philadelphians, afflicted by the tyranny of the Republican monopoly-machine, have the right, the duty—and the opportunity—to overthrow their oppressors." The paper charged that City Hall crooks had stolen from the municipal treasury, exacted illegal fees, conspired to cheat taxpayers, and neglected their duties.

Taking a different view, the *Philadelphia Daily News*—whose publisher, Lee Ellmaker, was a fierce foe of Dilworth—sided with Meade. "We do not believe that Richardson Dilworth is a Communist," opined the tabloid paper, "but we do believe he will take the aid of any Communist who wants to vote for him, or preach for him, or give him any help."

The main event in the hot summer of 1949 was a reprise of the debate between Dilworth and Sheriff Austin Meehan—this time with Meehan in attendance. The two men appeared before a capacity crowd in Philadelphia's red-plush Academy of Music, and their debate was beamed to a radio and television audience estimated at 200,000. With the two men hurling wild epithets at each other, the heavily publicized encounter on July 12 degenerated into what *The Bulletin* termed "one of the rowdiest exhibitions in Philadelphia's political history."

The raucous partisans, evenly divided in the staid music hall, interrupted the speakers with hoots and catcalls that the newspaper likened to "a crowd at a wrestling match." Dilworth, who had previously labeled the 250-pound sheriff the "fat sultan," accused Meehan of running a dishonest political machine in Northeast Philadelphia based on numbers-writing and horse-betting. City police, Dilworth claimed, were paid to look the other way as 10 syndicates took in "no less than $100,000 a day in bets." He named names and said the chief clerk in the sheriff's office administered the system.

Meehan dropped any pretense of civility, calling Dilworth a "chronic, dishonest liar" and a "political faker." Then, probing his opponent's personal life, he termed him a "perjurer" regarding his Reno divorce in 1935. Meehan argued, accurately, that although Dilworth had signed an affidavit, on August 6, 1935, that his wife divorced him on grounds of cruel and barbarous treatment, he had in fact been divorced in Philadelphia the day before on grounds of adultery. "And not only that," said Meehan, also accurately, "you ran off to Havana, Cuba, deserting your wife and four small children."

However valid the comments, they drew sharp criticism from *The Bulletin* as an invasion of Dilworth's privacy. "Fair-minded listeners felt only disgust," the newspaper stated, "at the sheriff's undertaking to make a political issue of his opponent's marital affairs, and at the unspeakably bad taste of his disregard of common decency in so doing."

In addition to slinging mud, both Meehan and Dilworth spoke candidly about themselves. Meehan, who was immensely popular with the GOP faithful, described his lack of education. "I only went to the sixth grade in public school, when I had to go out and work as a water boy," he told the throng. "I graduated from water boy to a laborer. My life is an open and honest one, and I am proud of it." He conceded that he was fat but said that his patrician foe was the sultan.

Dilworth, who enjoyed many of the material advantages that Meehan lacked, related what his father had told him on his graduation from Yale law school: "If all you are going to do with the great opportunities that you have had in this country is go out and pile up a little money, join some respectable church, and play golf on Sundays, then you never had any right to these privileges. If you can't and won't contribute something more to the community in which you live, then they ought to have gone to somebody who understands what it really means." He had taken his father's words to heart, he promised, and now he was being tested to see "whether I have got the courage and ability" to make Philadelphia "one of the really great cities of the world, both materially and, even more important, spiritually."

Dilworth also spoke of his wife's unflinching support. He described how one night during his run for mayor in 1947, when attacks on him were at fever pitch, he asked her if she was sure the fight was worth the effort. Ann, he said, had walked to a desk, picked up a Bible, and pointed to a line in the Book of Ruth. "And I will never forget this as long as I live," he told the audience. "She read the line, 'Whither thou goest, I will go.' And then she added a phrase of her own: 'Even to the end.' " Dilworth promised his supporters that he, too, would go on, "even to the end."

On election day, 79 percent of the city's voters went to the polls. Despite the Republicans' big lead in registration, their candidates took a shellacking. Dilworth, winning his first race at the age of 52, trounced a political neophyte, William Seiler, by more than 111,000 votes to become city treasurer. Clark, 49, beat William Linton Nelson, an investment banker, by almost as much in the race for city controller. Two other Democrats were elected coroner and register of wills.

The Democrats' sweep of the four "row offices" marked the first real crack in the Republican armor in Philadelphia. *Time* magazine noted that "after the exposure of graft, extortion, and embezzlement in nearly every city office, the smell from City Hall became too much even for torpid Philadelphians." *The Inquirer*, supporting the liberal reformers for the first time, said it wasn't a matter of party labels, but of "trying to redeem the city from those who had sunk it in the mire." For Dilworth, the victory had been essentially symbolic. Once elected, he announced that he didn't see any real need for the position of city treasurer, and he recommended that it be abolished: "There's no sense in paying me or anyone else $15,400 a year to serve as nothing more than a glorified cashier."

The fallout from the work of the Committee of Fifteen—and several other local and national investigations—continued to mount. On June 21, 1949, Ernest V. Wrigley, 71, the Philadelphia Water Department's superintendent of distribution, had killed himself by slashing his wrists in Fairmount Park. Wrigley, a principal witness in an investigation of the department, had admitted a racket in fee collection going back 17 years. The following summer, on August 29, 1950, Willard A. Severin, 58, a city plumbing inspector, leaped 185 feet to his death from the Henry Avenue Bridge over Wissahickon Creek. He was out on $1,000 bail at the time, facing charges of extorting $377.

Less than two months later, on October 17, 1950, a fourth city employee committed suicide. Police Inspector Craig D. Ellis, 51, commander of Philadelphia's police vice squad for 10 years, had been ordered to appear before a federal grand jury investigating the rackets. Hours later, Ellis drove to a remote area near Media, a county seat west of the city, and shot himself to death with his .32 caliber service revolver. On the back of his $169.37 semi-monthly paycheck, Ellis, who was in poor health, had scrawled a suicide note: "I have failed as a leader. My wife did not know of my laxity. . . . I pray God will help anyone I have caused regret." The note was kept secret for three weeks, leading Dilworth to suspect collusion with local racketeers. "The suppression of the Craig Ellis note," he charged, "shows the extent of the corruption of the Republican organization not only in Philadelphia, but reaching up as high as the state police." Two more police suicides would follow in 1951.

*   *   *

In 1950, Dilworth took a leave of absence without pay as city treasurer to run for Pennsylvania's governorship. His nomination was engineered by Pittsburgh mayor David Lawrence, who held vast power in Pennsylvania's Democratic Party. Convinced that his organization could easily deliver the western part of the state on election day, Lawrence wanted a candidate from Philadelphia to secure the pivotal vote in the east.

Lawrence picked Dilworth over Judge Michael Musmanno, an Italian American from Pittsburgh. Musmanno had wide support in the west and a high profile, having been a defense lawyer in the widely publicized Sacco and Vanzetti murder trial, a judge at the Nuremberg war crimes trials after World War II, and a noted novelist. He also happened to be a loose cannon and a virulent anti-Communist. To keep Musmanno from staging a primary battle against Dilworth, Lawrence slotted him in as the candidate for lieutenant governor. The Philadelphia liberal was extremely leery of joining forces with a red-baiter, but Lawrence convinced him that it wouldn't be a big issue.

Dilworth campaigned all over the state with a small caravan of loyal supporters and often with two or more of his children. His tiny cadre included Natalie Saxe, who served as advance agent and would remain with him throughout the rest of his career; former paratrooper John T. Hansen, who operated the speaker's sound truck; and insurance executive William B. Churchman, who handled publicity and served as the candidate's driver.

Churchman, who met Dilworth when both were serving with the Marines in World War II, took a leave of absence from his insurance agency and signed on with the campaign for $100 a week. "I loved every minute of it," he recalled. "I drove and phoned in stories as we crisscrossed the state." He said they made as many as 10 stops a day. Churchman estimated that the entourage traveled 20,000 miles between July 26 and November 3.

The opponent was John S. Fine, Republican leader of Luzerne County. As was usual with Dilworth, the fur flew. "There is no more corrupt political machine," he charged, "than the one presided over by John Fine. No racket is too low for this machine to protect—provided the price is high enough."

Dilworth knew the lay of the land in Fine's hometown of Nanticoke, having successfully defended the dramatic libel case brought by its mayor a decade earlier. Now he used the knowledge as a cudgel. In Nanticoke, he said on the stump: "...policemen on duty and in uniform visit every small businessman and merchant and collect the political assessments levied by John Fine's machine. In Nanticoke, it has been the practice to require an applicant for a teaching position to pay half the first year's salary for an appointment. In Nanticoke, the mayor represents the two leading slot machine operators, and heaven help any member of the police force who attempts to interfere with either of these gentlemen or any of the gangsters who work for them." He also alleged that Luzerne County's district attorney served as "the superintendent of gambling" for Fine's machine.

John Fine struck back, labeling Dilworth "a foul snooper who, with a flamboyant wave of his hand, screams from automobile tops with Hitlerism technique to tell a lie, often enough, with a hope that some people may believe it....Here is a man who has gone around the state vilifying me while at the same time, in his unbalanced zeal, insulting thousands of our citizens, including our school teachers and virtually everyone else in the Commonwealth. Irresponsible utterances flow from him like the waters of Niagara."

Dilworth's running mate did turn out to be a drag on his campaign. While the candidate was combating Fine, Michael Musmanno was going full tilt after Communists and fellow travelers—just as Senator Joseph McCarthy had begun to do earlier that year. By September, according to David Lawrence's biographer, Michael P. Weber, "Musmanno and Dilworth were conducting independent campaigns whose pronouncements often contradicted each other." Lawrence tried to muzzle the judge, but had no success. "The feisty candidate," Weber wrote, "spoke when and where he wanted."

Conditions in the state also began breaking the Republicans' way. Earlier in the year, the economy had been stagnant and unemployment stood at nearly 10 percent, providing leverage for Dilworth, who could tie Fine to the Republican incumbent, James H. Duff. But in June, with the start of the Korean War, orders for munitions and materiel flooded into the state. As election day approached, the economy was thriving and unemployment had plummeted to 4.7 percent.

In the end, Dilworth lost the governorship in 1950. The Republicans burnished their record in gubernatorial races, notching their 15th victory against one defeat in a string stretching back to 1895. But the 86,000-vote margin—out of some 3.5 million votes cast, an edge of two percent—was the slimmest Republican victory in 20 years. And the Democrats had come that close despite having 840,000 fewer registered voters in the state. Also, Dilworth had easily outpolled Fine in Philadelphia, thus becoming the first Democratic gubernatorial candidate since the Civil War to carry the longtime GOP stronghold. At last there was some hope among Democrats that the tide was beginning to turn.

CHAPTER TWELVE

The Reformers Arrive

*Born rich, reared gently,
they turned out hard as nails*

Early in 1951, it became evident that Joseph Clark and Richardson Dilworth would try to capture the top jobs in City Hall come November. What was unknown at the outset was the ticket. Who would run for mayor and who for district attorney? Dilworth biographer Joe Alex Morris wrote that long before the election the two reformers, so alike in family background yet so different in personality, "took a look at the staggering ruins of the City Hall machine and talked about what to do next." According to Morris, Dilworth told Clark that he should seek the mayoralty. And Clark responded, "What about you? You're the one who has the most support in the Democratic organization; what are you going to do?" Dilworth assured Clark: "As far as I'm concerned, you should run and I'll stick with you."

Dilworth's pledge in this account is consistent with what he had told his aides earlier. Natalie Saxe, his longtime assistant, said she heard her employer say, on election night in 1950, that he lost the governorship to John Fine and that he would "stick to his commitment to back Clark for mayor." Bill Churchman, the insurance man who worked for the campaign, heard something similar. He said that when he knocked on Dilworth's door that same night, the candidate said that although he had lost the governorship, he would run for district attorney in 1951, and Clark for mayor.

One person who strongly disapproved of this arrangement was Ann Dilworth. Dickie remembered that his mother had been "very upset" about it. She didn't like Joseph Clark, and she didn't want her husband to step aside for him. "The problem that Mother had in politics," he said, "was that she took everything personally. Whereas Dad didn't. There was going to be another election and you'd get going for that. You didn't worry about the last one. But Mother never could do that and she would form, during an election, real hates. And after the election, she wouldn't be able to drop it. She took all these things very personally."

Natalie Saxe said that Ann Dilworth's role in her husband's career was "enormous and extraordinary. She was a woman who was able to keep her husband's attention as well as respect, and there was nothing that I know of in Dick's life that he didn't solicit her views on," Saxe told Walter Phillips. "He, by and large, followed her advice, though not always, and they did disagree quite violently on one or two people in my experience with them—one of them being Joe Clark. Ann had no time for Joe. I think it may have partly been because she felt that Joe went out of his way to upstage Dick. She felt that Dick was the father of the reform movement in Philadelphia. [That he] should have been mayor in 1951 as well as going on to governor or whatever else he wanted. And that he was blocked in this by his commitment to Joe—a commitment she felt should never have been made. She felt that, were it reversed, Joe would have violated a similar commitment."

Natalie Saxe herself was hardly neutral. She said that Clark made her feel "very much like a paid flunky," while with Dilworth she was treated "rather more like a human being." Noting that Ann "very much wanted" Dick to run for mayor in 1951, Saxe added: "I did, too." But she said Dick had made a commitment, "and it didn't cross his mind to dishonor it." Beyond that, Saxe said Dilworth considered the office of district attorney to be a very good springboard for governor. And she added: "He always wanted to be governor more than he wanted any single thing."

By contrast, Joe Clark's lifelong ambition was to serve not as mayor or governor, but as a senator. In an interview with Walter Phillips, Clark stated: "It had been my ambition since I was 11 years old, believe it or not, to be a United States senator. It sounds incredible but it's true. American history was always my favorite subject." And Dilworth remembered that when the two met as teenagers in the summer, "Joe was always talking about going to the United States Senate. It was a weird thing. That was a passion with him. That's what intrigued him and what he enjoyed."

Stewart Alsop, the Washington columnist, took the measure of Clark in an article entitled "The Paradox of Gentleman Joe" that was published in *The Saturday Evening Post* when Clark was serving his first term in the U.S. Senate in

1957. "Joe Clark, Pennsylvania's new senator, was born rich, reared gently, and turned out hard as nails.... If he sets his sights on the Democratic presidential nomination, the fight will be fun to watch." The profile was illustrated with a photograph of three of the Senate's "eager new generation of Democrats": Hubert H. Humphrey of Minnesota, John F. Kennedy of Massachusetts, and Clark. Alsop dismissed Kennedy as a possible contender for the presidency in 1960 as being "a Catholic and too young." He ignored Humphrey altogether, but said Clark was a "proven vote getter." In Alsop's view, Clark, who had broken the GOP's hold on what was then the nation's fourth largest city, was "a man to be reckoned with."

Stewart Alsop was soon proven wrong on Kennedy, when he won the presidency in 1960, but also on Clark, who served two terms in the Senate without becoming the national figure that Alsop had foreseen. Actually, Clark had cautioned Alsop against expecting him to be more than a senator from Pennsylvania. He said that he was not temperamentally fitted for the presidency, and was not "dedicated enough." If Alsop's prognostications were shaky, he was very acute in characterizing Clark and Dilworth and in examining the "odd parallelism" of their careers. The two Philadelphia lawyers appeared to have much in common—"silver-spoon liberals" with impeccable Ivy League credentials who saw eye-to-eye politically, took turns helping in each other's campaigns, and together ended Republican hegemony in Philadelphia.

People likened them to Damon and Pythias, the friends in Greek mythology who were so devoted that Damon pledged his life as hostage for the condemned Pythias. But Alsop recognized that Clark and Dilworth weren't Damon and Pythias. They weren't even friends. Each had his own circle and they rarely socialized. He also pointed out what has since become a commonplace: that the two men's experiences in World War II reflected their dissimilar personalities. While Dilworth served with the Marines in the crucial and brutal battle on Guadalcanal, Clark was a desk-bound staff officer in the China-Burma-India Theater who never heard a shot fired. He told Alsop that he had "fought most of the war on the grass courts of Delhi." With this in mind, the columnist termed Dilworth "one of nature's combat men" and Clark "one of nature's staff officers." They were not, he emphasized, "two peas out of the same pod."

Stewart Alsop's take on Dilworth was brief and to the point: a "tall man with a pale, aggressive, handsome face." He said the former Marine was "gregarious and impulsive, a romantic, a man of action rather than a thinker, not really so tough as he seems, and a politician by instinct." By contrast, he said Clark was "a little lonely and withdrawn, intellectual, introspective behind the politician's mask of geniality, tough as nails, a politician by design." Dilworth had a "somewhat rambunctious personal history," Alsop noted, and he "has not always been the soberest and most discreet of men." That was putting it mildly. His over-the-top attacks on his political foes were what many people remembered about him, rather than his long record of accomplishments.

On the other hand, Alsop believed that Clark—"a short man, wiry, thin-boned, with a boyish smile" and a shy, unassuming manner—lacked "the natural politician's easy bonhomie. Unperceptive persons, noting his small stature and modest manner, tend to write him down as something of a lightweight. But to do so is to vastly understate the man." There was "a hard, inner assurance about Clark—the assurance of a man who has never known a moment of real financial or social insecurity."[12] And his friends and enemies used one word to describe him, according to Alsop. The word was "tough."

It was suggested to the columnist that Clark had much in common with liberal Democrat Adlai Stevenson, who twice lost the presidency to Dwight D. Eisenhower: similar family background, the same interest in ideas, the same articulateness, and "the same air of being an amateur and idealist among the professional political wolves." But another source rejected this notion: "Stevenson, hell. Little Joe's a left-wing Tom Dewey." In a letter to Alsop after the article appeared, Dilworth said he loved that characterization of Clark. "I wish I'd thought of it," he admitted. The reference was to New York's Republican attorney general, who made his name prosecuting leaders of organized crime and lost races for the presidency in 1944 and 1948.

Alsop contrasted the personalities of the second wives of Dilworth and Clark. Whereas Ann Dilworth loved the "rough and tumble of politics," he wrote, Noel Clark, "an attractive, gently reared Kentuckian, makes no bones about her extreme distaste for politics." And he went on to say, "It is not surprising that Noel Clark and Ann Dilworth, who have almost nothing in common, are by no means close personal friends."

In his letter to Stewart Alsop, Dilworth congratulated him on "the best summing up of what makes Joe tick that I ever read." But he took issue—or rather made clear that Ann took issue—with Alsop's characterization of Noel Clark as "gently reared." Dick's jocular letter quoted his wife: "She says 'gently reared, my eye. [Noel's] mother is the nearest thing to a stage mother I ever saw, and she and Noel spent years in Washington trying to unload Noel on every rich dope who came along. . . . If anyone was gently reared, it was I, right in the sweetest places in Palm Beach.' "

---

[12] Alsop may have been overstating the case. Dilworth, in an interview in 1972, noted: "Joe's father was damn well off and the Crash absolutely wiped him out. They had to sell that great big house they had in Chestnut Hill...and they lived in penury for quite a while." Clark's mother, Dilworth stated, was an impoverished southerner, a member of the Avery family. When they struck oil on Avery Island, "all of a sudden the Clarks became prosperous again, but the old man was absolutely defeated."

All this, of course, was almost certainly Dick Dilworth putting words in his wife's mouth. In conclusion, he wrote to Alsop, "I confess that your talent for sly malice leaves me green with envy." It's clear from the foregoing, however, that the Dilworths themselves were no slouches at sly malice. And in a later letter to the columnist that was full of good-natured disparagement of friends and foes, Dilworth declared, "I hope to see you soon so we can get malicious about a lot of people."[13]

Walter Phillips was the soft-spoken idea man behind the scenes in Philadelphia's reform movement. He served as Mayor Clark's commerce director and city representative, and later ran unsuccessfully for mayor himself. Ann Dilworth despised him because of his closeness to Clark. Phillips thought it logical that the reformers' assault on City Hall would be led by Dilworth, the fighting Marine, in 1947, and followed up by Clark, the staff officer, in 1951. "The fighter came in first and broke open the citadel," he reflected, referring to Dilworth's earlier race. "Then Joe came in as first administrator and Dick kept it going. And that was perfect for Philadelphia."

So it may have seemed after the fact. But the Democratic Party leadership hadn't planned it that way. Having carried Philadelphia in his losing race for governor the previous year, Dilworth was far better known than Clark in 1951. He had run a strong campaign for mayor in 1947, and the leaders wanted him to run again. They called a meeting at the Ritz Hotel to hammer out a solution. U.S. Senator Francis X. Myers was there. So were builders Matt McCloskey and Jack Kelly, real estate mogul Albert M. Greenfield, and Jim Finnegan, the respected city chairman. They planned to ask Clark to support Dilworth "for the good of the party." Clark would run for district attorney. But no sooner had the meeting opened than one man stood up to speak. It was Joe Clark, and he had no intention of backing Dilworth for mayor.

"Gentlemen," he said, "perhaps you would like to know that about an hour ago, I released a statement to the press. In it, I said that I intend to run for mayor. I'm going to run whether I have your backing or not, and I think our discussion here should proceed on that premise." Joe Alex Morris' account continued: "The group sat in stunned silence except for Dilworth, who said he would support Clark's candidacy. There was nothing the others could do but agree. They decided that Dilworth should run for district attorney."

---

[13] In 1967, after a *Philadelphia* magazine article alleged that the wives of Dilworth and Clark could not abide one another, Noel Clark sent a personal letter to Ann Dilworth. "I would like to say to you that this was never true on my side," she wrote. "I always liked and admired you. When, as sometimes happened, you seemed to not wish to speak to me, I told myself that it was not me personally that you disliked, but that you sometimes felt that Joe was not always fair to Dick and resented it, and that your attitude was a result of your most loyal and protective feeling for Dick." Noel said that her letter did not require an answer, and there is no record that Ann responded.

Although Clark was relatively unskilled and untested in back-room politics, he very neatly outmaneuvered the old pros. That private meeting in the smoke-filled hotel room set the course of reform government in Philadelphia for the next 10 years. But one can only imagine the earful that Dick got from Ann Dilworth when he returned home that night.

As events transpired, Joe Clark's brilliantly executed stratagem made good sense. Clark was not a trial lawyer, and he was not cut out for the DA's office. In fact, when Dilworth ran for mayor in 1947, he had asked Clark to join him on the ticket as the candidate for district attorney, and Clark had turned him down. "I'd never done any criminal work, and thought I'd make a perfectly terrible DA," he later told Phillips.

In the November 1951 election, Joseph Clark and Richardson Dilworth crushed their Republican opposition—Reverend Daniel Poling for mayor and Michael A. Foley for district attorney—winning 58 percent of the vote.

The break with the Republican past was immediate and pronounced. Earlier in the year a new city charter had been approved by voters, one that decentralized the city government, set up a merit system for hiring workers, and empowered the mayor to recruit talent from all over the United States. To the dismay of the Democratic organization, Clark proceeded to fill top positions in his administration with professionals, in such fields as finance, sanitation, and recreation, who lacked connections in party politics. Patronage was sharply curtailed if not entirely banished. Most city jobs went to those who scored highest on competitive civil service examinations. Under Mayor Clark, Philadelphia's wretched water was fluoridated and its wretched politics reformed. Public services were improved and public confidence restored. The city gained national recognition as a place that was cleaning up its act. He may not have been cut out for district attorney, but Joe Clark made a marvelous mayor, one of the finest in Philadelphia's long history. And his running mate, relegated to the DA's office, thrived there like few occupants it has ever seen.

CHAPTER THIRTEEN

Thrust and Parry

One of nature's noblemen in the DA's office

If Joseph Clark's cleverly timed press release served his own interests, it wound up serving Richardson Dilworth's—and the city's—as well. Dilworth loved the thrust and parry of litigation, and he was a brilliant natural leader. It was almost as though he had been born to be Philadelphia's district attorney. Under decades of Republican rule, the DA's office had been a sleepy, spiritless preserve staffed by part-timers. He transformed it virtually overnight into a professional organization of young, energetic, talented trial lawyers who worshipped their boss. With one exception, all the lawyers worked full time at starting salaries ranging from $4,500 to $10,000. The exception was Dilworth himself, who kept his link to his law firm. With a big family to support, he needed outside pay to supplement his $13,000 salary as district attorney. He hardly ever took time off, however, and was the first DA in 30 years to go into the courtroom and prosecute cases himself.

Even before taking office on January 7, 1952, Dilworth announced that Michael von Moschzisker would be his first assistant at $10,000 a year. Von Moschzisker, 33, was one of the youngest deputy DAs ever named. His father had been a chief justice of the Pennsylvania Supreme Court. Like Dilworth, von Moschzisker was a Yale graduate. His law degree was from Penn. He had enlisted in the Army one week after Pearl Harbor and rose to the rank of captain of artillery, serving in Western Europe.

Natalie Saxe remembered that when Dilworth and von Moschzisker reviewed the "pragmatic mix" of assistant DAs, city chairman Jim Finnegan pointed out the absence of Poles. That brought a prompt outcry from von Moschzisker. "What the hell do you think I am?" he protested. "That's not the kind I mean," retorted Finnegan, who knew that von Moschzisker was listed in Philadelphia's Social Register of prominent families. That exchange ended the issue of Polish ethnicity in the DA's office.

Michael von Moschzisker coordinated the activities of the staff, which Dilworth reduced from 110 part-timers under the Republicans to 86 working full time. Each staff member reported daily to the deputy and work was coordinated. Von Moschzisker, who remained for three years, had the time of his life. Interviewed years later, he termed Dilworth "one of nature's noblemen," and said working with him was "the most stimulating experience" he'd ever had.

To succeed von Moschzisker as his deputy, Dilworth chose 29-year-old Samuel Dash, who had been an assistant DA in charge of the appeals division. Dilworth had originally recruited Dash from the U.S. Justice Department. When asked about his party affiliation, Dash confessed that he hadn't found time to register. "Never mind," said Dilworth, "the politicians won't understand this appointment anyway. Don't say anything to anybody about it and just show up." More than two decades later, Dash would become the celebrated chief Watergate prosecutor in the investigation that led to President Richard M. Nixon's resignation, the first forced departure of a chief executive in American history.

Dilworth dramatically changed the makeup of the DA's office. In the process, he set an example of diversity for the entire city. When he took over in 1952, blacks were virtually invisible in Philadelphia's political, economic, and cultural landscape, and professional women were rarely heard from. This was the pattern in most of the nation's large cities before the civil rights movement. A few black lawyers with political connections had previously been hired as assistant district attorneys in Philadelphia, but their appearances were limited to minor cases in lower courts. There had been just one woman assistant DA, Hazel Brown, daughter of Judge Charles Brown. She was in domestic relations court. Dilworth hired Marilyn Gelb, a Temple law graduate, in 1952. She was followed by Evelyn Trommer and Lisa Richette. Both later became Common Pleas Court judges.

In hiring the assistant DAs, Dilworth made sure they were offered meaningful positions. "Before Richardson Dilworth became district attorney," said one of his African American hires, A. Leon Higginbotham Jr., "no black lawyer was ever permitted as an assistant district attorney to go into the major courts as a trial lawyer, whether they came from Harvard or Timbuktu. The door was closed.... Within one second after he took office, those centuries of oppression were wiped away by a man who put justice over political advantage, a concern for dignity over any momentary unpopularity."

Higginbotham, who became chief judge of the U.S. Circuit Court of Appeals, a Harvard professor, and a winner of the Presidential Medal of Freedom, said that he was hired "with no political background. I didn't know anyone, really." He held Dilworth in "special esteem" because "he never ran from a fight. Maybe he rushed to them! But I like what Richardson Dilworth stood for." Higginbotham maintained that Dilworth's "stature, his concern, his contributions...made him as significant as a Benjamin Franklin or Thomas Jefferson."

The quality of Dilworth's hires was consistently high. Christopher Edley, another of his black recruits, later became president of the United Negro College Fund. Two others, Curtis Carson and Thomas Reed, became Common Pleas Court judges. As an assistant DA, Reed faced blatant racism in the courtroom of President Judge Vincent Carroll. When Reed was assigned to his court, the vitriolic judge complained to the press and sent Dilworth a note telling him to "get your nigger out of my courtroom." Dilworth paid no heed to Carroll's fulminations, and the judge later conceded that Reed was a competent lawyer.

Another potential hire, William T. Coleman Jr., was recruited for the DA's office but took employment instead at Dilworth's law firm. A native Philadelphian, Coleman graduated from Penn in 1945, and three years later finished first in his class at Harvard Law School where he edited the *Law Review*. He clerked for a year in the Third Circuit Court of Appeals and then searched for work in the Philadelphia area. Despite his stellar credentials, no one in town was hiring. "I couldn't get a job," Coleman recalled. "Name all the big law firms; I couldn't get a job." None of the city's major law firms had ever employed a black attorney.

Coleman next clerked for legendary U.S. Supreme Court Justice Felix Frankfurter. Even after that prestigious assignment, no doors opened in Philadelphia. He finally found a job with a top law firm in Manhattan: Paul, Weiss, Rifkind, Wharton & Garrison. Three years later, when Dilworth became district attorney, he called Coleman, a registered Republican, and asked if he would become an assistant DA. Coleman said he would think about it. Dilworth called back two days later to say there was a snag. Four black Democrats who had supported Dilworth's election opposed Coleman's appointment on the grounds that he belonged to the wrong party.

Coleman met with the Democrats, who said they would support him on the condition that he formally ask for their recommendation. He viewed the demand as demeaning and refused. "I went back to New York," he would say years later, and "Dilworth called me the next day." This time he had a different proposal. "My partners and I very much would like to have you join our law firm." Coleman accepted the offer, thus becoming the first black lawyer hired by a major Philadelphia firm.

But Dilworth, Paxson's secretaries resented the hiring and threatened to leave. Dilworth told them it would be easier to find replacements for them than to replace Coleman. Walter Annenberg heard about the brouhaha and said he would pull his account from the firm if Coleman's hiring was rescinded. In the end, the secretaries dropped their threats and stayed. Annenberg's account stayed. And William Coleman stayed for 23 years, becoming one of the city's most successful lawyers. When President Gerald Ford named him Secretary of Transportation in 1975, Coleman became just the second black cabinet member in American history.

Dilworth gave his assistants free rein. "We were thrust right into the courtroom with no experience and very little guidance," said Leon Katz, another hire. "It was very exciting work." Katz went on to become chancellor of the Philadelphia Bar Association. In professionalizing his operations, Dilworth made minor changes as well as major ones. He discovered, for example, that there were no fewer than 27 doors that opened to various offices of the district attorney. All these doors offered easy access for fixers and other undesirables who had been accustomed to barging in uninvited. Dilworth had 26 doors sealed off, leaving only the main entrance, which was guarded by a policeman. Visitors were required to state their business in writing. Problem solved.

More significant was the transition Dilworth made in courtroom seating arrangements. Until he took office, the assistant DAs prosecuting cases sat alongside the judge, across the railing from the defense attorneys. This conveyed the impression that the prosecutors and the judge were in cahoots—which they may have been. At Michael von Moschzisker's suggestion, Dilworth moved his people back with the defense counsel on the far side of the railing from the judge. "This was bitterly resented by some of the judges," von Moschzisker remembered, "but the assistant DAs were never again inside the rail."

When Dilworth took office, he favored the death penalty. But before his first year was out, he opposed it. He studied the history of the death penalty and discovered that states that abolished capital punishment had no greater increase in murders than states that clung to it. Great Britain's murder rate remained unchanged after abolishing the death penalty. "History makes it clear that cruel punishments are self-defeating," he later wrote. Beyond that, Dilworth quickly learned that Philadelphia murder cases kept piling up because judges chose not to preside over first-degree murder trials and citizens preferred not to sit on such juries. "I found our backlog of murder cases was so great that it took more than two years to bring them to trial," he wrote. "This meant, of course, that the defendants had to sit in jail all during that time, as first-degree murder is not bailable."

Perhaps Dilworth's most important contribution as district attorney was his insistence on fair trials. He took special pains not only to prosecute the guilty but to protect the innocent. With big-city crime on the rise, prosecutors faced constant pressure to steamroll juries and keep piling up convictions. Dilworth ignored the pressure. "He wasn't just interested in a batting average," said Charles R. Weiner, another of his hires who later became a U.S. District Court judge. "He wanted to make sure that justice was done and if mistakes were made to admit them."

Sam Dash said that he was under instructions to review convictions and to determine whether cases had been handled properly: "Dick insisted if we found we'd violated somebody's rights, we were to go to court and ask for a new trial for the defendant, even if his own lawyer hadn't found the mistake. We were to vigorously prosecute for the people, Dilworth told us, but he reminded us we were also there to uphold the Constitution."

In one celebrated case, Dilworth was heavily criticized for defending the rights of a murderer. The facts were not in dispute: a black man had been convicted by the preceding DA and sentenced to death for the fatal shooting of a white taxicab driver. Because there had been a number of ugly incidents in which cabbies had been beaten and robbed, the public hailed the verdict.

In appealing the case, the district attorney went personally before the U.S. Supreme Court in an action that the Philadelphia *Bulletin* termed "almost without precedent." He argued that the defendant had never received a proper psychiatric examination and was not mentally competent to stand trial. Acceding to Dilworth's plea, the high court sent the case back to a "lunacy commission," which found that the killer was a "committable psychotic" and should never have been placed on trial. He was sent to an institution for the criminally insane. The DA got no plaudits from the public for saving the life of a deranged murderer; but he wasn't looking for any.

Much of Dilworth's time and effort as district attorney went into contending with the corrupt alliance between Philadelphia's police and politicians and the underworld. The underworld, in this case, consisted of runners, writers, and bosses involved in the illegal lottery known as the "numbers racket." It was a lucrative activity, so lucrative that the states ultimately took it over, legalizing the practice and setting up their own lotteries. In those days, however, to make it easy for people to "play the numbers," runners made house calls to collect bets on the day's lucky number. With runners collecting a dollar here and a dollar there in working-class neighborhoods all over the city, the money piled up for the men running the lotteries. Police generally winked at the racket; more often than not, they were paid off to do so.

At first, the numbers writers arrested in Dilworth's crackdown were merely fined. He pressed for higher fines and then jail terms. Some of the writers began to talk, and leaders of the racket were convicted. Joe Alex Morris, in his campaign biography of Dilworth, wrote that while the convictions did not "wipe out completely the alliance of crime and politics in Philadelphia," they dealt a "heavy blow to the racketeers." District Attorney Dilworth went into court himself to lead the assault. In January 1954, he personally prosecuted Magistrate Joseph J. Molinari on charges of subornation of perjury. Molinari was accused of inducing a confessed numbers writer to change his testimony to protect a higher-up.

The district attorney was near tears as he pleaded with the jury: "I'm putting it to you. I'm asking you to do your part to convict this man. There is a terrible connection between politicians and the lower courts. We've got to break up that connection—that alliance between corrupt machine politicians and the administration of justice in these courts. That's why this prosecution was brought and that's why we're asking you to convict Magistrate Molinari. If we don't convict this kind of man, how are we ever going to have a decent city in which to live?" Noting that he came from western Pennsylvania, Dilworth said that he had eight children and wanted Philadelphia to become the "finest city in the world." His efforts, he added, had resulted in "threats [and] anonymous phone calls. Cans of paint have been thrown through our windows."

The DA's emotional outcry registered with the jury, which convicted Joseph Molinari. However, the finding was later overturned by the Superior Court. A second trial ended in a hung jury when one juror held out against conviction. A third trial in 1957, after Dilworth had been elected mayor, ended in Molinari's acquittal. The verdict outraged him. He said it was "little short of willful" on the part of his successor, Victor Blanc. Dilworth had been galled when Blanc was backed by the Democratic Party to run for district attorney, and the Molinari acquittal only confirmed his low opinion of the choice:

"Convictions in cases of powerful political figures depend entirely upon the tone set by the district attorney himself. Where it is the district attorney's policy to cater to the worst elements of the political parties...and to give bail bondsmen, police court politicians and criminal court hangers-on free run of his office, convictions are not obtained in cases of political corruption. That is the way Mr. Blanc has seen fit to conduct his office, and the result has been a breakdown in effective prosecution all the way from organized crime and drunken driving cases to cases of political corruption." Clearly, the "heavy blow" that Joe Alex Morris said had been dealt to the racketeers had not been heavy enough. Dilworth's campaign against illegal numbers writing in the 1950s simply doesn't resonate in today's world of widespread gambling casinos, government-run lotteries, and off-track betting—all perfectly legal and wildly popular. What does resonate is his bold defense of civil liberties when they were being nibbled away.

Just as the threat of terrorism grips the nation now, so did the threat of communism in Dilworth's time. In March 1952, with fears of the "Red Menace" running high, the Pennsylvania legislature enacted a measure requiring public employees to swear fealty to the state. Governor John Sydney Fine took the so-called loyalty oath in ceremonies witnessed by officials of the American Legion and Veterans of Foreign Wars. Thousands of state workers followed suit.

Richardson Dilworth, himself a veteran of two foreign wars, refused to take the oath. No other public official had dared to challenge the law, which he termed an "outrageous" procedure. "This isn't a loyalty oath," he stated. "It will make possible witch hunts and inquisitions. If you don't conform to their idea of Americanism, they can crucify you." Dilworth charged that the "whole purpose and intent" of the loyalty oath was to "force people to conform to some cockeyed, unknown standard of behavior with the knowledge that if they deviate from it in some way, they're going to get walloped."

Dilworth cited a case in suburban Delaware County where an elementary school teacher, in discussing the Revolutionary War, told her class that the British had actually won the Battle of Bunker Hill. One of the students later told his parents what the teacher had said. "Within three days," Dilworth reported, "there was a delegation around to see her from the American Legion to find out whether she was a Communist."

The district attorney had frequent jousts with veterans groups. When an advertisement appeared in the Philadelphia *Bulletin* in January 1953 seeking funds for Julius and Ethel Rosenberg, a couple convicted of passing secrets concerning the atomic bomb to the Soviet Union, the local VFW chapter sprang into action. It took out a warrant for the arrest of a woman who had signed the ad, charging she was soliciting funds without a permit. She was subsequently indicted. In November 1953, Dilworth joined with the defense in asking the court to throw out the indictment. "Since there are no prior convictions against this defendant, we concede that the indictment should be quashed," read the brief prepared by Assistant DA Samuel Dash.

Colbert C. McClain, who represented the VFW, angrily assailed Dilworth. He said he intended to find out what "sinister influence" was affecting the district attorney's office. Dilworth had been "antagonistic and uncooperative" from the start, he charged, adding that it was "certainly unusual for a district attorney to usurp the functions of the court."

Dilworth's reply had a remarkably contemporary ring: "Unlike you, I think it is vitally important that we preserve our democratic processes," he wrote. "I have heard people suggest that Communists should get the same treatment from us that our people receive at their hands. If we ever resort to such tactics, we should very soon lose our war against Communism, for our strength lies in our integrity and in the courage to maintain our democratic processes. Unfortunately, there are some few people who attempt to play upon the natural fears of our people in these times of tension, hoping to create a wave of hysteria on which they may ride. Our office has no intention of helping you in this aim."

At Dilworth's behest, Henry Sawyer, a liberal lawyer who had defended teachers and others accused of Communist ties, was considering a race for City Council in 1955. John B. Capitolo, Philadelphia County commander of the Veterans of

Foreign Wars, warned him not to. In a private meeting with Dilworth and Sawyer, Capitolo said the district attorney's own "pro-Communist sentiments" had hurt him politically. Sawyer said that Dilworth "stood up, grabbed Capitolo and shouted: 'Listen, you little tinhorn Hitler. I don't need your vote or the VFW's either.'"

The encounter with Capitolo was little noted. By contrast, the one with U.S. Senator Joseph R. McCarthy two years earlier had made national headlines. McCarthy was then at the peak of his demagogic power. Few politicians dared to criticize him for fear of being labeled communists or fellow travelers. Dilworth was not deterred. After he attacked McCarthy in a Philadelphia speech in October 1952, the Wisconsin senator challenged Dilworth to repeat his charges on national television. He did so on April 14, 1953.

Their televised meeting was billed as a debate, but the moderator, Martha Rountree, had difficulty keeping order. McCarthy drew from his briefcase a photostatic copy of a Philadelphia *Bulletin* story of October 31, 1952. He read the headline: "1,000 Alger Hisses Hurt Less Than One McCarthy, Dilworth Says." Dilworth's reference was to the former State Department official who had been convicted of perjury in 1950 as the result of espionage charges made by Whittaker Chambers, a former Communist Party member. McCarthy asked Dilworth if he had made the statement and, if so, why. "I said it," Dilworth shot back, "and I'll say it again." The district attorney then uttered the words that made the debate memorable. "We can put traitors in jail," he told McCarthy, "but demagogues remain too long above and beyond the processes of the law."

The following year, on March 9, 1954, Edward R. Murrow had his famous showdown with McCarthy on *See It Now,* which contributed to his downfall. Nine months later, the Senate voted to censure McCarthy, and his career was at an end.

CHAPTER FOURTEEN

Running for Mayor
The last of the bare-knuckled aristocrats

Joe Clark faced a vexing decision early in his fourth year as mayor: whether he would run for a second term or leave office after one term and run for U.S. Senate. Because the Senate race was a year after the mayoral race, Clark could afford to take his time deciding. But with the primaries looming in the spring of 1955, Dick Dilworth, who planned to run for mayor if Clark did not, was eager to know his decision.

Clark had proved to be a superb mayor, recruiting professionals from outside the city to run major departments, virtually ending patronage (against the wishes of job-hungry Democratic bosses), and launching fresh initiatives to enliven the sleepy business sector. But the Senate was his ultimate destination. In a 1972 interview, Dilworth said of Clark: "He was a hell of a good mayor...but I don't think he ever really enjoyed it." Dilworth added that Clark, although he was a good administrator, "hated all the details of being mayor. The Senate was the one that he wanted."

Clark's senatorial aspirations were no great secret, and while he mulled his decision, the Democratic Party considered his replacement if he did not run for mayor. Dilworth, with a stellar record as DA, previous experience as a candidate, and a close political relationship with Clark, would seem to have been the clear choice. But he was unpopular with some Democratic leaders. They weren't convinced he could win. In an analysis of the reform movement, journalist James Reichley reported that organization heads "went a bit weak in the knees when they thought of sending [Dilworth] against the Republicans in November." They feared that he lacked widespread support. Critics considered him soft on criminals and communists.

Recognizing that he had work to do to achieve the nomination, Dilworth was eager to get started. But Clark kept deferring his decision. In a 1972 interview, Dick said that Joe "couldn't make up his mind." While his election to a second term in City Hall in 1955 would have been a "sure thing," he added, Clark's "chances of getting into the Senate looked very slim." That was because the incumbent Republican senator, James H. Duff, would be seeking reelection in 1956 on a GOP ticket headed by the immensely popular President Dwight D. Eisenhower. And Duff seemed likely to ride in on Ike's coattails.

Clark's indecisiveness led to "real coolness" between the two old allies. "I wanted to start making plans and I couldn't get any word from Joe," Dilworth recalled. "In fact, he kept ducking me." Instead of talking directly with Dick, Clark shunted him off to Walter Phillips, Joe's close friend and confidant. Phillips served as director of commerce and city representative in Clark's cabinet. And it was Phillips who had pitched the novel idea of street-corner campaigning to Dilworth in his race for mayor in 1947. He lost that race but found his signature style of campaigning. Ann Dilworth viewed Phillips as hostile to her husband, and Dick dismissed him as an insufferable prig. That was why he particularly resented Clark's directive that he talk to Phillips about the coming campaign. It was "just plain insulting," said Dilworth, and his relations with Clark became "quite strained."

Clark was still on the fence when the Democratic policy committee met to pick a mayoral candidate. Word got around that a judge named John Morgan Davis might be selected. *The Observer*, a gossip sheet that circulated in City Hall, reported that Joe Clark was out and John Davis was in. It made no mention of Dilworth. But Dick, losing patience with Joe, quietly lined up the support of three Democratic heavyweights: Congressman William J. Green, the party chairman; John B. Kelly, the millionaire builder and former mayoral candidate for whom Dick had campaigned in 1934; and Albert M. Greenfield, the powerful financier.

According to Dilworth, Greenfield's decision to back him was the result of a Machiavellian calculation. Dick said that Al had a "hand-picked candidate" for the Senate seat, and Al thought his man would have a better chance to beat out Clark for the nomination if Dilworth had already been chosen to run for mayor. In Dick's view, the policy committee wouldn't endorse "two so-called blue stockings." If Dilworth were selected, the committee would probably drop Clark, opening the door for Greenfield's unidentified candidate. "So I got Greenfield in my camp," Dick conceded, "not for any love of me, but because he was anti-Clark."

Not until the last minute did Clark declare that he wouldn't run for re-election. He never responded to Dilworth's entreaties, but finally sent word directly to the policy committee to withdraw his nominating petitions. "Things were quite cool between Joe and myself for quite a while after that," Dilworth noted. After he won the nomination there was a rapprochement with Clark, and "he was very helpful during the actual campaign."

Dilworth's Republican opponent in the mayor's race, W. Thacher Longstreth, was a 34-year-old political neophyte from Chestnut Hill chosen by the GOP hierarchy when they couldn't think of anybody else. In fact, it was a Democrat and Dilworth ally, Bill Churchman, who first suggested that Longstreth be the GOP candidate. "There's the fellow you want," Churchman told two insurgent Philadelphia Republicans at lunch one day at the Philadelphia Racquet Club. That night they paid a call on Longstreth, and he expressed interest in their idea. Not long afterward, he was named the Republican nominee.

For the first time in a Philadelphia mayoral race, voters were given a choice between two Ivy-Leaguers: Dilworth from Yale's class of 1922 and Longstreth, who had graduated from Princeton in 1941. Like Dilworth, Longstreth had played varsity football. Standing a gangly six-feet-six with his signature bow tie and horn-rimmed glasses, Longstreth had been an advertising man before entering politics, and James Reichley referred to him as a "disarming huckster." In a personal letter to *Inquirer* publisher Walter Annenberg, Dilworth termed his opponent "a big, good-natured…human replica of a St. Bernard puppy, the only drawback being that he does not have a keg of brandy hanging around his neck." (Definitely not; Longstreth did not drink.)

In the first of 18 debates scheduled over four months, Thacher Longstreth, a self-confessed "total novice in political campaigning," was humiliated. "I had never before been so aggressively attacked or insulted at a public meeting," he acknowledged in his memoir, *Main Line Wasp,* written with Dan Rottenberg. "I made an ass of myself. I remember coming home afterward so upset that I cried. My pride had been ripped apart and I felt totally inadequate."

Longstreth kept getting "clobbered"—his word—over the first half dozen debates. Still, the improvement in his performances astonished the Dilworth camp. It turned out that early on, he had hired Professor Edward Shils at the University of Pennsylvania for a crash course on urban government. They met for three, four, and five hours a day—more than 100 hours altogether. Shils imparted his knowledge of the field and Thacher learned fast.

In his memoir, Longstreth said Dilworth told him later: "It surprised us that you were such a quick study. We knew at the outset that you knew absolutely nothing about city government. It was quite obvious in our first few debates that I could eat you alive, because you were so ignorant and you didn't understand debating techniques. But by the fifth or sixth debate, you'd become so formidable that my people told me, 'Get out. This kid's showing you up.' So we canceled the last six."

In the campaign's most dramatic moment, however, Longstreth was a virtual bystander. It came at the Beth Zion synagogue in Center City on October 6, a month before the election. The candidates for district attorney, Republican Wilhelm Knauer and Democrat Victor Blanc, joined the mayoral contenders at the podium. On previous occasions, Knauer had goaded Dilworth in what he termed a "truth campaign." He would park his trailer on a corner where Dilworth was addressing the crowd and open up with a loudspeaker, accusing the Democrat of numerous transgressions. The tactic had been designed to make him lose his fiery temper, and it hadn't worked. At the synagogue session, it did.

Knauer spoke first, charging that Dilworth had been a "part-time district attorney" in a poorly run office. Blanc retorted that Knauer had failed to file tax returns until he was nominated for DA. Then Dilworth spoke. In measured tones, he said that he had taken off just 37 days in 39 months as district attorney, and he had not been paid for days when he wasn't working. He pointed out that he had been the only DA in decades to take regular turns in criminal courts and magistrates' courts.

Then suddenly, without warning, Dilworth launched what John C. Calpin, *The Bulletin*'s political writer, termed "the wildest, most vicious political [attack] in the city's recent history." Denouncing the Republican candidate for district attorney as a "mean, nasty, stinking little wretch," Dilworth said that when Knauer was director of supplies in the administration of Mayor S. Davis Wilson in the 1930s, the city had sold "rotten meat" to Philadelphia General Hospital and buried 2,000 unneeded fire plugs behind Municipal Stadium in South Philadelphia.

"I turned white," recalled Clifford Brenner, Dilworth's longtime press secretary. "The audience was dumbstruck." The allegations were new and they were never substantiated. But they were forgotten in the hubbub over the Democrat's next charges. He said that Wilhelm Knauer was "guilty of manslaughter by automobile and had the records destroyed."

"That's a contemptible lie," Knauer broke in. Twenty-five years earlier, he said, he had been driving in a blinding snowstorm with windshield wipers only on the driver's side when his car struck a snowplow. "My associate was killed," he added. "My client was killed but God spared me. Sometimes I wonder why." Knauer declared that records of the crash were kept, not destroyed as Dilworth had claimed.

Defending his running mate, Longstreth questioned whether his opponent was "emotionally and psychiatrically fit" for public office: "Mr. Dilworth has just demonstrated by his actions why he is not qualified to be mayor." Dilworth responded emphatically, saying he was "an emotional man" and "a fighter" and, if elected, he would "fight for the city because I love it." There would be no cities, he cried, "if there were not men like me to fight for them."

Furious at Dilworth's attack, Knauer sued him. Dilworth later admitted that he was mistaken in one of his charges, but Knauer did not collect the $50,000 he sought and his suit was withdrawn. Recalling his boss' performance at Beth Zion, Cliff Brenner said that he had clearly failed to keep his anger "within rational bounds," but even so "it played very well in the papers and galvanized the campaign."

On election day, Dilworth won with 59 percent of the vote to 41 percent for Longstreth—420,099 votes to 288,646. It was the most one-sided defeat any GOP candidate had ever suffered in Philadelphia. In the race for DA, Democrat Victor Blanc easily outpolled Wilhelm Knauer.

Thacher Longstreth reported in his memoir that one day after the drubbing, Dilworth took him to breakfast at the Racquet Club. They discussed their debates, and Longstreth expressed amazement at his opponent's grasp of the minutiae of city government. How could he keep so many statistics in his head? Dilworth replied that it had been easy; he just made up the figures. He believed—accurately, as it turned out—that neither his opponent nor the audience would know any better. "We both just died laughing," Longstreth wrote. He also said that Dilworth contrived many of his "famous rages" in the knowledge that "public displays of temper, properly directed, could be an asset." He quoted him as saying that, "In politics, politeness is weakness. Anything is OK to get elected. You never win playing the Queensberry rules."

Years after the race, Thacher Longstreth described the liberal Democrat who had given him such a shellacking as "the last of the bare-knuckled aristocrats," and said he displayed "the most instinctive thrust for the jugular of any man I've ever known.... More than any other mayor, he was ready to fight for what he believed in. He was a fighting mayor. Fight and feistiness backed up by a keen brain and a sharp tongue. I think he was the best mayor in my lifetime."

In the months following Richardson Dilworth's victory, with the race for the Senate approaching, Albert Greenfield continued to oppose Joseph Clark's bid for the nomination. According to Dilworth, at an important meeting of party leaders in Harrisburg early in 1956, Greenfield "gave a million reasons" why Clark should not be slated. And he appeared to be winning the argument. Dilworth described what happened next: "Joe Clark then spoke up and said to the group, 'Well, I don't give a goddamn what you do. I'm going to run and I'm going to win and I'm going to be able to collect enough money to do it. I'll lick your candidate, or even if I don't—and I'm quite sure I can lick him—I will louse him up so that he can't be elected in the fall.'"

On hearing Clark's passionate stand, Dilworth defied Greenfield and rallied to the side of his longtime running mate. "I spoke up and said, 'Well, I'll throw whatever weight I can as mayor of Philadelphia, and whatever assistance I can with the resources you have as mayor, in a primary fight for Joe.' " After what Dilworth termed a "long, very acrimonious meeting," the party leaders decided that Clark would be the candidate. And the following fall, Joe Clark, aided by Philadelphia's mayor and bucking the Eisenhower tide, narrowly defeated Jim Duff and won his cherished seat in the Senate.

CHAPTER FIFTEEN

Mayor Dilworth

Staid old Philly, recapturing the spirit of its precocious youth

After taking the oath of office before a packed house in Philadelphia's
Academy of Music on January 2, 1956, Mayor Richardson Dilworth was
nearly overcome with emotion. "It was a fight to stem the tears which welled in his
eyes and threatened to cascade down his cheeks," wrote *The Inquirer*'s John M.
Cummings. "He struggled for words which refused to come. There was a tremor
in his voice. The short period of emotion soon passed and the crowd gave him a
tremendous cheer."

The mayor's inaugural message was brief: "We must never forget that good
government is our strength. The moment we lose sight of that fact, the people of
Philadelphia will remove us just as decisively as they installed us. Good government cannot be a mere slogan. We must demonstrate our belief in it by deeds, not
just by words."

Dilworth delivered on the deeds, and the evidence was soon obvious across
Philadelphia—and around the country. "A beautiful new American city of two
million people is being born on the Delaware River in Pennsylvania," wrote
Leverett Chapin, a *Denver Post* editorial writer, in 1958. "Its name is Philadelphia.
If the name sounds familiar, don't be fooled. You're probably thinking of the old

126

Philadelphia. The old and new Philadelphias should not be confused. They're as different as night and day."

Dilworth's years in the mayor's office continued the remarkable resurgence begun by Joe Clark. Under their leadership, Philadelphia shed its stigma as a woebegone second-class city, a hotbed of inertia, and gained national recognition for the extraordinary quality of its governance.

Writing in *The Saturday Evening Post* in December 1958, author Roul Tunley reported that "staid old Philly" had been "building, tearing down, planting, uprooting, restoring, bulldozing, dredging, filling in and generally recapturing the spirit of its precocious youth." Tunley emphasized that Philadelphia's recovery went far beyond bricks and mortar. "There's a new spirit abroad," he wrote. "No longer are Philadelphians complacent. And their government is no longer corrupt. The baseball team may not have caught the spirit of things, but almost everybody else has."

Roul Tunley's piece was hardly investigative journalism. There were faults to be found under the rule of Philadelphia's liberal Democrats, and Tunley didn't find them. It was true, however, that during the Clark and Dilworth years most Philadelphians felt a swell of pride in their hometown. The reformers added parks and playgrounds, constructed new health centers, rehabilitated neighborhoods, and directed major renewal efforts. During their tenure, the Philadelphia Industrial Development Corporation rallied support for the city's shrinking industrial base, and the Philadelphia Redevelopment Authority helped private developers launch the largest building and rebuilding effort in the city's history.

Jeane Lowe, author of *Cities in a Race with Time*, reported that under the "superb leadership" of Joseph Clark and Richardson Dilworth, Philadelphia "spun off a dizzying number" of enterprises providing "unprecedented intervention by citizen leaders." According to political scientist Kirk R. Petshek, the achievements of Clark and Dilworth were determined by "their sequence in office" at City Hall. "Much that Clark had sown," wrote Petshek in *The Challenge of Urban Reform*, "Dilworth would reap." This was true in the case of two major projects in which both mayors participated. One was relocation of the city's sprawling, unsanitary, open-air food market, which had sat for nearly two centuries on Dock Street near the Delaware waterfront. Fruit, vegetables, and meat for restaurants and wholesale grocers throughout the region had been distributed over its narrow expanse, fouling the air. The market stood at the heart of the oldest part of the city, and in the years after World War II, big trucks jammed traffic there. Without a single public toilet, the market was a rat-infested sinkhole of filth and disorder.

In 1949, Harry A. Batten took action. Batten was chief executive of N.W. Ayer & Son, the city's largest advertising agency, whose offices were within smelling distance of the food market. With other executives he founded The Greater

Philadelphia Movement, which would become the city's most potent business organization. GPM set a goal of moving the market out of the historic district. Begun under Clark, the relocation was completed under Dilworth. What resulted was a modern, privately financed—for about 100 million dollars—food distribution center on 400 acres of city-owned land in South Philadelphia.

A second important project in which both mayors participated was Penn Center, a complex of new high-rise office buildings just west of City Hall. The Pennsylvania Railroad's eyesore of an elevated line, which provided a vital connection between 30th Street and Broad Street Stations, and which had been mocked as the "Chinese Wall" for the way it cut into the heart of the city, was finally demolished to allow for the new construction. Aesthetically, Penn Center's buildings fell far short of chief planner Edmund Bacon's dream of a development that would rival New York's Rockefeller Center. However, they offered the first dramatic sign since the war of fresh life in the aging city.

The reformers' ambitions were enormous, and so were their obstacles. The scale of the task they faced in transforming the city's department of recreation is representative of the battles they fought on many fronts. Formerly, recreation had been treated as a stepsister, functioning within the city's department of welfare. Under the new city charter, a separate department of recreation was established with the same status as other city departments.

Joe Clark's recreation commissioner, Fredric R. Mann, seeking a professional to run the new department, asked for names from the National Recreation Association. Heading the list was Oakland, California's recreation commissioner, Robert W. Crawford. He and his wife loved Oakland and didn't want to leave. But Mann was relentless, telephoning him at all hours of the day and night. Finally, Crawford told his wife that Philadelphia had a new mayor and a new charter, and it seemed an opportune time to work in a big city. "Would you be willing to take the risk?" he asked his wife. When she said yes, they decided to make the move.

The lengths Mann went to in recruiting Robert Crawford were typical of the Clark and Dilworth Administrations, which scoured the country to find the best possible candidates. The difficulties Crawford encountered in his new job were also typical of what many Clark and Dilworth recruits faced in trying to reform and energize a deeply flawed system.

"Never in our wildest dreams," Crawford told interviewer Walter Phillips, "did we think we would be here for 24 years." Nor did Robert Crawford in his wildest dreams imagine the dreadful conditions he would encounter in his new job. "Take swimming, for example," he recalled. "In 1952, Philadelphia, the third-largest city in the United States, did not have a filtering system in any swimming pool. That was against the law. Even Podunk, Iowa would not have allowed that. "There were no places for people to sit and there was no drinking water. Most of the areas were more or less dust bowls, and they had a lot of cinders for the surface areas of the playing fields and playgrounds…the recreation department in 1952 had two tennis courts."

Even more troubling was the department's personnel. "I was surprised to find how untrained many of the employees were and how lacking in education and background experience," Crawford noted. "Many of them told me frankly that they paid a certain percentage of their salaries to the ward leaders or to the committeemen before the Clark Administration, and got their jobs through their committeemen."

In Robert Crawford's first months on the job, 75 recreation department workers were fired. Dilworth later reported that from 1952 to 1958, 243 more workers were hired to staff 97 additional recreational facilities. According to Crawford, the incompetence he encountered in the recreation department extended to architects who had been chosen to design its buildings. He accused them of producing "stereotypical" construction with the same mistakes in every building. The architects shamelessly copied each other's hastily drawn plans, he said, repeating the same mistakes in building after building. In some buildings, entrance doors opened directly into shower rooms. Crawford blamed much of the incompetent work on the Republicans' rush to open new recreational facilities before leaving office. To the extent possible, he made necessary corrections, and he remained as recreation commissioner until his retirement in 1976. Nobody did the job better.

Despite all the fresh energy and spirit of reform, Richardson Dilworth got off to a shaky start as mayor. The troublesome issue was patronage. For decades the omnipotent Republican political machine had been oiled through distribution of municipal jobs to party members. The general expectation was that the Democratic Party, with their takeover of City Hall in 1951, would do the same. But the new city charter approved by voters that year tightened civil service rules, and Mayor Clark rejected his own party's pleas for patronage. District Attorney Dilworth agreed with him: "The voters elected us to office because they were sick to death of the big-city political machines and their bosses. We promised the voters good, clean, unbossed government, and now it is up to all of us in the Administration to defeat those who are seeking to repudiate these promises."

That was DA Dilworth on January 23, 1954. Two years later, Mayor Dilworth was more accommodating. Under pressure from Democratic city bosses, he pledged to work for revision of the city charter to open up about 500 of the 27,000 city jobs to patronage. In explaining Dilworth's about-face, writer John Guinther, in *Direction of Cities,* argued that patronage performed a useful function in giving politicians a "sense of self-worth." It made them feel "benevolent" and therefore "good about themselves." Maybe so, but patronage didn't make the voters feel good.

Dilworth had clearly misjudged the mood of his constituents. Philadelphians were proud of their new city charter and opposed changes in it. Amendments were denounced as "charter rippers." The press took up the cry, and the revisions

that the mayor sought were defeated. He also lost an effort to eliminate the requirement in the new charter that city officeholders resign before seeking another office,
a defeat that would come back to haunt him.

Abraham L. Freedman, a brilliant lawyer who had served as Clark's city solicitor and was expected to continue in that position, resigned in protest over
Dilworth's defense of patronage. David Berger, who succeeded Freedman as city
solicitor, rallied behind his boss. In a World War II meeting on a South Pacific
island, Berger and Dilworth had agreed to try to reform Philadelphia's corrupt
government. In a later interview, Berger argued that Dilworth was a reformer, but
also a pragmatist. Of the mayor's position on patronage, Berger commented, "he
studied the whole thing and concluded that the way to keep the charter from being
eroded by the politicians was to give them a bone...a few jobs." However, Dilworth
himself later acknowledged that the move had been an error. He told biographer
Joe Alex Morris that in seeking charter changes, he had committed "a real blooper,
a mistake in judgment."

Dilworth's political pragmatism was also reflected in his decision to replace
Edward Hopkinson Jr. as chairman of the City Planning Commission with financier and real estate mogul Albert M. Greenfield. Hopkinson, who was chief executive of Drexel and Company, the financial powerhouse, had been appointed to
the City Planning Commission at its founding in 1942 by Republican mayor
Bernard Samuel. Dilworth's decision to replace Hopkinson was loudly criticized—not so much because he removed Hopkinson, but because he appointed
Greenfield, whose companies controlled seven Philadelphia hotels, two department stores, the major taxi company, and huge chunks of downtown real estate.
C. Jared Ingersoll, a Democratic member of the City Planning Commission,
resigned in protest, charging that Dilworth had made "a dreadful mistake."
Ingersoll spoke for many when he said, "no real estate man should be placed in a
political position where he has so much to do with the value of individual pieces
of real estate." With such a man at the head of the planning commission, Ingersoll
noted, there would always be questions as to whether its decisions were influenced
by personal gain.

In response, Dilworth accused Jared Ingersoll of social class bias—and, by
implication, of anti-Semitism. Ingersoll, like Edward Hopkinson, could trace his
ancestry back to a signer of the Declaration of Independence. And the mayor suggested that Ingersoll apparently believed that appointments to the planning commission should be like appointments to the board of the Pennsylvania Railroad,
whose directors were drawn from the upper ranks of Wasp society. "I have great
affection and respect for Mr. Ingersoll, but I don't happen to agree with him." The
mayor's attack on "Proper Philadelphia" was one that Joe Clark, whose patrician
roots were deep in the city, would probably not have made. But as Dilworth told

Kirk Petshek, "I was never really part of the social structure. To many of the elite, a man from Pittsburgh is a semi-savage."

Philadelphia's top banker, R. Stewart Rauch Jr., though he considered Dilworth "the outstanding mayor of my lifetime," was also an opponent of the Greenfield appointment. Dilworth was unmoved. "I know your values," he told Rauch, "and I don't agree with them." Although Rauch lost the argument, he remained an admirer of the mayor.

The man who would work most closely with Albert Greenfield at the City Planning Commission was its executive director, Edmund N. Bacon. He held that post under four mayors, from 1949 to 1970, gaining an international reputation for the quality of his work. Such was his prominence that at one point *Time* magazine put him on its cover. Bacon said he went through some "fairly bitter soul searching," when Greenfield was appointed, but stayed in his post. In a later interview with Phillips, he was clearly of two minds about Greenfield.

"Albert Greenfield was a very difficult chairman, and I found it quite painful to serve under him, but nonetheless managed to do it," Bacon recalled. "He was very bull-headed and, of course, he was very much tied up with vested interests." However, Greenfield supported Bacon's enormously ambitious comprehensive plan for the city's long-term physical development—and found funding for it. "In fact, I have a strong suspicion that he was the only person who would have been able to do that. And although he certainly messed with the detailed zoning cases and made our lives miserable in that region, he never interfered with our comprehensive plan in any way, and I certainly gave him credit for that."

Dick Dilworth was well aware of the conflicts that Al Greenfield's appointment represented, and he knew he would take heat for the choice. Years later, he plainly explained the calculus behind it. Dilworth acknowledged that picking Greenfield to head the planning commission "wasn't in one sense a particularly good appointment, because he was always looking after his self-interest." But he noted that Greenfield played a critical role in helping him deal with the Irish bosses who were running the city's Democratic organization—Matthew H. McCloskey, treasurer of the Democratic National Committee; James Clark, trucking executive and the Philadelphia party's key financier; and most critically, Democratic city chairman Bill Green:

"God, I really needed somebody with some real power and some real muscle. And who could really talk and do business with Bill Green and Jim Clark and McCloskey. I knew I couldn't, because they were fundamentally antagonistic to me, you know. So it was really important for me to have Greenfield, and the price I had to pay for that was that he'd be chairman of the Planning Commission."

Joe Clark had made no such concessions to what some termed the Irish Mafia while he was mayor. He didn't have to, because he dealt with a far different party chairman, the affable Jim Finnegan. Writing years later in an essay in the landmark book, *Philadelphia: A 300-Year History,* Joe Clark and a coauthor, Dennis J. Clark, described how the Democratic City Committee was revitalized in 1948 under "the inspiring leadership of handsome, white-haired James A. Finnegan, a former Army colonel who was able for the time being to control the Democratic ward leaders who were no better and no worse than their Republican opposite numbers." The Clarks (who were not related) wrote that Finnegan "placed a somewhat reluctant Democratic organization squarely behind" the new city charter, which had been approved by the voters early in 1951. Finnegan, who was elected president of city council, worked closely with Mayor Clark, according to the ex-mayor's own account. He remained chairman of the Democratic City Committee until Clark's last year in office, 1955, when Finnegan left Philadelphia for Harrisburg to become Secretary of the Commonwealth and political adviser to the state's Democratic governor, George M. Leader. When Jim Finnegan left the chairmanship of Philadelphia's Democratic Party, he was replaced by Bill Green. How Joe Clark would have fared with Green in charge of the city's Democratic organization is unclear, but Dilworth's difficult relationship with Green would cause troubles throughout his time as mayor—and beyond.

Reflecting on his appointment of Albert Greenfield, Dilworth said that Greenfield gave him "at times damn good advice.... He was a fellow who knew every facet of the city. He knew virtually every political figure in it. He was enormously resourceful and he was not only a very attractive man, he was tremendously well read and very funny. A hell of a conversationalist. He was up on everything." But Greenfield was also, Dilworth added, "the most selfish son of a bitch who ever lived. . . . God, he was absolutely ruthless. He was only interested in making money. Very little else interested him. Oh, at times he could make gestures that were sincere. You know, nobody is completely avaricious. And there were times when he would do decent and generous things. But by and large his one interest was financial power."

Dilworth acknowledged the strength of Greenfield's hand in the administration, but said, "we did knock him down" on two major projects. One was the relocation of the food market. The other was the development of Penn Center. Both projects were carried out over Al's objections and without his participation. Dilworth said that he and Greenfield had a "serious falling out right after I was elected mayor because he wanted to harpoon the Food Distribution Center. So we had a really stormy meeting, just Greenfield and myself. I said that I was going to back it, and he said he thought he could defeat it in Council. I said that I didn't think that he could and that if he did, we would certainly line up the entire business community against him. And he finally did capitulate on that. . . . It was a terrible blow to his pride. . .and to his power."

Joe Clark would never have countenanced the compromises that came along with appointing a man like Albert Greenfield. Kirk Petshek wrote that Clark's most significant shortcoming was "his failure to appreciate politicians and his tendency to act as if they were beneath him. Too often he made it clear that he thought ward leaders [were] unimportant." Dick Dilworth, by contrast, seemed to take pleasure in the untidiness of politics. "Dilworth," Petshek wrote, "was interested in political strategy and felt at ease with politicians at any level." John Guinther made a similar point. He observed that while Clark was only willing to discuss issues "with those he considered his social equals," Dilworth understood "the importance of the broad-based colloquy." Guinther said that his "democratic receptivity may well have sprung from the sheer delight he took in people in all their varieties—which very much included politicians. Dilworth had studied them, had combated them, and understood them, well and sympathetically."

The mayor's relations with a South Philadelphia grain dealer named Samuel Regalbuto reflected his "sheer delight" in all kinds of people. Regalbuto had raised money for his bid for the mayoralty in 1947 and, said Dilworth, "I formed a great affection for him." Such was his affection that in 1956, he appointed Regalbuto as his commissioner of public property. Some of the members of his cabinet believed the grain dealer was totally unqualified for the position. That was the view of Vernon Northrop, who resigned as the city's managing director to protest the appointment. Northrop's departure infuriated the mayor.

"Oh, Vernon Northrop was so goddamn moral," Dilworth said in a 1972 interview, "he refused to serve if Sam Regalbuto was the commissioner of public property. And I will say—I have always held this against Joe—Joe [Clark] encouraged him. Joe said he thought it was an absolutely outrageous appointment." In retrospect, Clark might have been right. Dilworth himself disclosed in the 1972 interview that sometime after Regalbuto's appointment, an architect who had been awarded a city design contract reported that one of Regalbuto's staffers had tried to extort $10,000 from him. Dilworth summoned the public property commissioner to his office. "I said, 'Sam, if there's one thing you can't do, it's shake down architects. You just can't. You've got a goddamn good flour business, and you're going to fire that son of a bitch.... Sam, you either fire that guy and stop shaking these guys down, or I'm just going to have to sever relations with you.' " According to Dilworth, Regalbuto fired the staffer. "I'm sure he continued to do some shakedowns," Dilworth surmised, "but we never got another complaint. Sam was priceless."

His relations with Sam Regalbuto reflected Dilworth's enjoyment of his role as Philadelphia's chief executive. The City Council in the 1950s included a handful of upper-class liberals like the mayor. Most of the councilmen, however, were up-from-the-street types picked by ward leaders for their loyalty to the party. Whereas Mayor Clark had tended to ignore the councilmen, Dilworth reached out to them and got along well with most. Henry Sawyer, a Dilworth ally on City Council, noted that the mayor met with groups of councilmen for lunch every month to discuss matters of importance to the city: "Each lunch would have a theme, and it was very effective. He could be absolutely charming."

One of those charmed by the mayor was a South Philadelphia councilman named Paul D'Ortona, a native of Italy whose family immigrated when he was nine. Despite dropping out of school at 14 to take a nine-dollar-a-week job in a tailor shop, D'Ortona rose to become one of the city's most influential politicians and served 10 years as City Council president. D'Ortona's syntax was often skewed and his knowledge of foreign affairs was limited. When a representative from Nigeria visited City Council one day, D'Ortona welcomed him and spoke warmly of his homeland. But he pronounced it "nigger-ia." D'Ortona was hardly racist—he pushed for increased federal funds for programs designed for Philadelphia's minorities—but the malapropism angered the city's black population and made the councilman a laughingstock. Still, the gulf between D'Ortona and Dilworth in terms of education was no impediment to their working relationship. "Now, Dilworth was the type that I would place him as the greatest negotiator in the world," he told Walter Phillips. "He would give and take. He would compromise. He would respect your views. And if he made a mistake, he was the first to apologize. And that was great. It kept the city moving."

The differences in operating styles between Joseph Clark and Richardson Dilworth were delineated with great panache by Ed Bacon, who saw them close at hand:

"Joe Clark, in my opinion, had some very serious faults as an administrator," Bacon told Phillips. "His view of how to handle his cabinet...of simply putting the members in the gladiators' arena and he sitting in the emperor's box and turning his thumb up or down, encouraging his cabinet in every way to fight with each other to the death, was in my opinion not good public administration. . . . I invariably came away from those meetings with this overwhelming sense of guilt.

"With Clark, it was gloomier and gloomier, we've got to do better. With Dilworth, it was 'we're all together and we're gonna do great.' You'd go in there and you'd feel, 'My God, this is marvelous. I would die for this guy.'" (In another interview, Bacon said Dilworth was "an unbelievably witty man. . .about as funny as a person can be. . . . It was a tremendous pleasure to work with him.")

Bacon's positive assessment of Dilworth was not universally held. Certainly, Abe Freedman, Clark's city solicitor, didn't agree. Nor did Walter Phillips, whom the mayor dropped as director of commerce. And people like Vernon Northrop, whose principles were offended by Dilworth's actions, were not without ammunition for their complaints.

Shortly after taking office, the mayor made front-page news by favoring his former law partners with a juicy assignment over every other firm in the city. He made sure Dilworth, Paxson, Kalish & Green was selected as counsel in the issuance of more than $50 million in city bonds. Serving as bond counsel is well-paid and relatively easy work. Technically, the bond underwriters had the authority to name the counsel. But the mayor, who had resigned from the firm before taking office, wanted Dilworth, Paxson appointed, and he made no apologies.

"I expect to go back there when I complete my term as mayor," he told *The Bulletin* after it disclosed the deal. "I don't think there's anything wrong in getting them the bond business. The firm made it possible for me to be in politics. We lost business in 1947 [when Dilworth ran unsuccessfully for mayor]. They stuck by me. I think I have a right to stick by them."

Although *The Bulletin* printed Leonard Murphy's exclusive story above the fold on page one, there was no great public outcry over his conflict of interest. Dilworth's letter about the article, written the next day and addressed to Richard W. Slocum, the paper's executive vice president, was more in the nature of teasing than loudly complaining. "We have two unmarried daughters," the mayor informed Slocum, "and, like all fond parents, we want to make sure they find the best possible husbands. I am, therefore, deeply indebted to you for Leonard Murphy's article of yesterday...for this morning I have received any number of letters and quite a number of telephone calls from young lawyers evidencing an interest in marriage. When our daughters make their selection, I shall certainly see that you and Mr. Murphy are guests of honor at the wedding. Thanks very much for the boost." There was no response from Slocum.

While it's true that Dilworth embraced the quotidian tasks of governing, he always relished dramatic action most of all. This was a man who had fled college to serve in World War I and later cast off home life and prosperous lawyering to fight in World War II. In the courtroom, he was a tiger; on the campaign trail, he was a street fighter. Now, early in his first term as mayor, just as he was dealing with the outcry over his appointment of Albert Greenfield to the City Planning Commission and battling the backlash from his attempt to compromise the City Charter and restore a number of patronage jobs, Dilworth had a defining drama thrust upon him.

Late in June 1956, Dick and Ann Dilworth left on a European vacation. After a contentious first half year in office, he welcomed the time off. The Dilworths were away nearly a month, and concluded their holiday by boarding an Italian passenger liner, the *Andrea Doria,* in the French port of Cannes. The 30,000-ton vessel, with 1200 passengers and 600 crew, had been built after World War II to compete with Britain and France in transatlantic service. With 10 decks, three swimming pools, and over a million dollars in artwork, it was built for luxury.

The weather was fine on their crossing, and on July 25, the night before their scheduled arrival in New York, the Philadelphians hosted a small dinner party marking Ann's birthday. Just after nine p.m., they took a stroll around the deck and found the *Andrea Doria* wrapped in heavy fog not far off Nantucket Island. "It was impossible to see beyond the rail," Dilworth later wrote. He was surprised, given the weather, that the ship seemed to be traveling at top speed. He spoke to a young officer who said that thanks to radar, there was nothing to worry about. The Dilworths went to sleep.

At 10 minutes past 11:00, they were knocked to the floor of their cabin. Ann Dilworth, who had recently read *A Night to Remember*, Walter Lord's account of the sinking of the *Titanic,* exclaimed, "I think we've hit an iceberg." In fact, the *Andrea Doria* had been struck by the ocean liner *MS Stockholm* of the Swedish-American Line, which had been sailing at high speed in the opposite direction. The collision crushed the bow of the *Stockholm* and tore a large, deep hole in the *Andrea Doria*'s starboard side, about five cabins from the one occupied by the mayor and his wife. Almost immediately, the *Andrea Doria* took a 20-degree list, which made it almost impossible to stand. The Dilworths pulled on some clothes and crawled on all fours up a passageway to the starboard side of the boat deck. Once on deck, they discovered that all the starboard-side lifeboats there had already been deployed. The mayor then joined a group of men who formed a human chain to assist passengers as they crawled through the main saloon to the port side. They reached that deck only to discover that the port-side lifeboats could not be lowered into the water.

With their backs to the wall of the saloon, the Dilworths sat on the slippery deck of the sinking ship. Shortly before two a.m., a rescue vessel arrived. It was the famous French passenger liner *Ile de France,* which quickly put out lifeboats. Dilworth later termed it "the most welcome sight in our lives." Getting people into the lifeboats proved difficult. They had to slide down ropes or descend very wobbly rope ladders. When Dilworth sought to persuade Ann to go, she wouldn't leave him. By this time, the *Andrea Doria* was listing at about 30 degrees, and there was little time to offload the passengers. Still, Mrs. Dilworth refused to be separated from her husband. Taking matters into his own hands, Dilworth began pulling Ann across the deck, but she slammed into a glass door, bruising her right eye. He finally bundled his wife into a waiting lifeboat just after three a.m. It pushed off toward the *Ile de France* with the mayor himself still on the deck of the doomed liner.

A young Italian immigrant named Chiaramonti Miriello described what happened next: "There was a lot of confusion and most of the passengers had left the ship. I looked around, wondering what to do, and saw a tall man—a man in rumpled clothes, but I knew he was a *sindaco*—a man of authority. He was calm and confident, and he quieted some who seemed about to panic. He helped them to the lifeboats. Later I found out I was right; he was a *sindaco*—the mayor of Philadelphia." By dawn the fog had begun to lift. About 5:30 a.m., with the ship's list approaching 40 degrees, two lifeboats collected the last of the passengers, including Dilworth. His lifeboat circled the ship, looking for survivors, and picked up one man whose wife had died in the wreckage of their cabin. Suffering from shock, the grief-stricken husband was lowered to safety in a net.

Forty-six of the *Andrea Doria*'s 1,134 passengers were lost along with five from the *Stockholm*. When the *Ile de France* reached New York harbor about four p.m., all the ships in port blew their whistles and sounded their sirens in tribute to the rescue ship. The Dilworths were met by Cliff Brenner, the mayor's press secretary, and other staffers who also brought along the couple's two poodles. The Dilworths had lost all their luggage and returned home in borrowed shoes, having removed their own on the *Andrea Doria*'s slippery deck. Ann had a black eye and Dick was minus his socks, but neither seemed much troubled by the ordeal. In fact, Dilworth's brave performance after the collision at sea made Philadelphians proud of their mayor. *The Inquirer* wrote that his "great presence of mind" and "cool confidence" must have "helped enormously in the smoothness of the rescue operation." The barefoot mayor was photographed at home, resting on a sofa with springs and stuffing sticking out. The newspaper pictures led to numerous phone calls and letters from citizens—offering to repair the Dilworths' couch or to buy them another one. By public demand, they invested in a new sofa. Nor was the stricken ship forgotten. When their female poodle produced twins, they named one Andrea and the other Doria.

Years later, writing about the experience in the *Philadelphia Daily News*, Dilworth recalled that when he and Ann arrived in Cannes and picked up their tickets for the crossing, they noted that the tickets were stamped "*Andrea Doria, the unsinkable ship.*"

CHAPTER SIXTEEN

The Transparent Mayor
Potholes and penmanship

M ayor Dilworth made it a practice to respond with a letter to almost every article written about him or his administration—sometimes with a personal letter to the article's author, sometimes with a letter to the editor. More of his letters were published in the newspapers than those of any other Philadelphia mayor. Journalists covering Dilworth loved him for his willingness to comment—always candidly and often pungently—on any topic. But during his administration, you didn't need a press pass to get the mayor to answer your questions. As the city's chief executive, he was besieged with letters from Philadelphians, and he responded personally to an astonishing number of them. The result of all this penmanship was a continuing dialogue between the people of Philadelphia and a remarkably transparent city administration.

Dilworth once explained why he was so quick to respond to letters sent to City Hall when so many of them were sharply critical:

"First, we do not intend to be patsies for anyone with a four-cent stamp, a sheet of writing paper, and an envelope," he told Frank L. McBride, a *Bulletin* editorial writer, in a personal letter in September 1958. "When citizens complain, they will (and indeed, should) get a prompt answer to their criticism.

"Second, I personally believe that there cannot be too much public discussion of the conduct of city government. I think the decline of our city government in the past can be traced directly to citizen apathy and City Hall arrogance stemming from that apathy.

"Third, the people of Philadelphia are like people everywhere: They have short memories. I think it is well to remind them from time to time of the condition of the city's government and of the city prior to 1952. Not that I believe all is perfect now, or ever will be."

The letters the mayor received ranged from the banal to the sublime, and Dilworth took each one seriously—unless he saw an opportunity for a joke. Often his replies could serve as a model for how government officials should communicate with the taxpayers.

On August 8, 1961, the mayor received a letter from a patient in Room 817 at Jefferson Hospital at 11th and Walnut Streets in the heart of the city. The patient, Norman Geissinger, said he was writing at one o'clock in the morning to complain of being "kept awake by the jackhammer on the street corner below my window, working away at this hour of the night. What has happened to the spirit of brotherly love? Could not repairs be made in the daytime near hospitals?" One day later, Dilworth replied. He wrote that he could understand Geissinger's feelings and offered an explanation. The city, he said, must "completely resurface Walnut Street, and if we do so during the day, it will result in such bad traffic tie-ups and in such a loss of business to the merchants along Walnut Street that we agreed to do it at night. We are carrying out the work," he added, "as humanely as possible." How many of today's big-city mayors would go to such lengths to explain municipal policy to a single hospital patient with no political clout whatsoever?

Dilworth was just as quick and frank in responding to the more prominent, and he was not afraid to have an argument in public. In 1959, Philadelphia's police commissioner, Thomas J. Gibbons, an honest cop, had written an article in *The Saturday Evening Post* advocating legalized gambling. He argued that the profits from state-controlled betting could be used to strengthen the public schools. The mayor, in a letter to the *Post*, said that Gibbons had "fallen for the oldest fallacy of the human race—the idea that you can lessen an evil by legalizing it." Dilworth said that his experience as district attorney had "confirmed my belief that organized gambling cannot be tolerated in any large city." Under such conditions, he said, the "racketeers" who organized the games "would soon make honest and decent government" impossible. Within a few decades, of course, gambling was legal throughout much of the nation.

When Victor Blanc, Dilworth's successor as district attorney (and a man he despised), banned a French film starring Brigitte Bardot from Philadelphia movie houses, much of the populace applauded. "All decent citizens rejoiced that this blot on our fair City of Brotherly Love was removed," wrote a Catholic priest in Bucks County. Dilworth did not rejoice. He said Blanc had no right to "decide for two million people what movies they see." And for that comment, he was excoriated. "You and the rest of the Commies are no good," wrote one critic.

When a citizen complained that the pigeons on ledges at City Hall were an "absolute nuisance," the mayor agreed but pointed out: "Unfortunately, our city is absolutely loaded with pigeon-lovers, and all our efforts—including an anti-pigeon feeding ordinance—have met with failure." Although pigeon feeding in Rittenhouse Square is a "criminal offense," Dilworth continued, "old ladies, old gentlemen, and some younger people go in every day carrying paper bags full of crumbs and feed the pigeons as soon as the Park Guard has gone to the other side of the Square."

For the mayor, the pigeon war was a lose-lose situation. A subsequent disclosure that his deputy property commissioner had met with "some success" in reducing the pigeon population by raiding their lofts provoked an angry postcard writer to protest, "Your administration should be ashamed to waste taxpayer's money to make birds homeless during the winter months."

To alleviate chronic traffic congestion in South Philadelphia in 1961, the mayor proposed requiring residents to pay for overnight parking spaces in front of their houses. The proceeds of the $40-a-year licenses were to be earmarked for building off-street parking lots. Such a plan worked in Milwaukee, but Dilworth's scheme got nowhere. When he confronted his critics at a stormy public meeting, rock throwers targeted the building. A city councilman, Tom Foglietta, was cut by flying glass. As the angry crowd threatened to riot, the mayor's nervous aides urged him to sneak out the back door. But Dilworth being Dilworth, he walked calmly out the front, ignoring the boos and catcalls.

The mayor was unscathed, but the mail ran heavily against him. "When the day comes that Philadelphia makes me pay $40 a year to park my car on a street that I pay taxes to keep in good condition," wrote one irate resident, " that will be the day my wife and I leave this crummy city." "Dear Knucklehead," wrote another indignant citizen. "If everyone married money the way you did, they could afford to pay $40 a year to park in the streets. Instead of running for governor, I suggest you run for the next bus to Jersey. They deserve you." Dilworth took these jibes in stride. "I appreciate your taking the time to write and express your views on the parking situation," he wrote serenely to critic John J. Radke.

After a heavy snowfall in December 1960, Dilworth was barraged with complaints about snow removal. Such grievances are frequently heard in storm-tossed big cities, of course. But a Philadelphia resident, who had once lived upstate, suggested a novel solution. She said horses pulled snowplows up there and wondered why Dilworth didn't harness them in the big city. Instead of dismissing the idea with a form letter, the mayor asked the streets commissioner to look into it. "He reports that there are less than 50 horses in the entire city of Philadelphia which would be available for this kind of service, and we have 2,400 miles of streets and almost 5,000 miles of sidewalk." Motion denied.

Another resident observed that the mayor avoided snowstorms himself by heading south on vacation. "Not every Philadelphian," he wrote, "can afford to go to Florida or Bermuda in the winter, in the wake of a coming snowstorm." Dilworth wasn't apologizing. "For a number of years," he replied, "my wife and I have taken a 10-day vacation in the winter and four weeks in the summer. I work very hard at my job, and it is a job that requires seven days of work each week. I have found that in order to perform my task with vim and enthusiasm, it is important to take an occasional vacation."

A British visitor, Irene Gifford of Orpington in Kent, softened up the mayor by describing Philadelphia as "surely...the most perfect city in the world," but then termed its main bus terminal at 13th and Filbert Streets "utterly chaotic and dangerous, to say the least." She pleaded with him not to toss her letter aside as the work of "just another English crank! Do take a look for yourself." The mayor wrote back that he agreed with everything the "English crank" said and noted that a new terminal was planned for 17th and Market Streets.

On another occasion, a New Yorker who owned property in Philadelphia wrote that the city administration was applying "political pressure" to prevent him from acting against a tenant who hadn't paid rent for six months. "Should any political reprisals be taken against me," wrote Irving R. Neilblum, "I will immediately notify the various newspapers." Dilworth hit the ceiling. "What gives you the idea that you have any license to write insulting letters to me as the Mayor of the City of Philadelphia?" he asked. "From the tone of your letter, I am inclined to believe that you are the kind of person who makes it very difficult to properly govern a city.... In short, you are the type of person we can do without in our city." Dilworth sent copies of his letter to the papers and heard nothing more from the Manhattanite.

In 1956, Cereta M. Shockley, a registered nurse, suggested that the mayor curb crime by erecting a whipping post in the center of the city near City Hall. "This will make Philadelphia a safer place," she declared. Two years later, Lionel E. Doneson agreed: "I think the time has come when we have to start using again the old-style Public Whipping Stand" to make delinquents "think twice before they venture out again." Public lashings, he said, would teach juveniles that "we mean business."

Dilworth did not take kindly to the idea. "I am convinced, as is every thinking penologist in the country," he wrote, "that you never solve the crime problem by cruel and harsh punishment or by counter-violence. There is every difference between being soft and being firm." He said he was speaking not as a do-gooder or social service worker, but as a Marine combat veteran in two wars. Discipline is very strict in the Marine Corps, he added, "and I believe in discipline."

Center City crime was rampant in 1958 when a prominent Philadelphia banker and civic leader, Richard P. Brown, offered another idea that the mayor didn't like. Brown recommended calling out the Pennsylvania National Guard to "help patrol our streets until this reign of hoodlumism is stopped." Dilworth, who knew Brown personally, wrote that he was "frankly amazed to get such a letter from a man of your standing and character. If your suggestion were adopted, it would be nothing more than a token of surrender...we are living in an age of worldwide revolution and violence.... This is the time to be courageous and not panicky."

Another troubled Philadelphian, Irvin R. Barton, wrote in October 1958 that because of "muggings, stabbings, holdups, etc. by roving gangs of teenagers...it is not safe for folks to venture out at night, even in their cars." Dilworth responded that crime was not a "simple problem." Since the end of World War II, he said, Philadelphia's nonwhite population had increased by 250,000. "Most of these people "have little education, few skills, and little training for living in big cities. They are too often exploited, and they are the last hired and the first fired. They live in miserable housing and, unfortunately, have little control over their off-spring. The results of all this are bound to be explosive."

Dilworth correctly pointed out that the situation was worse in New York, Chicago, Detroit, and Los Angeles. He noted that Philadelphia was expanding its police force and adding two more courtrooms. "I am confident," he stated, "that this crime wave will recede...but there is no quick or easy solution...for we are living in an age of turmoil, violence, and tensions."

Dilworth was regularly denounced as a traitor to his race by some white Philadelphians. His support of an ultimately successful move to admit black students to Girard College, which had been founded by the 19th-century financier Stephen Girard as a boarding school for "poor white male orphans," produced a flood of derogatory letters. Although the case was in the courts for years and Dilworth was only peripherally involved, he was singled out for abuse. The mayor kept the correspondence in his "hate mail" file:

"I will be glad to vote for you as dog catcher. How can you be so blind?"

"What could one expect from a Nigger-Loving Skunk like you?"

"I am a white citizen of what used to be Philadelphia, but what is now known as Niggerdelphia."

"Are you the mayor of Philadelphia's jungle only? I wonder."

"Why in the hell don't you stop betraying your own people? We're sick of the Jews and the Niggers and the way you cater to them. There are a hell of a lot of Democratic voters looking for a White Man, and you are a Mulatto."

His critics on the issue crossed lines of class and education:

"I impugn your integrity and condemn your activities as contrary to public interest and indicating a selfish design to gain political advantage," wrote a suburban university professor.

"You have turned out to be an excellent example of a politically opportunistic charlatan," charged a Southwest Philadelphian. "Your appeal for votes, cloaked under a thick veneer of solicitude for a vociferous group of second-class citizenry, fools no one. You do not have the intelligence to keep your big mouth shut."

Dilworth always responded to white critics by writing that he received an equal number of letters from black residents blaming him for police brutality. "The fact that I am being accused by extremists on both sides of being unfair to their interests," he wrote in a kind of form letter, "makes me believe that the city government is in fact doing as good a job as can be done in a matter where feelings run so high." While condemning racism, the mayor called on blacks to play a larger role in improving American society. "There is a regrettable scarcity of leadership in the Negro communities in the large cities," he once wrote. "They must do more to help themselves and solve their own community problems."

Among the stacks of requests and complaints and the boxes of hate mail there were occasional admiring letters. Frederick W. Groff offered this salute: "I have lived in this city for 42 years and I have never known a mayor who worked for the city and its people as diligently and thoroughly as you have done. It is a good thing you have a sense of humor and a deep understanding of people." Dilworth responded with a single sentence: "Letters like yours are rare, indeed, in the life of a city official, and as a consequence deeply appreciated."

The Cold War was at its peak during Dick Dilworth's years at City Hall, and he didn't hesitate to express his views on international relations. After being admonished in one letter for welcoming a Polish Communist leader to Philadelphia in 1958, he defended his position on the grounds that it was important to "work out some effective means of communication between people of both countries." When *The Philadelphia Inquirer* ran a front-page editorial that same year urging President Eisenhower to invite the Soviet leader, Nikita Khrushchev, to Washington for face-to-face talks, Dilworth warmly supported the initiative. He had earlier recommended recognition of mainland China. Now he said that Khrushchev should be invited to address Congress and be given air time on American television and radio. "War is no longer a possible means of conducting diplomacy," the mayor told one letter writer who had been angered by his remarks. "If our way of life is good, and if our principles are sound, and we are sure they are, then we have everything to gain by putting all of our cards on the table and make Khrushchev do likewise."

The Philadelphia *Bulletin* also disagreed with Dilworth on this score. Instead of making a direct attack, however, the paper published a snide, one-paragraph editorial: "Mayor Dilworth says we ought to recognize Red China and invite Khrushchev to address Congress. The man next door disagrees. He says he wants the mayor to recognize potholes in Philadelphia streets and then invite the Highway Department to address them with a steamroller and a load of asphalt. Dilworth's reply was prompt:

> "Apparently, the point of your editorial is that mayors should stick to fixing potholes and collecting trash and garbage, and that foreign affairs are none of their business. Apparently, you also assume that no mayor is capable of having an intelligent opinion on foreign policy, and that this is the exclusive concern of heads of state, diplomats, and editorial writers.
>
> "In view of the fact that our great cities would almost certainly be the initial target if another war should occur, our foreign policy is of great concern to the mayor of Philadelphia. Therefore, as mayor of the nation's third-largest city, as a parent, and as a citizen, I shall continue to inform myself and to comment upon the steps our government takes or fails to take for peace in the world. You can be assured that in the process the potholes, trash, and garbage will not be neglected."

Nor would the mail.

CHAPTER SEVENTEEN

Philadelphia Black and White

The white noose and the problem of the color line

In 1830, there were only 15,624 Negro freedmen and slaves in Philadelphia's population of 204,585. Yet anti-black bigotry often led to violence. Race riots began in 1829 and continued sporadically until 1840. A visitor in 1842 wrote of Philadelphia: "There is probably no city in the known world where dislike amounting to hatred of the coloured population prevails more." An officially appointed riot commission—the first established in any U.S. city—reported in 1834 that the aim of the rioters was "destruction of the property and injury to the persons of the coloured people with intent…to compel them to remove from the district."

When Dilworth became mayor more than a century later, Philadelphia's black population was 26 percent of the total of just over two million, and race relations had not markedly improved. In February 1958, Mayor Dilworth sat down with a *Time* magazine correspondent to discuss what the magazine labeled "Philadelphia's New Problem." But it was an old problem, not a new one—and a national problem, not a local one. Back in 1903, the black intellectual W.E.B. DuBois presciently

145

defined it. "The problem of the 20th century," DuBois wrote in *The Souls of Black Folk*, "is the problem of the color line." His words rang truer with every passing decade. What was strikingly new was Dilworth's candor in speaking of the issue.

Dilworth employed a startling metaphor, telling *Time* that a "white noose" encircled the city. *Time* dramatized its article with a map of the region. Superimposed on the map, an artist had drawn a hangman's rope surrounding the heavily black city and separating it from the overwhelmingly white suburbs. The phrase "white noose" entered the language as a graphic description of Philadelphia's racial dilemma: Black families were blocked from leaving the city by a "growing collar of whites-only communities." And *Time*'s illustration sent the message nationally.

What got less attention in the *Time* article were the steps the mayor said were being taken to help balance the city's population. As a means of reducing "white flight," his administration was "deliberately making non-Negro apartments for older whites, pricing them out of the Negro range." The huge Eastwick housing development in Southwest Philadelphia was being designed with the hope that "no more than 10 percent of Eastwick will be Negro," he stated. "We have to give whites confidence that they can live in town without being flooded."

The newsmagazine noted that "Dick Dilworth is rated as the Negro's good friend," and that 30 percent of the City Hall workforce was black. That may explain why the mayor's incendiary comments drew little criticism in Philadelphia. His relations with black leaders and the black community were so solid that he could sound almost like a racist without being accused of racism. Another of his comments, however, may have cost Dilworth whatever support he had in the suburbs. "We're mighty anxious to get Negroes into the Main Line," he said, referring to the string of wealthy, nearly all-white suburbs stretching out to the west of the city. "We'd be happy to finance a house for somebody."

After the article was published, the mayor sent a telegram to *Time* charging that it had "misplaced the real emphasis" of his administration's efforts. "Our program is based on the fundamental policy that Negroes must have the same opportunity to purchase homes and select where they want to live as does any other American. We insist and have consistently insisted that in the City of Philadelphia Negroes shall have the right to buy homes and live wherever they desire." Dilworth asserted in the telegram that it was "virtually impossible" for black families to purchase new homes, and it was "extremely difficult" for them to buy "any kind of home" in the suburbs. "Unless that situation is ended," he argued, "the population of the big cities will soon be limited to low-income groups, with the well-to-do monopolizing the suburbs. Such a situation of class against class, of race against race, cannot long be tolerated in a democracy without destroying its moral fiber. That is why it is essential to put an end to the white noose of the suburbs, which is strangling our cities and threatening our basic concepts of equality and opportunity."

While making these points, the mayor did not deny any of the quotations attributed to him. He let stand his bald statements endorsing "non-Negro apartments" priced out of the range of blacks and, in effect, a quota system for black residency in Eastwick.

In March 1958, *Time*'s sister publication, *House & Home*, followed up with a long article entitled, "Inside story of Philadelphia's racial housing problem, as told by the mayor." The article was based on *Time*'s earlier reporting, and it included Dilworth's comments on "non-Negro" apartments as well as the "white noose." But *House & Home* went further. From a transcript of the original interview, it published incisive, often controversial comments by the mayor that *Time* had either condensed or omitted altogether. What now found its way into print was perhaps Dilworth's most outspoken examination of ethnic changes and the racial predicament bedeviling Philadelphia and other American cities:

"I moved here 31 years ago," the mayor began. "Then one-half the population was white Protestant. Neighborhoods were clannish and close knit—Irish, Polish, Italian. The population was stable. We were the only big city in the North with a majority of white Protestants. Now the Catholics are even with 'em.

"There are Negroes all over Philadelphia. The lowest income groups resent them the most—just as they did in the South—because they're competing for jobs. Also they think they're going to 'spoil' neighborhoods. The proud Italians think this especially and resist them in the southernmost part of South Philadelphia.

"We have about 75,000 third- and fourth-generation Poles in northeast Philadelphia. They clean the streets, tend their gardens, and keep up their homes. They really resent Negroes and damn well won't let 'em in. They even beat 'em up. The Negroes haven't hopped over the Poles.

"The tax base has really been hurt. Over the last 30 years, suburban income has tripled and the city income is just the same. Our real estate hasn't gone up the way New York's has. We had well-to-do properties of prosperous whites 30, 40, 50 years ago. There were so many white Protestants, who went from $6,000 to $20,000 and then got out of town to look good in the suburbs, that prosperous middle-class housing vanished.

"We're different from Chicago and New York. Chicago has ghettoized the Negro. There are damned few Negroes south of Harlem. There's virtually no Philadelphia section free of Negroes. Chicago and New York have managed to cling to their wealthy. In New York, particularly, the whites can stay in the city and be isolated from the Negro. Maybe it's because we were humane and had our tolerant Quaker tradition that this isn't true of us. In Chicago, too, they can live without fear of being infiltrated. But in Philadelphia, they're spreading out so rapidly that we're losing the whites. And remember: your white Protestant is apt to be your most prosperous person.

"This has been the best city in the country up to the last two years on race relations—due largely to the Quakers. Then there was the Supreme Court decision [*Brown v. Board of Education,* on desegregation of schools], Girard College, Little Rock, and Levittown. These have hardened things. The situation has become a little tense on both sides. You can't have reasonable meetings any more. Negro clergymen feel that to keep their congregations, they must keep attacking whites. Our white, low-income precincts give more trouble than the Negro ones, but there are more Negro precincts. There's more crime in the Polish and Italian sections. We have 130 to 140 murders a year, chiefly Negro."

Dilworth said he opposed an ordinance banning discrimination in the city alone, because it "would just drive people out faster." He favored instead a state-wide anti-discrimination law that would apply throughout Pennsylvania in all cities, suburbs, and rural areas. "We have to make it clear to whites that they can't run away." *House & Home* then carried the mayor's comments concerning black housing that were similar to those which had appeared in *Time*:

> "We are deliberately making non-Negro apartments for older whites— about 900—near the Art Museum, pricing them out of the Negro range. We're designing Eastwick the same way. We have to give whites confidence that they can live in town without being flooded.
>
> "Philadelphia has always been suburb-conscious, but we've got to get the whites back.... The trouble is that Eastwick—2,500 acres—is our last big chunk of available land."

In a subsequent letter to the editor of *House & Home*, Dilworth wrote that the magazine had distorted his views. Neither in the apartment project near the Art Museum, nor in Eastwick, he said, was there "any deliberate attempt at exclusion." Although insisting that there would be no discrimination, he did not charge that he had been misquoted.

Racial tension in Philadelphia rose further after a murder one Friday evening in April 1958. In-Ho Oh, a 26-year-old Korean graduate student at the University of Pennsylvania, left his uncle's apartment near the Penn campus in West Philadelphia to mail a letter. Heading back to the apartment, he was set upon by a group of teenage African Americans seeking money. A scuffle ensued. In-Ho Oh's assailants knocked off his glasses, shackled his arms, dragged him behind a parked car, and pummeled him with a blackjack, a lead pipe, and hard-toed shoes. When police arrived, his battered face was unrecognizable. He died 10 minutes later.

Oh, a political science exchange student at Penn, had been an interpreter for U.S. troops in Korea and an honor student at Seoul's National University. His murder shocked Philadelphia and outraged the mayor. At a simple Presbyterian funeral service two days later attended by two of the slain man's uncles and an aunt, more than a score of Korean and American college students and the Korean vice consul from New York, Dilworth was overcome as he spoke emotionally of the "tremendous courage" of Oh's family and friends.

"This is a dreadful and very mournful occasion for all us," he said as his eyes filled with tears. "It is a horrible thing that this could happen in our city." Stricken with grief, the mayor wept and said no more. But *Time* magazine reported that his tears were more eloquent than words. Dilworth returned to his office following the service and wrote a personal letter to Oh's parents.

After 11 black youths between the ages of 15 and 19 were charged with the brutal murder, the mayor wrote to the Korean ambassador to the United States in Washington: "That those who perpetrated this outrageous and senseless act of violence have been apprehended does not in any way minimize the shock that the entire law-abiding community has felt as a result of the murder of your country-man. It leaves us with the feeling that the world has some distance to travel before it can fully deserve being called civilized."

Two of the youths arrested in the slaying were sentenced to life in prison and five others served jail terms. Instead of demanding retribution, however, Oh's parents in Pusan appealed for leniency. They sent $500 from their savings for the kill-ers' "religious, educational, vocational, and social guidance." The family's gesture attracted national attention and inspired a motion picture on Christian love that was widely distributed.

Oh was buried in the graveyard of the Old Pine Presbyterian Church at 4th and Pine Streets in Philadelphia. In a visit in 1971, his parents placed a bouquet of red carnations and white daisies before his grave. The tombstone named their son and carried this quotation: "To turn sorrow into Christian purpose." Oh's father said he did not regret his pleas of leniency for the killers. "We don't think of it as a personal loss," he said through an interpreter. There is "purpose in every-thing Christian. We should show forgiveness and demonstrate this attitude to others."

Many Philadelphians were not as willing to forgive Oh's killers. Speaking on television a few days after the crime, Dilworth said he had been besieged with let-ters demanding "quick remedies" to the problem of juvenile delinquency. There were calls for a public whipping post, for a curfew keeping all those under the age of 21 off the streets at night, for ordering the police to "shoot prowlers on sight," and for the abolition of paroles and pardons.

Dilworth dismissed all of these ideas. He noted that juvenile delinquency had been a global plague since World War II. "We are living in a period of worldwide unrest and revolution," he added. "One of the inevitable consequences of that is the disturbance of our youth." He insisted, however, that juvenile delinquency was actually on the decline in Philadelphia, and delinquents accounted for less than two percent of the city's juvenile population.

With anti-black feelings at a fever pitch following the Oh murder, Dilworth spoke in general terms about the "juvenile situation." Not until page seven of his 12-page speech did the word "Negro" appear. "There is no question that the Negro incidence of crime is high in any city," he said. "But it is also important to emphasize that the Negro makes up the vast bulk of the population of our lowest-income wards. And the incidence of crime in a low-income, predominantly Negro district is no greater than the incidence of crime in an equally low-income, predominantly white district. The reason the overall Negro crime percentage is high is that there are so many low-income Negro districts."

Three pages later, the mayor got down to cases. "We should now take another look at the problem from the Negro's angle," he began. Dilworth spoke of employment discrimination against blacks, noting that virtually the only jobs open to them were in the "unskilled fields." They were generally excluded from the housing market, and the suburbs were "almost completely closed to Negroes.... What's more, the newly arrived, little-educated Negro is all too frequently seriously exploited in our big cities both by landlords and merchants.... All of this is bound to create deep resentments and tends to make the Negro family forget the enormous gains that have been achieved in the past 25 years."

In the most crucial part of his speech, Dilworth complained of a "regrettable scarcity of leadership in the Negro communities in the large cities." It was true, he noted, that there had been few opportunities for blacks in fields that create leadership. "But leadership must be developed and strengthened," the mayor pointed out. "I think the one real criticism that can be leveled at some of the important elements of the Negro community is that they demand, as they should, their rights as first-class citizens, but at the same time seek to retain the privileges and special considerations of a distinctly minority group. They must do more to help themselves, and solve their own community problems even though this is a most challenging and difficult task."

Only from Richardson Dilworth would black Philadelphians accept such a lecture without complaint.

An elated Joe Clark (*left*) and Richardson Dilworth on November 7, 1951,
a day after winning election as mayor and district attorney, breaking a
67-year Republican stranglehold on political power in Philadelphia.

Dilworth digs into the stacks of cases facing him as Philadelphia's newly
sworn-in district attorney in 1952. Helping out are the children of his second
marriage, Deborah and Dickie.

Thacher Longstreth (*left*), Dilworth's lanky young Republican opponent in
the race for mayor in 1955, took a historic drubbing but managed to smile
afterward. The dapper, well-born Democrat, Longstreth remarked, displayed
"the most instinctive thrust for the jugular of any man I've known."

Dick and Ann Dilworth were
among the passengers on the
Italian ocean liner *Andrea
Doria* when it was rammed by
another ship in the fog and
sank off Nantucket in August
1956. All but 46 passengers
were saved. Back at home,
Dilworth relaxes with one of
the family's poodles and *The
Inquirer*'s front-page story.

Pennsylvania governor George M. Leader (*right*), with Dilworth in Philadelphia for the St. Patrick's Day parade in 1957. Leader pushed for Dilworth to be the Democratic Party's pick to succeed him as governor in 1958, but was outmaneuvered by Philadelphia party chairman Bill Green, who secured the nomination for Pittsburgh mayor David Lawrence.

Photo: Special Collections Research Center, Temple University Libraries, Philadelphia, PA

The incumbent mayor with Philadelphia Democratic Party leaders Jim Clark (*center*) and Bill Green (*right*), monitoring election returns the night Dilworth prevailed in the Democratic mayoral primary in 1959. A year earlier, Clark and Green had been "vehement against Dilworth" as their party's candidate for governor, ruining his chances.

Photo: Special Collections Research Center, Temple University Libraries, Philadelphia, PA

Harold Stassen (*left*), former governor of Minnesota and former president of the University of Pennsylvania, was the Republican candidate for mayor of Philadelphia in 1959. Dilworth won in a landslide, 66 to 34 percent.

Photo: Special Collections Research Center, Temple University Libraries, Philadelphia, PA. Used with permission of *Philadelphia Inquirer* ©2014.

One of the most successful and far-reaching projects of the Dilworth era was the development of Society Hill, where dilapidated Colonial and Federal-era houses were renovated and interspersed with new construction. Here, Mayor Dilworth (in white suit) breaks ground on the project with (*from left*) developer William Zeckendorf, Planning Commission chairman Albert M. Greenfield, and City Council president James H.J. Tate, who would succeed Dilworth as mayor.

Photo: Special Collections Research Center, Temple University Libraries, Philadelphia, PA

The mayor and one of his wife's toy poodles out for a stroll—a familiar sight in Philadelphia.

Photo: Special Collections Research Center, Temple University Libraries, Philadelphia, PA

Ann and Dick Dilworth led the renaissance in Society Hill by building this Colonial Revival house there in 1961. In recent years, despite standing as a symbol of the rebirth of the area, the house has been threatened with demolition.

Photo: Special Collections Research Center, Temple University Libraries, Philadelphia, PA. Used with permission of *Philadelphia Inquirer* ©2014.

Billboards went up around Pennsylvania in 1962 when Dilworth resigned as mayor to run for governor.

Photo: Special Collections Research Center, Temple University Libraries, Philadelphia, PA. Used with permission of *Philadelphia Inquirer* ©2014.

President Kennedy stumped for Dilworth (*to left of podium*) in 1962 as Pennsylvania's next governor, and for Joseph Clark, who was running for re-election to the U.S. Senate.

Photo: Special Collections Research Center, Temple University Libraries, Philadelphia, PA

Joe Clark (*far left*) and Dilworth may have been the Pennsylvania Democratic Party's candidates for senator and governor, but Clark's expression sums up the pair's misgivings about Philadelphia party chairman Bill Green (*far right*). Outgoing Pennsylvania governor David Lawrence (*second from right*) had helped derail Dilworth's nomination for governor in 1958, paving the way for his own.

William Scranton—wealthy, well-educated, moderate, and analytical—proved a formidable Republican opponent in Dilworth's run for governor in 1962.

Ann Kaufman Hill met
Dick Dilworth in the early 1930s
when both were married with
children. When they divorced
their spouses and married each
other, it caused an enduring
scandal in Philadelphia.

Ann and Dick Dilworth at home in Society Hill in 1970, Dilworth's last
year as president of the school board. By all accounts, their marriage was
a happy one, and Ann's support for Dick and her interest in politics were
powerful drivers of his public career.

CHAPTER EIGHTEEN

Sick Transit

One gauge of a city's health is its mobility

Although he almost never rode in a bus or a streetcar, Richardson Dilworth believed that public transportation was as vital a public responsibility as the supply of water. And he crusaded longer and more successfully for public transit than any mayor before or since. In his first weeks in office, Mayor Dilworth, declaring that traffic was strangling the city, denounced the "ridiculous" size and "lavishness" of American cars. He vowed to "get people out of the automobile and back into the use of mass transportation." He even expressed hope for an eventual ban on vehicles in the center of the city. His concept was to create a restricted area that would comprise some 400 blocks, from 8th Street west to the Schuylkill River and from Spring Garden Street south to Lombard and South Streets. Within that area there would be free bus service. "I think we are going to come to that," Dilworth predicted, "and I think it will re-attract people to the city. But I know it's going to take a long time to work anything like that out, because it's got a lot of bugs in it."

Under the mayor's leadership, Philadelphia became the first city in America to subsidize commuter rail service provided by private carriers. He then led the fight for creation of a regional public entity, the Southeastern Pennsylvania Transportation Authority, or SEPTA, to take over privately run transit facilities in the city and four suburban counties. Getting the state and the suburbs to fork over money for a service primarily focused on Philadelphia took all of his skills of persuasion.

Dilworth provided the impetus for later extension of the city's Broad Street Subway south from Snyder Avenue to the sports complex at Pattison Avenue, and for a new railroad line taking riders from Suburban Station in Center City to Philadelphia International Airport. But his attention on improving mass transit was not only focused on the larger policy issues; in one instance, he insisted on installation of escalators at Suburban Station, whereas City Council favored sticking to cheaper stairways. Dilworth's passion for transit and his growing expertise were obvious, and after leaving office, he was picked by President Kennedy to head the Eastern Railroad Authority, whose job was to strengthen ridership from Boston to Washington; the creation of Amtrak can be traced, in part, to his work there.

The effort to improve mass transit was late in coming, however, and Philadelphia lagged behind other cities in delivering transportation services. Prior to the triumphs of Clark and Dilworth, the city had honored what historian Lloyd M. Abernethy termed a "long tradition of reverence for private enterprise." And the result, he wrote, was "an abiding resistance to the expansion of government programs and management even into those areas of essentially a public-service nature."

As an example, Abernethy cited the 50-year contract that the city awarded to a private firm, the Philadelphia Rapid Transit Company (PRT) in 1907. Founded in 1901 by traction magnates Peter A.B. Widener and William L. Elkins, the PRT had quickly been brought to the brink of collapse by rising expenses, stock manipulation, and a shortage of investment capital. "Under similar circumstances, other cities had put the transit system under municipal control," Abernethy stated, "but this alternative was never seriously considered at the time in Philadelphia." Instead, the PRT was awarded a monopoly over all existing transit operations in the city and over all new construction within time limits set by the city. Critics charged that under "this latest municipal crime," Philadelphia gave up regulation of the transit system and essentially agreed to subsidize the private company, as Abernethy noted. The PRT did little to improve conditions after that, and its decisions led to one of the worst labor strikes in Philadelphia's history. Endless disputes with the PRT finally led to its dissolution in 1940 and the formation of a new private entity, the Philadelphia Transportation Company, or PTC.

When Clark and Dilworth took over the city government in 1952, the PTC was running all of Philadelphia's buses, streetcars, and subways. It was the nation's largest privately owned transit firm, and its goal was to make money for its shareholders. That meant operating on the cheap while raising fares as much as possible. The PTC couldn't raise fares, however, without permission from the Pennsylvania Public Utility Commission. And when the transit company sought increases from the PUC in May 1953, it faced formidable opposition from the reform administration.

Mayor Clark appointed District Attorney Dilworth's brilliant law partners, Harold E. Kohn and Bill Coleman, as special deputy city solicitors to fight the fare rise before PUC Examiner Jay Eiseman. Their duel with the PTC's attorney, Hamilton C. Connor Jr., dragged on for months with the two sides quarreling over increases of a few pennies. Kohn and Coleman's hard-fought contest with Connor over such esoteric matters as the PTC's "depreciation reserves" and "fair value" was like a chess match of masters, each seeking to close out the other.

In retrospect, the PTC rate case may seem inconsequential, but it wasn't. Hundreds of thousands of workers depended on the company to get them to and from their jobs. Many were chronically short of money in those difficult days, and even a tiny increase in transportation spending would pinch. Most significantly, by opposing the fare rise, the city launched the battle that led to eventual public control of transit in Philadelphia.

On November 13, 1953, the rate case ended seven months and 19 days after it began. The long fight had been over PTC's request to raise its 15-cent base fare to 17 and a half cents. On the final day, financier Albert M. Greenfield, who was chairman of the PTC's executive committee and a major stockholder, attacked Harold Kohn. "You've done a good job of destroying," Greenfield declared. "You're a good wrecker." He dismissed as a "lot of bunk," the city's charges of PTC "gouging" and "juggling its books." Although Kohn stuck to his guns, the PUC granted the fare increase. And the PTC kept running Philadelphia's transit system.

The Philadelphia Transportation Company won that battle but lost the war. When Dilworth succeeded Clark in 1956, he moved to take over the company, which he said was in business to enrich its investors rather than to serve its riders. In a 1958 television broadcast, the mayor explained his position: "My forbearers were all great believers in private enterprise, and God knows our nation was founded on it." But he noted that "public transportation in the cities today has arrived at the same stage that water and sewage did 100 years ago," when these utilities moved from private to public ownership in Philadelphia. And he strongly favored the same shift for transportation.

On August 31, 1956, the mayor predicted that the city would take over the transit system within a year. "These babies are not going to be operating after June 30—that's my firm conviction," he said of the PTC. His timing was off, but he accurately foresaw the end of private ownership of Philadelphia's transit system. It was not until 1968 that the Southeastern Pennsylvania Transportation

Authority, or SEPTA, the public entity Dilworth had helped put together, bought the PTC for $48.2 million plus $17 million in pension obligations. The City of Philadelphia guaranteed SEPTA's bonds, which were sold to finance the acquisition. Although out of office by then, Dilworth was deeply involved. "He was the single most important person" in the acquisition, said Harold Kohn, who represented the city. "He carried the day."

Nevertheless, Kohn criticized his old mentor as a "somewhat inept negotiator" who was inclined to "give away the store to get his paramount interest, a public system. He realized it had to be done, and he would have paid twice as much as he ultimately paid. I thought he was overly generous in the settlement." He noted that Dilworth's law firm ended up as counsel for SEPTA. But Kohn added that whatever SEPTA's imperfections, it was better than having private enterprise running the trolleys. "Without it," he said, "we would have nothing."

In the 1950s, most of the railroad trains that carried commuters to Philadelphia were old and inefficient. And the companies that operated them, the Pennsylvania Railroad and the Reading Company, were struggling financially and had little interest in commuter service. Passenger operations for both railroads had sunk into the red in about 1950, and conditions steadily worsened. From 1963 through 1966, they reported combined losses in passenger service of about $210 million.

With commuter rail travel in peril, the mayor took an unprecedented step. "He offered public money to improve the service rather than letting it die," recalled William H. Polk, who was assistant administrator of the Passenger Service Improvement Corporation. PSIC was created by the Dilworth Administration to subsidize the PRR and Reading commuter lines. John A. Bailey, who enjoyed national repute as a transit expert, was named director of PSIC, and Edwin Tennyson, almost equally renowned, became the city's transit engineer. In 1958, Philadelphia began underwriting some of the cost of the Pennsylvania Railroad's Chestnut Hill line and the Reading's run as far as Torresdale in the far Northeast section of the city. One year later, the Reading's service to Levittown in lower Bucks County was subsidized. In 1963, the subsidy covered runs out of the city to Reading stations in Glenside, Hatboro, and Lansdale. Fares were reduced and trains were added. In three years, passenger volume grew by 44 percent to more than six million riders per year. Clifford Brenner noted that some critics thought Philadelphia's experiment merely helped rich suburbanites, but he disagreed: "If the city government had not moved with alacrity to preserve the commuter lines, I think this city would have been sunk." William Polk concurred: "Those subsidies did the job. They forced the railroads to stay in business."

New York state followed Philadelphia's example in 1965, purchasing the failing Long Island Rail Road for $65 million and creating the Metropolitan Transportation Authority, which was similar to SEPTA. But the subsidies were no panacea for the railroads, which had far deeper problems. The troubles might have been glimpsed in the 1968 merger of two once-great companies, the Pennsylvania Railroad and the New York Central Railroad, which together became the Penn Central.

Penn Central's disdain for commuter service was clearly illustrated in an impromptu exchange between Harold Kohn and Stuart T. Saunders, the new line's chief executive, on February 4, 1970. Kohn, who regularly rode the Penn Central's Paoli Local, was fed up with its failure to run on schedule. When his Devon-bound train was more than an hour late that evening, Kohn phoned Saunders to complain of slave-ship conditions on the rattler. Saunders recited the railroad's woes and then surprised Kohn: "I would be delighted to give it to you lock, stock and barrel," he said, referring to the 219 red coaches and 64 stainless-steel cars in suburban service. Asked if he meant it, Saunders replied: "Of course, I mean it. It's a drag and a drain."

After the Philadelphia *Bulletin* published a story based on Kohn's account, an abashed Saunders conceded that he had no authority to give away the railroad's rolling stock. But it hardly mattered. The Penn Central, just two years after the great merger, was near death. Less than five months later, on June 21, 1970, it filed for bankruptcy. SEPTA subsequently took over its commuter service and Amtrak its long-haul passenger runs. Both the Penn Central and the Reading disappeared as corporate entities.

Public transportation in Philadelphia remained alive if desperately under-funded. It got a huge boost in 1975, and Dilworth's protégé and law partner William T. Coleman supplied it. As President Gerald Ford's transportation secre-tary, he signed papers providing federal funding for the $300 million tunnel link-ing commuter trains east and west of Broad Street. The Center City Tunnel gave coherence to the entire commuter rail network and made possible the successful development of Market East and the Gallery shopping district.

In 1963, when President Kennedy chose Richardson Dilworth to head the Eastern Railroad Authority with responsibility for developing high-speed rail ser-vice from Boston to Washington, it was clear to Dilworth that Kennedy was "intensely interested" in the project. He appointed a good committee to work with the former mayor, and in six months they presented an informal plan providing comfortable train service between New York and Philadelphia in 55 minutes, and between New York and Washington in two and a half hours flat.

If Kennedy had lived and the plan had been executed, Dilworth believed, "it would have been a hell of a big help to this area." But the committee's effective-ness ended with Kennedy's assassination. The Philadelphian had "no influence" with Lyndon B. Johnson, and was forced to wait six months for a meeting with the new president. When the meeting with LBJ finally came, Dilworth recalled, "It was very clear that he just couldn't be less interested. He just sat there wondering what the hell we were talking about. All he could envision was where he lived. And he would either get a helicopter or an airplane or else get in that enormous Lincoln and drive on a straight road to Austin at 95 miles an hour. So who needed or wanted a train?"

Dilworth's role in transit improvements drew comparatively little attention from the press, which was bored by the topic and fascinated with his flamboyance in other areas. Clifford Brenner believed that the media missed the story. In his opinion, Dilworth's achievement "in working out the beginning of a unified transportation system of the city, state, and county governments was probably his major accomplishment as mayor."

CHAPTER NINETEEN

Reviving Society Hill
The heart and soul
of the colonial city

While Richardson Dilworth was mayor, Society Hill, the oldest and most historic part of Philadelphia, was the focus of a dramatic transformation. It had been a dilapidated slum. Today, with its attractively restored Federal and Georgian brick row houses offset by striking modern buildings, its wide brick sidewalks and cobblestoned streets, its shade trees, gaslights, and landscaped greenways, Society Hill feels both organic and charming. It's a section of the city that clearly works.

Society Hill owed its original settlement to a real estate speculator named William Penn. In 1682, the year of his arrival from England with the largest land grant ever given by the Crown, Penn formed a stock company called the Free Society of Traders to stimulate the economy of his colony. The Free Society was given an allotment of about 100 acres running roughly from the Delaware River to present-day 7th Street, between Walnut and Lombard Streets. Penn persuaded about 200 backers, most of them well-to-do Quakers, to invest a healthy total of about £6,000 in the venture. They planned to build houses in the designated area and engage in maritime commerce through trading stations along the Delaware.

Their plans were thwarted, however, when the Pennsylvania Assembly refused to confirm their company's charter. By 1686, four years after its formation, the Free Society of Traders was headed for bankruptcy. And by 1723, the last of its real estate holdings were dispersed.

The Free Society's former plot was at the very heart of the colonial city, home to many of the wealthiest and most prominent Philadelphians during and after the Revolution, and in the 18th and early 19th centuries it was replete with superb architecture. But after that came a gradual worsening of conditions as the old housing deteriorated. By the end of World War II, Society Hill was rife with seedy boarding houses, rat-infested warehouses, and vacant lots littered with trash. Many of its dwellings lacked plumbing and electricity; squatters inhabited some of the buildings, and others were empty.

The first positive step for the area came with the formation of Philadelphia's Redevelopment Authority in 1945. A state law allowed this new agency to acquire land by eminent domain in blighted areas and to sell or lease the properties for renewal purposes. Enter the United States Congress. In 1949, it enacted legislation giving cash to cities like Philadelphia that were clearing out slums. The Redevelopment Authority qualified for two dollars in federal aid for every dollar expended locally. In the two succeeding decades, it would pour about two billion dollars into the citywide effort. The hard-won relocation of the old Food Distribution Center cleared the way for development of the neighborhood.

Most evidence of Penn's Free Society of Traders had long since vanished by the 1950s, but a Free Society flag still flew on a tiny hill above Dock Street. Charles E. Peterson, one of the founders of the nation's historic preservation movement, dubbed the area Society Hill. And seeing the possibilities of the place, he moved into the 300 block of Spruce Street in 1954, thereby helping to launch the revival.

It took many hands to make Society Hill work. The Redevelopment Authority, led by Mike Von Moschzisker, was deeply involved. The Old Philadelphia Development Corporation helped coordinate the ties between public renewal and private investment. A key role was performed by John P. Robin, who came from Pittsburgh to head up redevelopment for the mayor. Supporting players included Richard J. McConnell, the city's finance director during most of Dilworth's tenure, who later headed the Food Distribution Center; development star William L. Rafsky, who served in the cabinets of both Clark and Dilworth; and Richard Graves, former executive head of the California League of Cities, who was recruited as the first director of the Philadelphia Industrial Development Corporation.

The two men whose involvement in Society Hill spelled the real difference between success and failure were Ed Bacon and Dick Dilworth. Bacon's vision coupled with Dilworth's persuasive powers proved to be an unstoppable combination. The innovative urban planner had advanced the idea of "revitalizing" Society

Hill in 1947, when a huge exhibit for remaking downtown Philadelphia opened in a department store. Bacon's many ideas dominated the display. Nothing much happened before his appointment as executive director of the City Planning Commission in 1949. After that, a great deal happened.

Under William Penn's surveyor-general, Thomas Holme, Philadelphia had been America's first planned city, and Edmund Norwood Bacon, whose Quaker antecedents had emigrated in Penn's time, followed in that tradition. In the 1950s, "urban renewal" often meant leveling poor black neighborhoods; critics termed it "Negro removal." But Bacon believed in reviving rundown sections by restoring the best architecture and replacing the rest with modern buildings. His approach was "exceptional for that period," wrote Christopher Klemek in *Urbanism as Reform*, originally his doctoral dissertation at the University of Pennsylvania.

In giving Bacon its 1971 distinguished service award, the American Institute of Planners cited his role in "the rebirth of Philadelphia as a vital city." When he received the prestigious Philadelphia Award in 1984, he was described as "a pioneer in urban revitalization." And the University of Pennsylvania, in giving him an honorary degree in 1984, hailed his "major impact on the design of cities in the 20th century." Inga Saffron, *The Inquirer*'s architecture critic, wrote in 2005 that in Bacon's 21 years as executive director of the City Planning Commission—from 1949 until his retirement in 1970—he "dominated all discussions about the city's form and function."

Although Edmund Bacon's place in planning's pantheon seems assured, not all of his plans have stood the test of time. His attempt to block off traffic and make Chestnut Street the city's "pedestrian spine" fizzled, and his support of converting commercially viable South Street into a crosstown artery linking the Schuylkill Expressway and Interstate 95 was, fortunately, scuttled.

But if Bacon was wrong on certain specific issues, he was totally correct in his overall vision of a livable city. Partly because of Ed Bacon, central Philadelphia has enjoyed population growth in recent years. Family homes have increased. New hotels and restaurants have proliferated. It is now a dynamic, walkable place with so many pleasing aspects. Bacon first advanced the idea of "revitalizing" the center of the city in the 1947 exhibit. In *The Saturday Evening Post*, writer Roul Tunley described what the planner had in mind for Society Hill:

> "Since the area was really the heart and soul of the colonial city at its greatest, the planners decided to develop it in a wholly new way. No one, except a few diehards, wanted to make the section into a mere museum of early Americana.... Such fake colonialism would merely have created what Lewis Mumford, author and architecture critic, once called 'a dead beauty preserved in embalming fluid.' Besides, there was not enough money for a project involving such uneconomical use of the land. Consequently, it was

decided to preserve the things that were genuinely worthwhile and add to them the best that modern architecture and landscaping could offer. The result would be a living area, rather than a museum, that would look both to the past and the future, and above all to the present."

Eventually, that is what happened. But it didn't happen overnight. And it might not have happened at all had it not been for Richardson Dilworth.

Bacon said that after the 1947 exhibit, he "continually worked on the [Society Hill] plan, trying to get citizen support for it," but without success. "Finally, I got Dilworth's ear, which was very important in making the whole thing move." Gustave G. Amsterdam, for an extended period one of Philadelphia's most influential civic leaders, said Dilworth "understood planning" and "beat heads together" to get things done: "Dick had a capacity for pushing things forward, I think, that was unusual among the mayors of Philadelphia. Many of us would have done almost anything to make Dick successful in his administration."

Mike Von Moschzisker, whose Redevelopment Authority chose the developers of Society Hill, spoke of a "gigantic tug-of-war" between competing interests. He cited Dilworth's "tremendous leadership" in overcoming obstacles. Former City Councilman Henry Sawyer recalled that the Society Hill development "just barely got through the Council," and that the mayor made the difference. Dilworth himself took no credit for Society Hill's concept or design. Asked about his role in implementing the development, he told *The Inquirer* in 1970: "Yes, I did push hard, but it had been planned and I was lucky enough to be in office when the program got started."

The mayor was also fortunate that prominent Philadelphians bought rundown housing in Society Hill because they believed in the neighborhood's future. One of the early settlers was C. Jared Ingersoll, who had resigned as a member of the City Planning Commission to protest Dilworth's appointment of Albert M. Greenfield as its chairman. Though no fan of the mayor, Ingersoll shared his faith in Society Hill. He and his wife bought a decrepit row house at 217 Spruce Street. It had been built by a carpenter named James Davis in 1750, and was enlarged by David Lenox in 1784. Lenox, who fought in the Revolutionary War, later served as president of the First Bank of the United States and as U.S. representative to the Court of St. James's in London.

"It was a lovely old house," Ingersoll recalled, but had "gone completely to ruin" when he and his wife purchased it from the Redevelopment Authority. "The filth was beyond belief. The fleas were such and the stench was such that you couldn't stay in the house over 10 or 15 minutes.... There were two dead cats found in the bathtub. The front door was just partly open all the time." Ingersoll said the place apparently functioned as a boarding house, "but I don't think anybody made money out of renting the rooms." The Ingersolls paid $8,000 for the house and spent more than $80,000 restoring it. They lived there for 18 years. A plaque now identifies the elegant three-story brick residence as the Davis-Lenox House. The block it stands on, like much of Society Hill, is lined with shade trees, wide brick sidewalks, and gaslights. James Davis and David Lenox would feel right at home.

One unfortunate consequence of the widely heralded revival of Society Hill was the relocation of numerous low-income residents, most of them African American. How many were forced out is unclear. Christopher Klemek wrote that of 2,197 buildings that stood in Society Hill when the project began, 726 were retained; the other two-thirds of the houses were torn down. Urban redevelopment projects throughout the country in the 1950s and 1960s led to relocation of countless poor, often black families. In some instances, great bitterness resulted and race relations deteriorated. This was not the case in Society Hill. Protests were muted. In some quarters, however, Dilworth was labeled a racist because of what happened in Society Hill. His record provides ample evidence of his progressive views on civil rights, but the charge still hangs in the air.

In addressing this issue in 2005, John Andrew Gallery, executive director of the Preservation Alliance for Greater Philadelphia, said that the federal urban renewal program gave "insufficient consideration" to its impact on low- and moderate-income residents, who were "usually African American." He said that "inattentiveness to dislocation" was an aspect of the federal government's urban renewal policy, and "Philadelphia followed the federal guidelines." Gallery continued: "This is not to say that was good or appropriate, simply to say that if the city wanted the federal money, these were the guidelines that applied. The dislocation of African American families from Society Hill was not a policy Richardson Dilworth created." And, he added, it would be "inaccurate and absurd" to label the mayor racially discriminatory because of it.

Perhaps the single most significant step in Society Hill's rehabilitation came in 1957, when Philadelphia's first family built a house there. Instead of just promoting the project, Mayor Dilworth and his wife moved in. At the time, the nearby Independence Hall area was being rehabilitated, but not much had yet happened in blighted Society Hill.

In 1956, Ann Dilworth had inherited just over a million dollars in the distribution of a $20 million trust left by her grandfather, Chicago financier Otto Young. After that inheritance, she began scouting for properties and "fell in love" with two that were for sale on Washington Square, according to her youngest daughter, Deborah Dilworth Bishop. "They were beautiful 1810 Federal houses with wrought-iron second-floor windows." Her mother bought them for $60,000, Deborah recalled, and planned to restore them into a single house:

"I was there when she got a letter from City Hall saying that the houses were condemned and had to be torn down. She never got angry at my father, but this time she was so angry that fire was coming out of her nose. 'What is this!' she said. He said, 'I'll see what I can do.' " The mayor got his wife an appointment with City Hall officials, probably in the Department of Licenses and Inspections. But they were not accommodating. "She was told the houses were unsafe and would have to be torn down."

Ann Dilworth offered a different version with the same outcome. She said she was advised not by the city but by her architect, G. Edwin Brumbaugh, and by her builder, John S. Cornell, that the two houses had to be demolished. Wherever the edict came from, the houses were torn down. And using Ann Dilworth's inheritance, Philadelphia's first couple then constructed, for about $150,000, a three-and-a-half-story, red-brick, Colonial Revival house with white trim on 6th Street near Walnut.

In May 1957, Dilworth told his former comrade-in-arms, Marine Corps General W.O. Brice, that he and his wife were "building a small house for our old age down on Washington Square, which is immediately adjacent to Independence Square." He noted that "The building of a house is a terrible headache nowadays." However, he expected their house to be "a very pleasant place when it is completed." And their 50-by-190-foot lot would allow ground for "a nice garden right in the heart of the city." He noted that Philadelphia was "making a great drive to revive the old Revolutionary [War era] part of the city" and was getting "considerable help" from the federal and state governments.

Ann Dilworth, in an interview with *The Bulletin*, said that "Dick and I feel that we are in a sense pioneers. We both love Old Philadelphia, and we both felt we would like to have a home here, right in the very heart of it. We may, quite possibly, be the first to build here at a time when the city is embarking on a program for the revitalizing and rehabilitating of Old Philadelphia." Deborah Bishop, who said the house was "perfectly beautiful," lived there for four years, from the age of 19 to about 23. "It was not Monticello," she said in reference to Thomas Jefferson's estate near Charlottesville, Virginia, but she viewed it as a symbol of her parents' faith in Philadelphia.

The new Society Hill house was wedged between the three-story Athenaeum of Philadelphia, a private, special-collections library founded in 1814, and the six-story home of J.B. Lippincott, the publishing company founded in 1792, the nation's second oldest. There was a general consensus that the Dilworths sparked the revival by actually moving into Society Hill rather than just promoting it. As a longtime resident of the area said of the mayor, "He put his money where his mouth was." And Henry Sawyer, recalling the struggle to get the Society Hill plan through City Council, said it wasn't just Dick Dilworth's charm that pushed the legislation through; the fact that the mayor and his wife moved directly into the area impressed even jaded councilmen: "That electrified them," Sawyer remembered.

Dilworth pushed hard not only for Society Hill, but for nearby Independence National Historical Park, which was also undergoing restoration. In a 1958 letter to Judge Edwin O. Lewis, who headed the project, he expressed his displeasure with M.O. Anderson, the park superintendent: "It does seem to me that Mr. A is moving at a snail's pace with regard to restoration of all the buildings actually on Independence Square. Each morning and each evening when I drive past Independence Square, I am struck by the outward shabbiness of all these buildings."

If the Dilworths' move was one catalyst for Society Hill's revival, who were the pioneers who followed in their wake? It was widely believed that only the wealthy could afford the thousands of dollars needed to rehabilitate ramshackle housing. But such was not the case. Franklin S. Roberts, a playwright who moved to Society Hill in 1961, said the "shock troops" were "more middle-class than upper-crust, newlyweds with infants rather than oldsters with college kids." There was a sprinkling of artists and writers seeking a quiet place to work, but the majority of the diehard pioneers were people who planned to make this place their permanent home, people of limited means who could not afford to lose the sums they would commit. Perhaps that is why the "brilliant concept" succeeded so brilliantly.

CHAPTER TWENTY

Dilworth for Governor
Red China and the Blanc slate

Richardson Dilworth relished his days as mayor of Philadelphia. Unlike many other idealistic reformers, whose best efforts are spent critiquing the ills of government from without, Dilworth was effective from within as well, displaying a passion for the nuts and bolts, the push and pull of governance. The toughness that he and Joe Clark evinced in office, combined with their idealism and Ivy League educations, led one wit to describe them as "hardboiled eggheads." Dilworth's commitment to his adopted city was the bedrock of his political career.

But if the mayor gave everything he had for Philadelphia while in City Hall, he also had an abiding aspiration to be governor of Pennsylvania. Having run unsuccessfully for the office in 1950, Dilworth was seriously considered for the Democratic nomination again in 1954, while he was making headlines as Philadelphia's hard-charging district attorney. Pittsburgh's four-term mayor, David Lawrence, long a Democratic power-broker in the state and the man who had orchestrated Dilworth's nomination in 1950, urged him to run again in 1954. *The Bulletin*'s Earl Selby wrote in the fall of 1954: "Early this year it was obvious that in every county except one, Dilworth was the party's No. 1 choice for governor. But that one was the king-sized job: Philadelphia."

Dick Dilworth's problem in Philadelphia in 1954—and for years afterward—was with Democratic Party chairman Bill Green. The immediate difficulty was a rancorous dispute between Green and Joe Clark. Clark, who had been a vocal leader in the movement that culminated in the reformist rewriting of Philadelphia's City Charter in 1949, staunchly defended the new document while he was mayor. The new charter completely closed the door on patronage. All 27,000 city jobs were to be civil service positions awarded on the basis of merit. Bill Green, responsible for keeping the city's Democratic organization running, was desperate for some patronage jobs to grease the machinery. He was relentless in pushing Clark to get the charter revised to permit at least some jobs to be distributed as patronage. Clark refused to consider such a move, and his intransigence on the issue caused a bitter rift with Green.

Dilworth, too, was frustrated by Joe Clark's lofty refusal to compromise. Like Clark, Dilworth had been involved in the charter reform movement; but Dilworth took a more pragmatic view of the new document. He thought that a healthy party organization was essential if any administration was to serve for more than a single term, and he felt that conceding a few patronage jobs was a fair price to pay for that stability.

As support grew for Dilworth's candidacy for governor in 1954, Clark promised to back his old friend. But the would-be candidate knew that his endorsement, valuable as it might be in many ways, would antagonize Bill Green and therefore lose him the critical support of Philadelphia's ward leaders. Left with no room to maneuver with Green, and calculating that in any case President Eisenhower's popularity would make it an uphill battle that year for any Democrat, Dilworth announced that he would not run for governor. "In '54," he stated years later, "it just looked to me hopeless." And it did turn out to be a strongly Republican electoral year in the state. Yet the man selected in his stead as the Democratic nominee, George M. Leader, an obscure 36-year-old chicken farmer and state senator from rural York County, won the governor's race comfortably.

Over the next four years, while Leader served as governor, Dilworth completed his term as district attorney and then won the mayor's office. As the 1958 governor's race approached, he was in the third year of his term and deeply engaged in his duties as mayor. But his gaze gradually turned toward Harrisburg, and the view was favorable. At the time, Pennsylvania's governor was restricted to a single term. Governor Leader, who was planning to run for the U.S. Senate, favored Dilworth as his successor. David Lawrence backed Dilworth again, as in 1950 and 1954. Calling him "colorful and capable," Lawrence said Dilworth was the strongest candidate the party could field. Other mayors around the state, including Altoona's Robert Anthony, pleaded with Dick to run. And Joe Clark, by then in the middle of his first term in the U.S. Senate, pledged his support.

Pennsylvanians weren't the only ones who liked Dilworth's chances for higher office. John F. Kennedy, as he laid plans for his run for the presidency, kept a watchful eye on his friend in Philadelphia. In a 1965 biography of Kennedy,

Theodore Sorensen, JFK's longtime chief counsel, wrote that the late president had viewed Richardson Dilworth as potentially the most dangerous of his rivals. The Kennedy team calculated that if Dilworth were elected Pennsylvania's governor in 1958, he would be "an obvious choice for the presidency in the same Northern and Eastern states to which Kennedy appealed," wrote Sorenson, "and would also be more acceptable to Westerners and Southerners." He added that Dilworth had "none of Kennedy's liabilities and many of his assets—a photogenic appearance, a heroic war record, a name for idealism and integrity, and a background of wealth and education."

Other Washington insiders had the same thought. In January 1958, Dilworth received a letter from William Benton, a former senator from Connecticut and publisher of the *Encyclopedia Britannica*. A classmate of Dick's at Yale, he was close to Adlai Stevenson, the Democratic candidate for president in 1952 and 1956. "I suppose you know you are being gossiped about as a presidential possibility," Benton wrote. "I had a three-hour lunch with Adlai on Monday and we talked much about you. Here is one piece of 'gossip' I can report. The story goes that you walk in as governor with a tremendous margin, and this will give you a key springboard for the presidential nomination. I shall wait until I see you firmly ensconced in Harrisburg before I pursue this subject further."

Dilworth's relationship with Bill Green remained an obstacle to entering the race for governor. His attempt, in his first months as mayor, to broker a charter compromise that would have delivered 500 patronage jobs to Green had blown up in his face. The harsh public reaction to the idea—Dilworth was vilified as a "charter ripper" for the suggestion—had ended his honeymoon as mayor and left Chairman Green resentful that he was still without the jobs he coveted.

But if his failure to deliver patronage jobs rankled Green, another Dilworth maneuver absolutely infuriated him. In 1957, the mayor had bitterly opposed the re-nomination of Victor H. Blanc for district attorney. Blanc, a former city councilman, had been elected DA as Dilworth's running mate in 1955. Green favored running Blanc again in 1957, but the mayor strongly disapproved of his performance in the office. Having done so much himself to clean up and invigorate the DA's office, Dilworth was loath to see it slide back into its former murk. "I was just determined we had to have a decent district attorney," he said years later. "So I went in and really fought in the policy committee." He declared in the meeting that Blanc was a party hack who "would do just as he was ordered." If Blanc remained DA, Dilworth predicted, the district attorney's office would be "worse than it had been even under the Republicans." Bill Green, he said, "got awfully sore about that and so did Jim Clark."

Dilworth, usually willing to compromise on political issues, was adamant. To give in on this, he said, "was more than I could take." If the party pushed Blanc's nomination through over his objections, "I would not support Victor Blanc or work for him in any way, shape or form." Then the argument "got really acrimonious," he recalled, "and it left very bad blood. Very bad. I said that Blanc was a no-good son of a bitch." Green, ignoring Dilworth's threat, forced Blanc's nomination through the policy committee.

The dispute over Blanc's nomination wasn't an isolated incident. According to Dick's aide Cliff Brenner, the episode illustrated a longstanding point of contention between Dilworth and Green. His boss, Brenner said, had made it clear that Green's input on matters of policy would be considered. In return, Dilworth felt that as mayor he deserved a voice in matters of politics. But Bill Green and Jim Clark had consistently shut Dilworth out of party decision-making. And now the mayor, in no mood to extend himself for a roster of candidates he'd had no hand in selecting, made good on his threat and abstained from campaigning for the Democratic slate. Even without his support, Blanc was re-elected.

In spite of the ongoing discord with Green, Dilworth felt confident as the 1958 gubernatorial primaries approached. Everything seemed to be lined up for a successful campaign. Looking back years later, he recalled that he "really did want to run, and I seemed to have the [nomination] sewed up. I really thought I did."

In early February, David Lawrence arranged for Dilworth to speak to a group of Democratic women in Washington, D.C. The mayor had not officially announced his candidacy for governor, but he was clearly shifting into campaign mode, and he gladly accepted the forum. The talk he gave was nothing memorable, but a single question afterward changed the course of the campaign. One member of the audience asked Dilworth whether he thought it would be possible to achieve world disarmament if Red China were not included in the agreement.

To have a chance of success, Dilworth responded, any such agreement would need to include China, and he indicated that admitting China to the U.N. would make sense. "We must establish some genuine communications between the Western and Communist worlds, and we must not fear such communications. If ours is the best way of life—and none of us doubt that it is—we should be delighted by the opportunity to show that way of life to the Communist world, and engage in the freest possible exchange of ideas."

Dilworth noted that after the talk, he "didn't think anything" about his remark. But the next morning, the Pittsburgh newspapers carried big headlines reporting the incident and implying that he was soft on Communism. Later in the day, David Lawrence and Joseph M. Barr, the state Democratic chairman and a Lawrence protégé, jointly issued a statement asserting that Dilworth's remark "hurt his chances" for the governorship; what they meant was that he was now a liability to the ticket and must be dropped.

A group of 82 prominent Philadelphians—including labor and business leaders, lawyers, physicians, architects, and artists—immediately wired Lawrence, saying that it would be a terrible mistake to dump Richardson Dilworth from the ticket. The telegram described Dilworth as "the most effective, inspiring mayor this city has ever had," and it concluded: "The accomplishments of his administration have brought worldwide recognition to Philadelphia as a well-governed, most progressive, dynamic, and honest city."

But David Lawrence showed no signs of changing his mind. And then Bill Green made his opposition to Dilworth plain. With Green and Lawrence against him, and with Jim Clark being "just impossible at that time," the mayor announced on February 15 that he wouldn't be a candidate for the nomination. But George Leader continued to be a strong supporter, favoring Dilworth over his own lieutenant governor, Roy Furman, who was seeking the nomination. Major labor unions also backed Dilworth. And of course, Al Greenfield was in his corner.

On February 26, the mayor met with Governor Leader in Harrisburg. They talked for 40 minutes in the Capitol and then walked three blocks to the Democratic headquarters for a climactic meeting of the state committee. Green and Jim Clark were there. They made a point of standing across the street while Dilworth and Leader posed for photographers. The governor, grim-faced, entered the building arm in arm with the mayor.

Before he went in for the meeting, Bill Green was asked whom he liked for the nomination. "I like everybody," he replied. "Dilworth?" Green was curt: "No, he took himself out." Behind closed doors, Green and Jim Clark were, according to Leader's aide David Randall, "vehement against Dilworth, and vented their vehemence on Leader." They championed David Lawrence, who won the endorsement of the committee. At the meeting's conclusion, Green was asked whether Dilworth was still under consideration. He ridiculed the mayor:

"I thought he took himself out of the picture. What did he do, change his mind? Besides, he ought to serve out his term. When we put him up for mayor, he said he would serve out his term. He gave us his commitment. He never serves out a term. What's he going to do, run out on it again?"

Lawrence, who had previously claimed to have no interest in running, had apparently changed his mind. Joe Clark, in sizing up Lawrence in an interview some years later, called him "as shrewd and astute a politician as I've ever known. Like all good politicians, he likes to keep a foot in every camp—like a centipede." Dilworth concluded that the game was over. "I couldn't have raised enough money to conduct a primary fight," he remarked in 1972. "I would have had virtually the whole organization against me. There's no doubt about that." David Lawrence then gained the Democratic gubernatorial nomination. And as it had in 1954, the time turned out to be ripe for a Democratic candidate. Lawrence easily defeated his Republican opponent, Arthur McGonigle, a Reading pretzel manufacturer.

Dilworth's aide Cliff Brenner acknowledged that Dick wanted "very much all during his political career to be governor," and that he "originally probably viewed the mayoralty of Philadelphia as a stepping-stone to the governorship." But by 1958, he added, Dilworth "was a very happy mayor of Philadelphia," and perhaps as a result he approached the gubernatorial nominating process with a "casualness" that led to mistakes. "I think that Dick was somewhat relieved," Brenner suggested, "when his governorship possibilities collapsed in '58. I don't think he wanted to leave Philadelphia at that time."

CHAPTER TWENTY-ONE

Retaking City Hall

Glorious victory,
then egregious embarrassment

Mayor Dilworth's relations with Philadelphia's Democratic Party were never smooth, and in the aftermath of the fracas over the 1958 gubernatorial race, as his administration continued to earn national notice for quality government, his dealings with party chairman Bill Green only became more vexed. Green would have been happy to put forward an alternative candidate to run for mayor in 1959, but, as Dilworth pointed out, "By that time things were going pretty well.... They would have liked to oppose me, but they just didn't see any way that they could."

Since he couldn't replace his foe, Green's strategy was to tie his hands. Green and the party, Dilworth noted, "had Blanc in the district attorney's office and a lousy City Council, so they knew they could make life...miserable for me." Of his relations with City Council's president, James H.J. Tate, Dilworth remarked: "We had a terrible time with him." Tate held the purse strings, he conceded, and if the party organization wanted money spent on something, "Tate would make sure it happened. But anything else, no...they're not going to spend any money." According to the mayor, Tate opposed spending on highways, transit, a badly needed traffic signal system, and the entire field of redevelopment.

Despite the internal tensions, when Dilworth was endorsed for a second term in March 1959, there was no hint of disharmony among the Democrats. The mayor put out a statement declaring that he was "honored to receive the unanimous endorsement of the Democratic Policy Committee for re-nomination.... We have a City Council which, under the fine leadership of Jim Tate, has supported every important project and policy decision which has had to be made." For Dilworth, this was a rare lapse from his characteristic candor. Continuing in this vein, he added: "We have also had the complete support of our city chairman, Bill Green, and of Jim Clark and the Democratic City Committee in every one of the important policy decisions we have had to make. And many of these required real political courage."

Early in 1959, Philadelphia Republicans found an impressive candidate to run against Dilworth. Harold E. Stassen brought impressive credentials to the campaign. Often mentioned as a possible Republican candidate for president, Stassen was well known in GOP circles from his days as the youthful and progressive governor of Minnesota in the 1930s. He had served as president of the University of Pennsylvania from 1949 to 1953, and later became disarmament advisor to President Dwight D. Eisenhower. After failing in a bid for the Republican nomination for governor of Pennsylvania in 1958, he plunged energetically into the mayoral race against Dilworth, making walking tours of the city and introducing himself to residents and small businessmen.

Stassen accused the Dilworth Administration of deliberately encouraging black migration from the South to strengthen the Democratic base in Philadelphia. He pledged to form a "special commission of men of all races with funds to pay the return transportation of those who voluntarily wished to return." His charge got headlines, but Dilworth took little notice of his opponent's allegations. He dismissed the Republican's candidacy: "Mr. Stassen is no more interested in serving as mayor of Philadelphia than he would be in serving as mayor of Yonkers. He sees the Philadelphia mayoralty solely as the first step in a walk he hopes will lead to the White House."

In their first joint appearance, Stassen sharply criticized the mayor. Instead of launching a counter-attack, as his backers expected, Dilworth took a deep breath and counted to 10. He then proceeded calmly to recite the accomplishments of his administration. He said later that in deliberately keeping his temper in check, he was following his wife's advice.

In September 1959, two months before the election, Dilworth presented his 1960 budget to City Council. Stassen had accused him of excessive spending, and the mayor noted that the budget was the largest in the city's history. He made no apologies. Instead, he said that there might be a tax increase in 1961. "Make a choice," he told the voters. "Do you want retrenchment or progress? The choice, however difficult, is a free one."

Late in the campaign, it was reported that Stassen had failed to pay the city wage tax for four years. He argued that as a member of Eisenhower's staff in

Washington, he was exempt from the tax, but the disclosure damaged his candidacy. Harold Stassen's name on the ticket had initially excited Republicans, but as election day neared, it was apparent that he was doomed to defeat. A group of 30 prominent citizens, most of them Republicans, took out full-page newspaper advertisements endorsing Dilworth.

The Republican-leaning *New York Herald Tribune* reported that Stassen was making "reckless" charges but getting nowhere. All three local dailies—*The Bulletin, The Philadelphia Inquirer* and the *Philadelphia Daily News*—came out for the incumbent. *The Inquirer*'s needle was especially sharp:

> "Stassen has been running for president almost continuously since 1940. Given a severe jolt by the Republican Party in 1956, when his attempted dislodgement of Vice President Nixon from the national party ticket ended in dismal failure, he recovered the limelight by running last year for governor of Pennsylvania. Having lost that fight, he now undertakes to run for mayor. His next bid, if this backing-away pattern is repeated, might well be for a job as magistrate or writ-server in the sheriff's office."

When the ballots were counted in November, Dilworth had crushed Stassen by a record-breaking margin of 208,000 votes, carrying 66 percent of the vote to Stassen's 34 percent. In *The Sunday Bulletin*, political columnist John C. Calpin addressed Dilworth and his victory, writing that it had "put a capstone on the efforts you have made for the city, which you love so much. Your love is not a pose, it is genuine amour."

If the populace and the media celebrated Dilworth's triumph, so did those who knew him best. One of the letters he received after the election was from his first wife, Bobbie, who congratulated him on "your glorious victory." Two decades after their divorce, Bobbie still followed his career closely and rooted for him. "It must be a great satisfaction to you," she wrote, "to know that the blood, sweat and tears you have expended on Philadelphia are being appreciated. Best wishes for the next four years."

The victory was glorious but the glow was brief. The start of Mayor Dilworth's second term was tarnished by a scandal arising from extensive repairs to the Frankford elevated rail line. A New England firm won the low-bid contract but failed to perform the specified work. After bribing three key employees on the city payroll and two executives of the Philadelphia Transportation Company to keep them quiet, the firm completed only a portion of the repairs but presented a bill for the full amount, defrauding the city of more than a million dollars.

In his 1972 interview, Dilworth spoke of the matter as a "tremendous embarrassment." He said his administration "had gotten so busy with planning and a whole lot of things that we were getting a little sloppy on details." The firm that got the contract had a "respectable" reputation, he claimed, but was somehow persuaded to engage in wrongdoing by a man whom the mayor termed "a drunken little bum from Massachusetts." He added, "I don't know how he managed to do that. I never found out. But the things he was doing were obviously damn flagrant, and we should have been able to spot them and pick them up."

Making matters worse, he charged, was the treachery of the city's very ambitious comptroller, Alexander Hemphill. A protégé of Bill Green's and, in Dilworth's opinion, a "pious phony," Hemphill dressed in tweeds, smoked a corncob pipe, and made his name as a relentless pursuer of corruption and wrongdoing. He was among the first to get wind of the bribery and to understand the scope of the scandal. But he downplayed its significance to Dilworth. When the first inkling of irregularities on the Frankford El job reached the mayor, he and his wife were on the point of leaving for a vacation in the Far East. The day before their departure, he called Hemphill to his house to discuss the Frankford El situation.

Years later, Dilworth recalled saying to Hemphill that night, "I won't go if there's any indication that there's any criminality in this thing, because I just don't think I can afford to." The comptroller assured him there were no indications of criminal activity, just "very sloppy work," which the city should have uncovered. "There's no criminality involved," he quoted Hemphill as saying, "although we will severely criticize the managing director and Licenses and Inspections for not having picked up this stuff." Reassured that the case was under control, Dilworth departed as planned. "God, the day after I left," he recalled, "Hemphill put out this release [describing] how this fellow had bribed everybody right and left."

The story caused a sensation, and Dilworth was nowhere in sight. Walter Annenberg, *The Inquirer*'s publisher, phoned the mayor, who was by then in London, urging him to return home immediately to address the issue. Dilworth got the same advice from his managing director, Donald C. Wagner, who was handling the mayoral duties. "So we took a plane back the next morning," Dilworth recalled. His administration moved swiftly to put the scandal to rest. The employees in the case were fired, and City Solicitor David Berger recovered all the money that had been taken. Questioned by a reporter about the scandal, the mayor defended the 10-year record of Joseph Clark and himself, saying, "I don't think there is any city in the United States better governed than Philadelphia."

Clark and Dilworth's achievements notwithstanding, there was now support in Philadelphia for a comprehensive investigation of City Hall. The Republicans called for a special grand jury probe of the entire city government with particular focus on the offices under Dilworth's jurisdiction. Even some of his friends urged him to agree to a grand jury investigation. The mayor opposed the petitions for such a probe. Appearing before Common Pleas Judge Raymond Pace Alexander, he presented the record of each city department, describing what he saw as high achievement and superior performance. After more than one month, Alexander denied the petitions for a probe. And on appeal, the state Supreme Court sustained the decision. Dilworth's worst misadventure as mayor was officially over, but reverberations from it would persist. If he had succeeded in closing off the investigation, he had also opened himself to charges of a cover-up.

The mayor prided himself on running an open and honest administration, and he might have been expected to allow the investigation in the spirit of transparency. As it turned out, he may have opposed it not so much to protect his reputation as to ensure his ability to govern. When he was asked in 1972 why he opposed the grand jury investigation, Dilworth said his aim was to shield City Council. "I had to get a hell of a lot of things out of City Council," he remarked, "and I knew I could never get them if I agreed to a grand jury investigation."

The councilmen were "terrified," he believed, that if the grand jury poked into their activities, they would find evidence of a "great racket" involving zoning variances for gasoline service stations. It had been standard practice for some years, Dilworth added, that when oil companies sought to open gas stations in Philadelphia, they were forced to make payoffs to City Council in exchange for the required variances: "They had a fixed price. It ran from $1,500 to $2,500, depending on the location."

Dilworth stated that at one point an oil company executive urged him to put a stop to the payoffs. But when the mayor asked if he would testify about the corruption in court, the executive demurred: "He said they did business in…something like 20 fairly good-sized cities, and in 11 cities they had to pay off. And if they squealed here, it would be impossible for them to do business in any of these other cities." Without the executive's testimony, there was no way to end the payoffs. Presumably, the kickbacks continued until Philadelphia had a surfeit of stations.

Joe Clark's administration, the spearhead of the reform movement after so many decades of deep corruption, was notable for its refusal to compromise its ideals under any circumstances. Dilworth, by contrast, throughout his mayoralty, showed a willingness to go a distance toward letting the ends justify the means. If conceding a few hundred patronage jobs would help keep reform—and his administration—alive for another term, he was agreeable. If countenancing the conflict of interest posed by appointing real estate baron Albert M. Greenfield as chairman of the City Planning Commission was the price Dilworth had to pay for a better bargaining position in the power struggle with the Democratic Party organization, he would pay it. And if, in order to get his reform agenda through City Council, he had to ignore the gasoline company payoffs to City Council members—and in fact work to keep the payoffs from coming to light—he would do that, too.

Yet Dilworth was no less an idealist despite his penchant for realpolitik. His vision was focused not so much on perfecting the system—he didn't assume it could be made perfect—but on delivering the most beneficial changes and services to the city. In the aftermath of the Frankford El case, Dilworth's impassioned defense of his administration succeeded in averting the grand jury probe and in preserving his working relationship with City Council. But it also left him vulnerable to charges of a cover-up. And although this didn't hurt him in the short run, it would come back to haunt him in time.

* * *

While on the local front the first year of Dilworth's second term was consumed with scandal, on the national stage it was dominated by the presidential primaries and the general election. Dilworth was an early supporter of JFK, and he became co-chairman of Pennsylvania Citizens for Kennedy during the 1960 campaign. Dilworth had met John Kennedy in 1956 and had been "tremendously struck by him." He frequently traveled to Washington while he was mayor, and each time he did in the late 1950s, he would stop in to visit Kennedy. "It was always an enormous pleasure to see him," Dilworth said in an oral interview conducted in 1965, "because his conversation was tremendously stimulating...he had a delightful—almost pixieish—sense of humor...and was a great master of understatement."

There was strong resistance to John Kennedy among members of Americans for Democratic Action in Philadelphia, because Kennedy had never taken a stand against Joe McCarthy; the great majority of ADA members supported Adlai Stevenson instead. But Dilworth, who described himself as "bitterly anti-McCarthy," still came out strongly for Kennedy: "One of the reasons I decided to be for [JFK]...was that in addition to being a bona fide intellectual and a fine politician—and it seemed to me you could not be an effective president unless you were both—he had enormous toughness of fiber."

In his role with Pennsylvania Citizens for Kennedy, Dilworth reported to Bobby Kennedy nearly every month during 1960. He was also president of the U.S. Conference of Mayors that year, and in that capacity he worked frequently with JFK and his staff on urban matters. When Kennedy campaigned in Pennsylvania, Dilworth and Bill Green joined him in his open car for two days. They "were hardly speaking" at the time, the mayor recalled. "But by noon each day, we three would be extremely friendly." Kennedy had "an amazing fund of good anecdotes, and an ability to warm people up and bring them together," Dilworth remembered. "Those two days riding with him were an absolute delight."

After his victory in November, the president-elect, who was working out of offices in the Hotel Carlisle in New York, asked Dilworth to meet with him there. He had advised Kennedy on housing issues, which would come under the purview of the planned Department of Housing and Urban Development (HUD), and

Dilworth had high hopes of being named Secretary of HUD in the new administration. At the Carlisle, he and Kennedy "talked at some length about housing, and I was beginning to think I was going to be offered it." But the offer was never made. Kennedy said he wanted to appoint Dilworth, but gave the job instead to Robert Weaver, an administrator from New York. A new life chapter that was not to be.

CHAPTER TWENTY-TWO

One Last Race

Little Lord Fauntleroy
with a bucket of whitewash

R ichardson Dilworth never lost his yearning for Pennsylvania's governorship. He had been defeated in 1950, had chosen not to run in 1954, and had been denied the nomination in 1958. Now, two years into his second mayoral term, as Governor Lawrence's single term was winding down, Dilworth began considering another run for governor. Philadelphia's new City Charter, whose anti-patronage provisions he had stumbled over, also included a requirement that a serving politician resign his current office if he chose to run for another post. He had tried and failed to have that language amended.

Dilworth sought to keep things quiet, but word got around about his intention to run, and late in November 1961, Robert L. Johnson, former president of Temple University and head of the Republican Alliance, a group formed to combat Dilworth, demanded that the mayor make his plans public. "If you are a candidate [for governor], then you should announce it and resign from your position as mayor, as demanded by the City Charter," Johnson wrote to him. "If you are not a candidate, then you should say so and give your full attention to 'minding the store' and stop using your high office as a platform for invective, insult, and political advancement." The mayor declined to make an announcement about his candidacy.

At a press conference the day after receiving Johnson's letter, Dilworth made light of it: "I am very much flattered by the concern being evidenced by the Republican politicians over the possibility that I might be a candidate for governor on the Democratic ticket." Then he toyed with the GOP, saying that George Bloom, the Republican state chairman, had "shown signs of nervous collapse" and that two other party operatives, William A. Meehan (the son of Sheriff Austin Meehan) and Joseph C. Bruno, had "waxed hysterical."

Meanwhile, Dilworth's former running mate, Joe Clark, was campaigning for reelection to the Senate. When President Kennedy came to Philadelphia for the Army–Navy football game in December 1961, he asked Governor Lawrence about the proposed slate. "It's in a mess right now," Lawrence told the president. Kennedy said he thought that "a Dilworth–Clark ticket would be a winner, and I hope it works out." The president also talked privately with the mayor. Asked if he was getting "enough backing," Dilworth stated: "There are problems but I'm going to run anyway." Kennedy replied: "Good for you. That's the way I did it."

Finally, on February 12, 1962, Dick Dilworth left City Hall after six years to run for governor, saying: "I don't claim to be a politician's politician, but I do believe I have the experience and the ability to meet these great challenges which confront Pennsylvania in the second half of the 20th century. I'm in this race to stay, and I shall give it the very best I have." He had kept his team of advisers virtually intact throughout his time as mayor, and many of them had served under Joe Clark as well. When Dilworth gave his farewell speech to his cabinet, there were, according to longtime aide Cliff Brenner, "grown men crying in the commissioners' meeting…it was a terribly moving, emotional scene."

Two days later, Democratic leaders met in Harrisburg and agreed to endorse Senator Clark for a second term, but they couldn't agree on a choice for governor. The problems that Dilworth alluded to in his conversation with John Kennedy could be personified in William J. Green, who was once again resolutely opposed to a Dilworth candidacy. Green insisted that he would support "anybody who can win." But if the party were to select a Philadelphian, he added, his choice would be not Dilworth but "my good friend" John Morgan Davis, who had been lieutenant governor in the Lawrence Administration.

Green's opposition to Dilworth led to deadlock at another meeting of the Democrats on February 22. It was reported that while the state's 14 Democratic congressmen from outside Philadelphia all supported Dilworth for governor, the six Philadelphia Democrats in the House opposed him. Word leaked out that Green had sought commitments on state patronage, but Dilworth turned him down.

Party leaders around the state had come to resent Bill Green's tactics. Back in November 1961, Bruce R. Coleman, the Democratic chairman in Berks County, had warned Dilworth to "disassociate" himself from the Philadelphia city chairman: "My statements on Green are the sentiments of the people here—not my personal sentiments. I'm a friend of Bill Green. Politically, he has done a good job. He has done a good job as congressman. I think he has a good organization. But the people resent him being a political leader who seems to dominate the political atmosphere of the state."

Dilworth finally won the endorsement of the Democratic policy committee on March 2, 1962. Before the vote, one of Green's aides spoke of the 1,800 state patronage jobs controlled by the Democratic city committee. "All we want," he said, "is an understanding from the mayor that the people who elect him aren't going to be replaced by his ADA friends." In other words, the machine politicians feared losing out to affluent liberals in Americans for Democratic Action if Dilworth became governor. Green was clearly unhappy. "No comment, none at all, no comment," he remarked after Dilworth's endorsement. He shook hands with Judge John Morgan Davis and left.

In the 1972 interviews, Dilworth said that Bill Green sought to keep him from getting the nomination by spreading scurrilous stories about him in western Pennsylvania: "The stuff he said to them—that I was a most ungrateful son of a bitch, that they'd find that I'd cut their throat in an instant, that they wouldn't get anything, and if they elected me, they'd elect a monster—did a lot of harm." But Dilworth added that Green worked hard for him in the general election: "Actually, he did. I never had any doubt about that. I don't think that he put his heart into it the way he would have if he'd had a candidate that he knew he could really push around. But he certainly didn't dog it at any time. He really didn't. I was quite surprised. I think he did what he could for me."

At a $25-a-plate dinner for Dilworth on May 9, 1962, Green first quoted Shakespeare—"This above all: to thine own self be true, and it will follow, as the night the day, thou canst not then be false to any man"—before adding, "And as the night follows the day, Bill Green will be in there all the way to elect a great Democratic ticket headed by a great Democrat, Richardson Dilworth." Despite such oratory, *The Bulletin* reported that it had required pressure from President Kennedy to make sure that Green publicly endorsed Dilworth. To guarantee that Green carried through, JFK had sent three of his staffers, including Myer (Mike) Feldman, his special deputy counsel, to the dinner.

Before the event, Green and Dilworth posed for photos. "Good luck, Dick," Green said brightly. "You know I'll be for you all the way." "Thanks, Bill," Dilworth responded, "I sure appreciate that." But Joe Clark remained skeptical. "We want no ticket-splitting in the coming elections," he cautioned. "We want

Democratic levers pulled from top to bottom. I don't want any split tickets, and I know that you don't either."

To oppose Dilworth for the governorship, the GOP nominated a man that historian Michael Weber described as their "best candidate of the century," William W. Scranton. Scion of the family that helped develop the upstate city that bore his name, Scranton held liberal positions on social issues including civil rights, Social Security, increasing the minimum wage, and the creation of the Peace Corps. He had worked in the State Department and had been a leader in his hometown's rebuilding effort before being elected to Congress in 1960. A conservative on fiscal issues, he was viewed as a candidate who could appeal to Pennsylvania's business community and would not be beholden to party bosses. Like Dilworth, he was a Wasp, a patrician, a graduate of Yale and its law school, and heir to a fortune made in iron and railroads (as well as water and natural gas). But unlike Philadelphia's mayor, he lacked experience in raucous urban politics. For much of the state, the absence of such infighting was seen as an asset.

Scranton may have been unsullied by political deal-making, but he was far from unconnected politically. There had been several U.S. congressmen on his father's side of the family, and Scranton's mother, Margery, known as The Duchess, was the state's most prominent Republican woman, having served on the Republican National Committee for more than 20 years and as vice chair for four of them. Her son, who at 45 was 19 years younger than Dilworth, had been an Air Transport Command pilot in World War II, delivering combat planes from Brazil to North Africa and flying General George Marshall and Senator Harry Truman on defense missions. Before the war, Scranton had dated Kennedy's sister, Kathleen, and met the future President. And after the war, he served as press aide to Secretary of State John Foster Dulles before winning his seat in Congress. It was yet another heavyweight who convinced Congressman Scranton to run for governor in 1962.

Former president Dwight D. Eisenhower, on seeing the preliminary slate drawn up by the GOP for the 1962 gubernatorial race, called it "a miserable ticket" and "a goddamn rotten setup." He invited Scranton to his farm in Gettysburg and urged him to run for governor. Scranton demurred repeatedly, but finally acquiesced when Eisenhower reportedly told him, "Bill, this all comes down to a four-letter word—duty."

Polls showed Dilworth was hundreds of thousands of votes behind at the start, and making up ground against Scranton proved difficult. Dilworth aide William Klenk said years later: "Scranton was an excellent candidate, and he had a good staff. He adopted the policy that no matter what Dilworth said, he would agree with it up to about 99 percent, and just leave himself a little bit of room so he wouldn't be accused of being a me-too-er." Historian Paul Beers was less charitable, writing that Scranton "campaigned on nothing but hot air, good looks, and lots of money. The Republican platform was meaningless. The tactics called for Scranton to be a celebrity. Said Dilworth later, 'It was like trying to pick up a drop of water. When you had it in your hand, there was nothing there.' That is exactly what Scranton's strategists designed."

A reporter for *Time* magazine who covered the race described Dilworth as "second to no one as a slashing speaker. Now shouting, occasionally weeping, he can carry an audience along with him on rolling waves of emotion." By contrast, he wrote, "Scranton on the stump is far less flamboyant and eloquent than Dilworth. But he is much more controlled. He has an analytical mind that travels fast to the major points."

Dilworth kept demanding that Scranton agree to a series of debates, and they met at last in a televised one on September 18, 1962. Dilworth might have been expected to benefit from the economic records of the previous two governors, Democrats George Leader and David Lawrence, who had taken the state's coffers from deficit to surplus. But Scranton waved that away, saying that in Pennsylvania, "we have the highest rate of unemployment in the Union," and pounding Dilworth for his ties to the machine politics that Lawrence—and Bill Green—represented. Over and over in the debate, Scranton decried the "power politics" of the Lawrence Administration and those "playing a political machine job in Philadelphia." Scranton also did a little digging into Dilworth's personal life and accused him of having been "fired—or forced to resign" a state job in 1935. Dilworth didn't respond to the charge during the debate, but afterward said that he had "quit a job as deputy Attorney General in Harrisburg...to return to private practice in Philadelphia." His former father-in-law might have disagreed.

The debate didn't have a clear winner, but Dilworth's team judged that their man had gained ground. The Democrat decided to keep after Scranton to engage in additional debates. On October 9, he poured it on: "The public gets tired of hearing my opponent describe me as 'the crown prince of failure.' And I know the public is tired of hearing me call him 'Little Lord Fauntleroy.' I don't blame them. I want debates. My opponent refuses to meet me. I hate to say this, but his basic lack of integrity would be exposed in a series of debates." Scranton ignored the challenge.

A week later, in a move recalling his debate years earlier with an absent Austin Meehan, Dilworth said that he would be in his opponent's hometown of Scranton on October 20, and if Scranton didn't show up, he would debate an empty chair on live TV. As late as October 19, Scranton said he would not participate. Dilworth went to the TV station at the appointed time and was preparing to debate the empty chair when, with a minute to go before air time, Scranton burst onto the set with a brush and a bucket of whitewash. The ground rules for the debate forbade the candidates from bringing notes or props, but Scranton had never signed off on the rules, since he'd never said he would participate.

Once the cameras were rolling, Scranton held up his bucket and brush and said, "I would suggest that he use this to try and make up for the whitewashing that he has been doing of the graft and corruption in Philadelphia, and likewise the record of the Lawrence Administration on which he is running." Dilworth was rattled, and remained on the defensive through the debate. Scranton hammered away at him for the Frankford El scandal, and particularly for having squelched the grand jury investigation. As Philadelphia's mayor, Scranton charged, he had presided over a "nest of squalor and corruption." And to avert the investigation, he had "whined and cried and fought tooth and nail to protect the grafters and corrupters who ran rampant in his administration."

After the debate, Dilworth turned to aide William Klenk and confided, "Bill, I've got to break up Scranton's press conference." When Dilworth entered the room where Scranton was talking to reporters, one of Scranton's aides, Walter Alessandroni, stepped between Dilworth and Scranton. According to an oral history account by Klenk, "Dilworth looked at him in a very stony way and said, 'Get out of my way, you little creep.'" Alessandroni did step aside, and Dilworth and Scranton had a heated exchange. At its climax, Klenk recalled, Scranton was shaking his finger and "Dilworth said, 'If you shake that little effeminate finger at me one more time, I'll separate you from your skinny ass.'" Klenk, who knew that his boss often manufactured his public rages, said of the incident, "I believe that Dilworth was trying to get Scranton to take a punch at him in front of the press." The cool-headed Scranton didn't swing.

The debate was a decisive victory for Scranton. With election day just two weeks away, Dilworth's reliable advantage in political debates had failed him, and his opponent's lead in the polls looked insurmountable. The electricity of the previous campaigns seemed to have drained away. One campaign event had Dilworth shaking hands with shoppers in Philadelphia department stores. In Snellenburgs, he was mistaken for an employee. A shopper shook his hand and asked, "Where are the new fall hats?" When Dilworth identified himself, the woman said: "Well, I wouldn't know about that. I'm from New Jersey."

Even the presence of the charismatic President Kennedy hadn't seemed to help. For two days earlier in the campaign, Kennedy had accompanied the candidate and Lawrence as they drove around the state, and they drew large crowds. But according to Dilworth, when they made a campaign stop and Lawrence would introduce him as "the next governor of Pennsylvania," the crowd would shout, "Sit down, you bum. We want Jack."

Having Kennedy there was "almost a drawback," Dilworth believed. "I wasn't really getting any exposure at all because they just regarded me as an interference to hearing Kennedy." Still, he would have welcomed Kennedy's help in the last weeks of the campaign. And JFK was scheduled to make another trip. But when, on October 14, 1962, the United States observed missile sites under construction just 90 miles offshore and the Cuban Missile Crisis erupted, the president's return to Pennsylvania was canceled.

In the final week of the campaign, Dilworth lost the support of *The Bulletin*, Philadelphia's largest daily. The paper, which had backed his two runs for mayor, charged that Dilworth had "ceased crusading for clean, unbossed government" and had done nothing about "entrenched corruption," which he formerly fought. In *The Bulletin*'s opinion, "the Commonwealth's best hope seems clearly to lie in the fresh approach promised by Mr. Scranton."

The Republican candidate's hometown paper, *The Scranton Times*, did not agree. "We're for Dilworth," it announced, saying that the Democrat had "demonstrated his capacity for executive leadership" and was "far better equipped" than Scranton to "direct the destinies of our great Commonwealth during the next four years." Dismissing Scranton's "sorry record in Congress," the paper denounced its "fellow townsman" as an "opportunist" who was "reckless in his campaign speeches and promises." Moreover, Scranton "lacked the knowledge of state government required of any man aspiring to the office of governor."

On election day, Bill Scranton carried 60 of Pennsylvania's 67 counties and defeated Dilworth by nearly half a million votes, taking 55 percent of the vote to his opponent's 45 percent. Remarkably, due to widespread ticket-splitting, Joe Clark won reelection to the Senate by 107,000 votes over Republican James E. Van Zandt. Clark carried Dave Lawrence's Allegheny County by 108,000 votes, while Dilworth, whose family was so big a part of Pittsburgh's industrial history, lost his native county by 52,000 votes, despite a 250,000-voter registration edge for the Democrats there. In Philadelphia, Clark outpolled Dilworth by more than 70,000 votes.

Reflecting in 1972 on his defeat, he credited Scranton with doing "a hell of a good job," and termed his opponent "an amazing politician. I think he just outmaneuvered me at every turn." Scranton did "a really effective job in playing up all the irritations the public has—the chronic unemployment, which really goes back more than 50 years; the natural antipathy of the voters of the state for the big city; the grand jury, and the so-called corruption." And he added, "It is clear that I never got off the ground. I don't remember a single good day during the whole goddamn campaign. I really don't. Not a single damn thing."

Asked what the difference was in this campaign, Dilworth replied: "I was beginning to get older. I was 64. My wife hadn't really wanted to get into it. She was wonderful, worked like hell on it, but it was just a terrible drudge for her. And by that time the children, who had been very helpful in 1950, had all grown up and gotten to work. So we had a very hard time setting up a really good campaign staff."

Late in the campaign, Joe Clark had been asked at a kaffee klatsch in Levittown whether Dilworth was "mature." The senator said the question was hard to answer. "I would agree that he is impulsive, that he sometimes shoots from the hip," Clark responded. "But you can ask any objective businessman in Philadelphia, and he will tell you that Philadelphia is the best-governed city in the world. In a way, I rode into office in Philadelphia on his coattails. And if you will just get behind some of these words of his—which I sometimes deplore—you will find a man of unimpeachable integrity."

As he always did when things went badly, Dilworth took all the blame: "I lost this election, not the Democratic Party." Politics was in his blood, he said, and he hated to leave the arena. "Believe me, this is not something I am doing of my own free choice. Nobody in elective politics ever gets out willingly. But as of now, I am out."

On the morning after his crushing defeat, Dilworth called a meeting of his campaign staff. Cliff Brenner was one of the aides in the room that day and wrote about it some years later. He and the rest of the demoralized staff were beginning to talk about the drubbing they'd just endured, "when in strode a smiling Dilworth. He'd been up late the night before but was his impeccably groomed self. Setting his briefcase down, he clapped his hands together and said, 'This morning we are opening the Dilworth Employment Agency.' Whereupon, he proceeded to interview every single staff member...and spent the better part of a month on the phone helping us all get placed in new jobs. About the debacle that had sent him back to private life for the first time in 15 years, not a word."

To those who knew Dilworth best, this would have come as no surprise. For longtime aide Cliff Brenner, his "most outstanding characteristic was his complete lack of self-pity. He did not look back; he was a man who always kept his eyes forward."

CHAPTER TWENTY-THREE

Sensation at the School Board

An influx of idealists, smart as hell and absolutely fearless

On December 6, 1965, Richardson Dilworth embarked on what many considered a hopeless mission: reforming Philadelphia's woebegone public school system. He took charge of the city's schools just as racial, ideological, and generational conflicts were beginning to rip the nation apart. He might as well have taken the helm of a creaking, century-old ship in the midst of a typhoon.

During his four years as Philadelphia's district attorney and six years as mayor, Dilworth had paid little heed to the city's public schools. With all his zest for municipal reform, he had never tried to reform the schools. Nor had his predecessor in the mayor's office, Joe Clark. In fact, in Philadelphia, education was considered off-limits to politicians; any involvement was construed as meddling. A strict separation of the school system from the municipal government had been effected in 1912 when, in order to end blatant political interference, the Pennsylvania legislature established Philadelphia's Board of Education as an independent entity. Before that, teachers had often been forced to pay aldermen for jobs, and ward leaders had the last word on the location of new schools.

Although this insulation from City Hall ended the worst abuses, it also cut the schools off from healthy political processes. Members of the school board, who were appointed by the city's judges, could generally serve as long as they wished. One woman lasted more than 25 years; at one point, the average age of the school directors exceeded 65. The board was dubbed the "House of Lords," and likened to an "arthritic turtle." The separation from City Hall had failed to remove all political pandering. Philadelphia's school taxes were set by the state legislature, and to buy the support of upstate politicians, the school board decreed that 250 of its 265 school buildings were to be heated with "fresh-mined anthracite" from the coalfields there.

From the mid-1930s through the early 1960s, virtually all the district's financial decisions were made by its business manager, Add B. Anderson, whose own schooling had ended in the 10th grade. The schools were relatively scandal-free under Anderson's tight control, but his priorities could be eccentric—he made sure that some school janitors were paid more than veteran teachers, for example—and his draconian economies came at the cost of educational quality. As a result, achievement scores in Philadelphia's elementary and junior high schools in the 1950s were substantially below national norms. Philadelphia's high school dropout rate was the highest among the nation's 10 largest cities, while one-sixth of the city's teachers were permanent substitutes. A higher proportion of school-aged children attended parochial and private schools in Philadelphia than in any other major city except Pittsburgh, and 63 of its aged elementary schools were classified as fire hazards.

American education came under the microscope after the Soviet Union beat the United States into space in October 1957. Russia's successful launch of Sputnik, the 23-inch aluminum ball that circled the earth, led to a nationwide clamor for improvement of the public schools. In Philadelphia, a call for reform of its sluggish system in the early '60s was headed by a coalition of downtown civic groups. William H. Wilcox, executive director of the Greater Philadelphia Movement, and Robert W. Blackburn, who headed the Citizens Committee on Public Education in Philadelphia, effectively rallied public opinion. Joining them was one member of the school board, Albert M. Greenfield's wife, Elizabeth. In time, virtually all business, labor, and civic groups with a stake in education pitched in.

Hearings were held. The process seemed interminable. But on May 18, 1965, Philadelphia voters approved an educational supplement to the city's Home Rule Charter that mandated much closer ties between the public schools and the city government. The hoary, 15-member school board was replaced by a nine-member board named not by judges but by the mayor, with input from a citizens' nominating panel. And this new school board was given a stronger voice in managing its own affairs.

Mayor James Tate's choice as first president of the reconstituted Board of Education was Richardson Dilworth. The selection was welcomed by the civic groups, even though neither the mayor nor his appointee had any personal experience of public schooling. Tate was a product of Philadelphia's Catholic schools, and Dilworth, who had received an upper-class private education, had provided the same for all of his children. Ann Dilworth was appalled that her husband took the "ghastly job," but Dilworth, who was 67 years old, relished the challenge.

It was a tempestuous time in urban America. The civil rights movement was in full cry. Ghetto blacks were demanding better schools, housing, and jobs. Frustrations mounted. "The streets are going to run with blood," Malcolm X had warned in January 1964. "Whole cities will be bright with flame. Black people are going to explode. It'll be like a war." Rioting erupted in cities across the country. The trouble began in Harlem in the summer of 1964, and spread in bloodier, more destructive uprisings in black sections of Detroit, Cleveland, Newark, and Los Angeles. Rioting in North Philadelphia in August 1964 resulted in one death, 600 arrests, and more than two million dollars in property damage.

Taking his new post just as tempers were boiling over, Dilworth saw the schools as central to the looming crisis. He agreed with James B. Conant, Harvard University's former president, who had warned that the large numbers of unemployable dropouts building up in urban slums constituted "social dynamite." Dilworth feared that Philadelphia would fall further and further behind if its schools were not improved and its teaching made more relevant.

He wanted to take decisive action, and he needed a school board that would follow his lead. Mayor Tate was never a friend; in private, Dick often spoke dismissively of his successor. But in forming the new school board, Tate consulted with Dilworth and, in effect, did his bidding in appointing the other eight directors. The result was the selection of a "Dilworth board" that generally supported his initiatives and annually renamed him as president.

Soon after taking office at the end of 1965, Dilworth began looking for a new superintendent of schools to replace the incumbent, C. Taylor Whittier. He was still searching the following June when, in a letter to his friend Mike Von Moschzisker, he wrote of Whittier, "I do not know when we are going to be able to get this school board running smoothly...in addition to everything else, our superintendent is a perfectly nice, big, overgrown teddy bear who does not seem to be able to get anything moving."

Dilworth's opinion of Whittier had become embarrassingly public the month before, when he first met Richard de Lone, a 27-year-old *Bulletin* reporter assigned to cover the school board. De Lone, both bright and brash, had graduated magna cum laude from Harvard, where he was also a varsity shot-putter, and had gone on to earn a master's degree in English at the University of California. He and Dilworth hit it off instantly, and Dick, thinking their conversation was off the record, spoke scathingly about a session he'd just had with the superintendent and his top aides. "Jesus Christ, we've got to get rid of half the administrators over there," he told de Lone. He likened talking with Whittier and his staff to being "on the board of Oliver Bair," Philadelphia's best-known undertaker. The remarks typified Dilworth's brand of hyperbolic disparagement, and he assumed they would remain between him and de Lone. But his assumption was wrong. Rick de Lone's exclusive story reporting that Dilworth wanted to remove dead wood at the school administration building ran on *The Bulletin's* front page.

The story caused a minor sensation, but when Dilworth next saw de Lone, instead of complaining, he started laughing. Soon thereafter, the reporter quit *The Bulletin* to work for Dilworth at the school board. He became an important player on Dick's team, and his new boss made an indelible impression on him. Looking back years later on his time with Dilworth, de Lone recalled the "incredible spark, verve, energy—the fun of the man." The people who worked for Dilworth, he said, "appeared better with him than they ever did before or after. He got the best out of people. One of his marks was that he surrounded himself with bright, energetic people and gave them license to do what they would."

Dilworth took his new hire into his confidence as he searched for a successor to Whittier. De Lone was a close friend of Theodore R. Sizer, a noted educational theorist who was then dean of Harvard's Graduate School of Education. At de Lone's suggestion, Dilworth talked to Sizer. And based largely on Sizer's recommendation, he chose a 40-year-old New England native and Methodist minister's son named Mark R. Shedd as Philadelphia's new superintendent of schools. Shedd had earned his bachelor's degree from the University of Maine and his doctorate in education from Harvard. When Dilworth tapped him to lead the Philadelphia school system—with its 280,000 pupils and nearly 300 schools—Shedd was superintendent of schools in Englewood, New Jersey, with 4,000 pupils and six schools.

Outwardly, Richardson Dilworth and Mark Shedd could hardly have been more different. Where Dilworth was often hot-tempered, occasionally explosively so, Shedd rarely showed emotion. Dilworth spoke his mind on controversial issues, but Shedd was generally more cautious. Dilworth's off-the-cuff comments were frequently priceless, while Shedd relied on carefully prepared speeches, some of them superb. The two men were alike, however, in believing that Philadelphia's school system needed a good shaking. They proceeded to shake it.

Shedd set the tone for his administration in a speech to his principals in May 1967, before officially taking office. It was a speech—almost certainly written by Richard de Lone—the likes of which had never been heard at school board headquarters. "It should be perfectly clear to anyone who reads the daily roster of violence, hatred, and despair which fills the newspapers," Shedd declared, "that this country needs a social revolution—a revolution in human values and human relationships. If this does not occur, I see no reason for bothering to educate our children. And if it is to occur, the schools must be the cauldron, whether we like it—or consider it our traditional role—or not."

The incoming superintendent promised to decentralize the schools, to stir a "lively dissatisfaction," to encourage teachers and principals to take risks, rock the boat, and "try the way-out idea."

"It is this sort of person we need in the school system at all levels," he declared, "and it is precisely this kind of lunacy which we must reward and we must stimulate in the system. No one can sit on his hands—or whatever else he sits on—if his responsibility is clear. And it should be clearly understood that anyone who takes risks may experience some failure. The system must develop an expectancy—even a hope—that there will be some dramatic failures. But it is part of my job, and part of the job of central office staff in general, to make sure that those who fail... are not punished. With the uncertainties we all face in education today, there are no safe bets, and we must all be gamblers."

Mark Shedd was adamant that Philadelphia's schools serve as the "cauldron" of a "social revolution," but it was a role they were unprepared for. In fact, it ran counter to the original aim of America's public schools, which were meant to serve as agents of social control during a period of heavy immigration from Eastern Europe at the turn of the 20th century. "We tend to think of our American system of public schools as having been founded out of great zeal for the welfare of the common people," wrote historian Merle Curti. "But actually this zeal was tempered by the zeal for the welfare of the employers of labor, by zeal for maintaining the political and social status quo."

Certainly, Philadelphia's schools had long upheld the status quo. And both teachers and administrators generally reflected the conservative values of the population at large in this working-class city. Given the disconnect between what the schools stood for and what Shedd was calling for, a reckoning was inevitable. Such was Dilworth's strength, however, that for a time the school system made enormous changes, one after another, under his inspiring leadership.

Just as he had when he was district attorney and mayor, Richardson Dilworth attracted remarkable people to work with him at the school board. "It was Dilworth who drew a bunch of us," said educator Bernard C. Watson, who came from Chicago and later was named head of one of Philadelphia's largest charitable foundations. "He was a mythic figure, smart as hell, and he wasn't afraid of anything. The man was absolutely fearless."

In Dilworth's first 10 months on the job, more than 15 top administrators were hired and their average age was 35. They lacked backgrounds in pedagogy, but they were strong in liberal arts. They were tagged the "Ivy Mafia," and their arrival marked the first takeover of a major American school system by lay reformers. "Education today," said one of the new breed, "is too crucial to be left to the educators."

Besides Mark Shedd and Richard de Lone, four of the new administrators came with degrees from Harvard and three had attended Yale. Others were drawn from Dartmouth, Princeton, Amherst, Antioch, Oberlin, and the University of California at Berkeley. Dilworth's magnetism convinced such diverse talents as entrepreneur L. Daniel Dannenbaum, planner Graham S. Finney, civic agency head Bob Blackburn, business executive Harry M. Perks, lawyer Gillian Gilhool, and Price Waterhouse partner Donald Rappaport to sign on with the city schools.

Daniel Dannenbaum, who had been captain of Yale's swimming team in 1943 and two-time national backstroke champion, sold his frozen-food distributorship to become the school district's business manager. Harry Perks, who got his master's degree in engineering from Yale after graduating from The Citadel, left a vice presidency at Day & Zimmermann, a major engineering firm, to take charge of school construction.

Bob Blackburn, after leading the battle for school reform in Philadelphia in the early 1960s with the Citizens Committee on Public Education, had joined the Peace Corps and spent two years as a regional director in Africa's Somali Republic. Returning to Philadelphia, he was hired by Dilworth as the school district's director of integration and intergroup education. Blackburn actively recruited former Peace Corps teachers into the city schools, and soon Philadelphia could claim more teachers with Peace Corps experience than any other city or state. Blackburn, who is white, and Marcus Foster, an African American, worked together at the school board and were dubbed "salt" and "pepper." In 1970, Foster, who had earned a towering reputation as a principal and administrator in Philadelphia, was recruited to be superintendent of schools in Oakland, California. He persuaded Blackburn to be his assistant there, and the two of them instituted sweeping changes and made impressive progress.[14]

Donald Rappaport was a 38-year-old partner in the Philadelphia office of the international accounting firm Price Waterhouse in 1965 when his life changed. Before even taking office, Dilworth formed task forces to study the schools and tell him what needed to be done. He was looking for someone to head up a task force examining the school district's finances. He didn't know Rappaport, but a friend of the accountant recommended him. He phoned and explained the purpose of his call. Rappaport met Dilworth and was immediately won over. Taking

---

[14] Tragically, in 1973, the radical group calling itself the Symbionese Liberation Army (famous for abducting Patty Hearst) murdered Marcus Foster and left Blackburn critically wounded. A rambling "communique" from the SLA claiming responsibility for the attack revealed that the group had completely misunderstood Foster's program and killed him for policies he had not supported.

a leave of absence from Price Waterhouse, he headed the school board task force on finance and later became deputy superintendent for administration.

"He was the most influential person in my life," Rappaport said of Richardson Dilworth. "He had the greatest leadership qualities of anyone I've ever met. He could get anybody to do anything for him. People would drop everything to do what he wanted." One of Dilworth's striking qualities, Rappaport recalled, was the trust he put in subordinates: "He expressed complete confidence in people working for him. I would go through accounting gyrations to produce surpluses when there weren't any. He would say, 'I don't know anything about accounting. Anything you want to do.' That would motivate me to knock myself out. But actually he knew exactly what was happening. He understood the issues. He was getting the most out of people with this approach."

Rappaport remembered that when he and Dick Dilworth paid calls on City Council President Paul D'Ortona, pleading for money, Dilworth always made sure to be five minutes early: "He'd be wearing his double-breasted suit and he'd just sit there, courteously waiting for his audience. He had the courtesy of kings."

Graham Finney had been working as a city planner in Boston when Ed Bacon recruited him for Philadelphia's City Planning Commission in 1961. Bacon was nationally known at that time and so was Mayor Dilworth, then in his second term. Finney found such leadership irresistible: "Clearly, Philadelphia was a Mecca for urbanists and planners. It was the city getting the most federal dollars, doing the most in urban renewal." He served as Bacon's deputy at the planning commission until 1964, when he left to run a North Philadelphia civic agency funded by the Ford Foundation.[15]

Finney was still at the civic agency in early 1966 when Dilworth asked him to serve on a task force examining the school district's capital building requirements. After the task force recommended heavy spending on the decrepit physical plant, Dilworth told Finney to draft the building plan, and get it done in 30 days. "We met our deadline," Finney recalled, "and came up with a half-billion-dollar building program." He drafted it on his dining room table.

But his work was just beginning. Dilworth told him: "Listen, you drafted this plan, and now you've got to get it implemented." The implication was that he should come work for Dilworth. He told Finney to dream up his own position— "whatever you want to be." So Finney left the civic agency and designed a job for himself at the school board—"Director of Development."

When Graham Finney began work at the school board, Taylor Whittier was still the superintendent of schools, but "hanging on by his teeth," and he didn't

---

[15] One of Finney's hires at the agency was a claims adjuster for Sears Roebuck whom everyone called Willie Goode. W. Wilson Goode would later serve two terms as Philadelphia's first black mayor.

make the newcomer feel welcome. "I had to bring in a card table from home and my own Olivetti typewriter because no one was going to help," he remembered.

Finney was young and green, but Dilworth gave him a free hand with the $500 million building program. His responsibilities did not extend to the engineering and architectural work, but he laid out the program, gradually staffed it and, over the next several years, pushed it forward. He noted that federal aid was readily available in those days: "Washington would phone on a Thursday and say, 'Here's $25 million. Where shall we send it?' That made it easier to move along."

Like Donald Rappaport, Graham Finney emphasized Dilworth's skills at delegating authority, empowering people working under him, and defending them from criticism. Early in the reform period, one of Finney's ideas caused an uproar. Teachers recruited from all parts of the country needed housing and, as a stopgap measure, some were staying at the Benjamin Franklin Hotel in Center City. Finney suggested a long-term solution. He pointed out that the 50-acre campus of Lincoln High School in Northeast Philadelphia was largely unused. Why not build "modest apartments" for teachers there? Logical enough, but in making that proposal, Finney had overlooked the racial implications. The Northeast was an all-white enclave, while many of the incoming teachers were black. Northeast residents who already distrusted the educational reformers viewed Finney's scheme as an integrationist plot. "All hell broke loose," he recalled. "The people were mad as hornets." A protest meeting attracted about 2,000 "very angry people." Dick and Ann Dilworth picked up Finney and drove him to the meeting. Within five minutes, Dick had "defused the situation and stuck up for me. He charmed the audience and drove me home." No more was heard of the modest apartments for teachers.

Despite that setback, the Dilworth board's early accomplishments were staggering. In the first 12 months alone, it opened 14 new pre-kindergartens, 100 kindergartens, and 100 school libraries. It doubled the money for books, increased overall spending by $145 per pupil, and launched the record building program overseen by Graham Finney by putting $66 million worth of school construction under contract. Dilworth, viewing teacher recruitment as crucial, personally visited Penn State and other universities, urging their best students to teach in Philadelphia. His board reduced class size and virtually wiped out the teacher shortage by hiring 3,000 new teachers and putting their salaries in the top rank nationally. The average Philadelphia teacher's salary rose during Dilworth's tenure from $7,200 in 1965 to $12,500 in 1971.

The reformers also proved to be remarkably innovative. Following an idea of John Patterson, one of Dilworth's key advisers, they set up a network of "magnet" schools with high-quality programs to draw students from the entire city. The special schools gained national attention, and "magnets" were established in school districts throughout the United States.

One aim of the Philadelphia magnets was to encourage racially integrated student bodies in the predominantly black school districts. Black enrollment in the city's public schools had topped 50 percent in 1961 and was climbing steadily. Skeptics in the civil rights movement had suspected that public school spending in Philadelphia would decline once black enrollments exceeded 50 percent. But they were wrong. Instead, at Dilworth's behest, education expenditures increased dramatically just as black enrollments rose.

Another idea that was hatched in Philadelphia under Richardson Dilworth and spread nationally was the "school without walls." The idea for this alternative school originated with Cliff Brenner. He had been Mayor Dilworth's press secretary and went on to work for him at the school board. Brenner's proposal was that the new kind of school, instead of operating from a traditional building, hold classes in the city's central library, its museums, cultural organizations, newspapers, and other institutions. Many of the sites were clustered along the Benjamin Franklin Parkway, the boulevard that connects City Hall with the Philadelphia Museum of Art, and so the school became known as the Parkway Program.

The program arose, Brenner wrote, from "a sea of emotion—of protest against war, against discrimination and against political dishonesty." Its mission was to "provide an environment which encouraged rather than stifled student creativity, to promote rather than discourage independent thought and action, an opportunity and a place for the turned-off, the tuned-out, the students who considered themselves lost, unhappy and confused, to pursue their education."

The Parkway Program was an imaginative scheme, and soon curious high school students from the suburbs were riding buses into the city to enroll there. Over the succeeding years, it went through numerous incarnations, but it's still alive in Philadelphia.

A federally funded report in 1967 found Philadelphia's schools undergoing "the most dramatic reform in urban education since World War II." A Philadelphia citizens group agreed: "Probably no large school system has ever moved so far, so fast, and in so many ways as has Philadelphia's during the past 12 months."

Vast sums were needed to finance the reformers' ambitions, and Dilworth lobbied constantly for money from Washington, Harrisburg, and City Hall. He formed an alliance of city schools throughout Pennsylvania to persuade the state legislature to increase school spending. He did the same nationally, allying Philadelphia with America's biggest school districts to encourage increased federal funding for schools. While it was common for city politicians to engage in such lobbying, it was very unusual for school officials to get involved. Dick Dilworth was a trendsetter in that regard as in so many other ways. He and Mark Shedd developed close ties with U.S. Office of Education officials, who were much impressed by Philadelphia's efforts to revitalize its big-city school system.

In its first year in office, Dilworth's reform board picked up $66 million in new money through additional state and federal aid and tax increases. In succeeding years, it maintained this fast pace. Over six years, it persuaded the state to increase its annual cash allotment to the school district from $50 million to $165 million. And City Council contributed $40 million in new money. Overall, the school district's annual operating budget more than doubled in those six years, going from $151 million to $365 million.

Despite the increased financial support, the school system soon started spending more than it was taking in. Both as mayor and school board president, Dilworth spent lavishly. He was so committed to action that he sometimes ignored costs. Now, as his board ran big deficits, he turned to Philadelphia's conservative bankers for help. Largely because of their faith in Dick Dilworth, they began lending the district tens of millions of dollars.

Meanwhile, the reformers took steps to open up the school system. Just as transparency was Dilworth's byword in City Hall, so it was at school board headquarters. For the first time, nationally standardized tests of basic skills were administered in every city public school. And, for the first time, school-by-school results were published. The picture was not pretty. With results in hand, Philadelphia parents and taxpayers could see how far behind national norms the district ranked in reading and arithmetic. It was clear that much work needed to be done. And this was a message that the reformers wanted delivered.

To improve communication with the public, Dilworth's board put its show on the road—and on the air. Formerly, all board meetings had been held on midweek afternoons at the school district's imposing headquarters, known as "the Palace on the Parkway." Rarely would more than a handful of citizens watch these pro forma proceedings. There was little reason to attend, because the board reached all major decisions behind closed doors and simply ratified them in public with little or no debate or disagreement.

Dilworth's board met at night in schools around the city. And the meetings were carried live by the city's public television station, which received a subsidy from the school board. Debate was encouraged at these televised sessions, and there was no shortage of it. Dilworth, his white hair in place but his voice rising in anger, would sometimes attack his critics in the audience, and they would strike back at him as the TV cameras rolled. It made fascinating viewing for spectators at the meeting and for those watching at home. "Only somebody like Dilworth could have run those meetings successfully," Graham Finney remarked, "because they were sometimes very explosive. He liked it, and with his sense of humor he could diffuse a lot of angry situations."

One night, the cameras turned to a black high school student who had received permission to address the board members. She was articulate and beautiful, and she was furious. In denouncing Dilworth's team, she uttered an expletive which was carried live into countless homes by TV, but which the newspapers declined to print the next day. The word was "motherfucker." No doubt the lovely young woman employed it to shock and horrify Philadelphia's white community and to bring shame on the school board. If board president Dilworth was flustered, he didn't show it. But the incident would be cited by critics as evidence of the board's loss of control over its student body, especially its African-American component.

Such anger did not deter the reform board from reaching out to alienated black students. Rick de Lone marched with a summer school class to protest all-white housing in the city's Northeast section—the same neighborhood where Graham Finney's idea of apartments for new teachers had been shot down. Black militants were invited to address high school students at assemblies. Mark Shedd supported a "bill of rights" giving all students a voice in school governance. He set up weekend retreats held in private facilities where students were allowed—even encouraged—to tell principals exactly what they thought of them. Some of them did just that, vilifying white high school principals as racists.

Community activists were sometimes invited to the retreats as well. According to a report submitted to the school board after one of the retreats, one principal, an older, unmarried woman who headed a high school for girls, was asked if she knew what students meant when they shouted, "Fuck the system!" Before she could answer, a community activist broke in: "What's the matter, white woman? Don't you understand black folks' talk? Or don't you know what 'fuck' is because you're a maiden lady?" The principal broke down in tears.

Shedd defended the "sensitizing workshops" as a "critical first step for ventilation of feelings which inhibit true communication." While some principals supported the workshops, most were appalled. A group of principals protested to the board, calling the sessions "denigrating, humiliating and demoralizing." They charged that only "black power advocates" were invited as community representatives, while "the great majority of Negroes who consistently strive for understanding and concerted effort is ignored." Speaking of themselves, the principals concluded: "Never before have those who have given their lives to the education of deprived children felt less appreciated." The result, they said, was "extreme polarization of staff and a lessened sense of dedication." Although the workshops were quietly dropped, bad feelings lingered.

In September 1967, Mark Shedd addressed more than 10,000 teachers and administrators in Philadelphia's Convention Hall. Although he had been commuting from Englewood since the first of the year, his official appointment had just taken effect. In his talk, Shedd took the position that cracking down on misbehaving kids was not the way to attack mounting absenteeism and truancy. "We cannot meet discontent with dogmatism," he declared. "What we should not do is tell these alienated youngsters to cut their hair."[16]

Two months later, on November 17, 1967, some of Philadelphia's "alienated youngsters" staged a demonstration outside school board headquarters. They were demanding black studies courses, more black teachers and principals, and the right to wear African clothing and Afro hair styles. Shedd had specifically encouraged students to petition their schools for urban studies classes, and to take their requests right to the school board if their schools were not responsive. When the students gathered on November 17, he agreed to meet with their leaders. "We heard their demands," Shedd was quoted in *The Bulletin* as saying, "and then went into conference session to give them an answer."

As Mark Shedd and his board members conferred inside, the crowd outside was getting restive. With some 3,500 students trampling on the landscaped court-yard and shouting "Black Power! Black Power!" the small police detachment grew nervous. As the noise and movement increased, Police Lieutenant George Fencl, respected head of the civil disobedience squad, put in a call for help. The police commissioner, Frank L. Rizzo, who had been appointed by Mayor Tate just two months earlier, was attending the swearing-in of 111 police sergeants and lieutenants at City Hall. When Fencl's call came in, Rizzo rushed the newly promoted officers into buses, which sped them to the scene less than a mile away. He placed his men in a military formation across from the demonstrators and then ordered them, he later claimed, to "move in and disperse." Others alleged that Rizzo's order was "Get their asses!" or "Get their black asses!" Whatever his words, close to 200 club-wielding policemen charged the unarmed black students, who fled in disorder. The confrontation lasted only a few minutes. But afterward, some of the demonstrators ran through Center City bowling over pedestrians, overturning lunch carts, and disrupting subway operations. Some 18 people were hurt, none seriously, and 57 were arrested, mostly for disorderly conduct.

In the aftermath, public opinion divided sharply—and predictably. The Philadelphia branch of the American Civil Liberties Union called for Rizzo's removal, while the Catholic War Veterans demanded the ouster of Dilworth and

---

[16] I was in the hall that day, not as a reporter but as a substitute teacher. With the blessing of Dilworth and Shedd and with a grant from the Carnegie Corporation of New York, I had taken a leave of absence from my job at *The Bulletin* in order to teach elementary school kids in poor sections of the city and write a book about urban education. My plan was to spend one semester in a predominantly white school in Kensington and a second semester in a mostly black school in North Philadelphia and then describe what happened in my classroom. What happened was humiliating. I lasted less than a week as a fourth–grade classroom teacher at the Lewis R. Elkin School in Kensington before being routed by kids who were far wiser than I in the ways of that world. However, I remained as an observer in the schools and came away with renewed respect for inner–city Philadelphia's sore–beset teachers. (See *Whitetown USA*, Random House, 1970.)

Shedd. Richard de Lone insisted that he had witnessed a "police riot," and the former mayor said that the demonstrating "children" were blameless. By contrast, board member William Ross, who would later succeed Dilworth as board president with Rizzo's support, declared that there was "no pattern of violence on the police force."

James Tate, vacationing in Florida, briefly considered using the incident as a pretext for firing Frank Rizzo. The mayor had enthusiastically embraced Rizzo and his tough-guy tactics that fall while campaigning, and two weeks before the school board protest, Rizzo's working-class supporters had helped Tate to a very narrow victory over Republican Arlen Specter. But he saw Rizzo as a potential political rival and wondered whether the moment had come to remove him. Yet even as left-wing groups condemned Rizzo's actions and called for his ouster, City Hall was swamped with calls supporting him. Loath to buck public opinion, Tate hailed Rizzo's performance and suggested that Dilworth should "quit meddling in the activities of the police department over which he has no jurisdiction."

Although Richardson Dilworth and Frank Rizzo had not clashed publicly before November 17, a collision of these two highly visible public figures—the patrician liberal reformer and the tough cop from the streets of South Philly—was inevitable. They despised each other.

Rizzo, who once pledged to "make Attila the Hun look like a faggot," rose to the top of the police department despite his penchant for controversial actions and inflammatory statements. Even flunking a highly publicized lie detector test did not impede his ascent to become the department's first Italian-American commissioner. In Joseph Clark's opinion, Rizzo was a "stupid, arrogant son-of-a-bitch." And in a 1972 interview, Dilworth, who never trusted Rizzo and viewed him as a demagogue, offered this evaluation of him as a police captain in Center City:

> "He was a very well-organized man. He knew every area of the city. He knew who was in every area. He knew the racketeers and all that. But we were also firmly convinced that he followed what the old-time inspectors had done. He would say to one group, 'You people can operate, but you've got to turn everybody else in to me. And if you get out of line, if you start any violence, I'll chop your balls off.' "

Ironically, Frank Rizzo received several important promotions on Clark and Dilworth's watch. One promotion, to acting police captain, came just days after the two men took office in 1952. Captain Rizzo frequently courted controversy in the 1950s, but his superiors on the force consistently backed him. When Emlen Etting, a wealthy artist, complained that Rizzo's men had used "Gestapo tactics" in breaking up a late-night post-theater party in his pad on tiny Panama Street in

1958, Mayor Dilworth ordered an investigation. The Associated Press sent the story of Rizzo's "Cossacks" across the country. But the word from Police Commissioner Thomas J. Gibbons was that "the officers behaved in gentlemanly fashion."

In 1959, Rizzo led raids on Center City coffeehouses where young people played chess, listened to records, read poetry, and drank Italian coffee. There was no evidence of drug use or alcohol or of any criminal behavior, but the coffeehouses stayed open late and annoyed some nearby residents. It was the Beat era, and there was a growing generation gap. Most of the downtown apartment dwellers were older than the coffeehouse patrons, and they feared a decline in real estate values if their neighborhood became another Greenwich Village.

The raids were condemned by the American Civil Liberties Union and other groups, but there was no great outcry. Mayor Dilworth kept silent, and his managing director, Donald C. Wagner, defended Rizzo, saying that the police had sufficient grounds for a crackdown. Instead of a reprimand, Rizzo got a promotion to police inspector.

While Dilworth was mayor in 1958, he created a civilian agency to oversee the police department. Its job was to investigate reports of police brutality, false arrest, and other instances of wrongful police conduct. Philadelphia's Police Advisory Board, or PAB, was the first such civilian agency in any American city. The mayor created the board by executive order after City Council refused to act. The Fraternal Order of Police bitterly opposed Dilworth's action, charging that the PAB was part of a "communist plot to undermine law enforcement." But Dilworth was convinced of the need for the agency.

In a national television interview with Chet Huntley in 1961, Dilworth said that payoffs to the police were "a real problem," and he bluntly cited specific dollar amounts. Patrolmen, he said, could pick up $25 to $50 a week, house sergeants $100 to $200, police captains as much as $500, and police inspectors $1,000 to $1,500. "And of course all of that is tax-free," Dilworth noted, "so it is a tremendous and continuing temptation." He never said where his figures came from, but his charges did not endear him to the men in blue.

Through the 1960s, the PAB heard about 1,000 cases. Although Dilworth created the board to control graft, as racial tension increased, it became an instrument mostly for investigating allegations of police brutality. While the black community strongly supported the PAB, police officers continued to hate it.

By the late 1960s, the Police Advisory Board had come to be seen as a political liability for the party in power, and on December 22, 1969, Dilworth's successor, James H. J. Tate, terminated the agency. "In spite of the sincere emotional support," he said, "the board's activities and procedures have been negative." No one was happier than Frank L. Rizzo, who had urged Tate to act. The police commissioner described the termination as a "Christmas present" for the cops.

The police action of November 17, 1967, a day that came to be known as Black Friday in Philadelphia, was the most significant flash point between Dick Dilworth and Frank Rizzo and a momentous event in the city's history. It came to symbolize dramatic divisions in American society. Four days later, Dilworth, in a letter to *Philadelphia Inquirer* publisher Walter Annenberg, warned that the city was at a "crossroads," facing a rift between the white and black communities "so wide and so deep as to be almost beyond repair." He said that "we must make a determined effort to channel the present energy and drive of the militant young black leadership into a constructive rather than a destructive course."

"I know this has its risks," Dilworth wrote, "and it would be safer to lay down rigid rules of law and order, and have them enforced by the police." With Rizzo's tough tactics in mind, he added: "However, if we are forced to do that, and we may yet be, then while order may be restored, the underlying situation will, in my opinion, be worse than ever, as we will then be dealing with thousands and thousands of sullen, uncooperative young Negroes, watching and waiting for another chance to explode."

Dilworth's reputation and that of Mark Shedd suffered in the aftermath of November 17. Certainly their relations with Rizzo were irreparably damaged. And it wasn't simply a war of words. Dilworth and Shedd both charged that the police commissioner had them followed. "Immediately after November 17," Dilworth maintained, "we both had shadows put on us. These were what the police have always described as rough shadows.... This was a shadow to impress you with the commissioner's power. He wanted you to know that you were having a shadow put on you and that they were there all the time." Shedd contended: "There is no doubt that I was tailed. Two plainclothesmen in an unmarked car parked outside the administration building and followed me wherever I went. After work, they'd park in front of my house."

The surveillance later became less obvious, but it continued for many months, according to Shedd. Then, in the summer of 1968, while he was vacationing in Maine, his house in Philadelphia was burglarized. Shedd said that while nothing of value was stolen, "I especially noted that the files and records in my office at home appeared to have been carefully examined." He said he believed that Rizzo "ordered the break-in."

"There was never any doubt," Mark Shedd stated, "that Rizzo was out to get me from the time I first arrived in Philadelphia." Rizzo conceded that he wanted Shedd ousted, but he denied ordering the police shadows and the break-in. "Not true," he responded in a *Bulletin* interview. "It didn't happen. We don't do things like that. These guys are seeing cops and robbers in their sleep. What's his proof? We don't break the law, we obey it."

Several weeks after November 17, Shedd, Dilworth, and other school board members met with Mayor Tate and Commissioner Rizzo to discuss the latter's request that the police be allowed to enter troubled schools without first getting permission from school authorities. According to Dilworth, Rizzo at one point warned the school officials that the police had collected dossiers on each of them with enough damaging information "to run you out of the city."

Dilworth aired the charge on the TV program *CBS Reports*. The commissioner denied it and threatened to sue but never did. Shedd confirmed his friend's account: "Rizzo made it clear he was keeping a close and careful surveillance on board and administration members, and that he had sufficient information on each one of us, on our personal lives, that could be incriminating. I saw a veiled threat toward me."

Between Black Friday in 1967 and the end of Dilworth's six-year term as school board president in 1971, the city was filled with tension. Racial conflicts often broke out, and Rizzo made a point of personally visiting every school where police were called to deal with trouble. Dilworth thought the police commissioner had an ulterior motive. "He seems to want to stir up trouble in the predominantly Negro high schools," the former mayor wrote to Joe Clark, "just so he can put it down with a club."

During Mark Shedd's tenure, Philadelphia actually lost fewer school days because of student disruptions than other big-city school districts and some much smaller suburban districts. And teacher assaults, which had risen sharply in the years before Shedd's arrival, leveled off. But when Rizzo accused reformers of "permissiveness," many working-class white parents agreed with him. When he called for stricter discipline, he won support.

In truth, Dilworth himself was not uncritically supportive of Mark Shedd's reforms. He sided with those who believed the schools were not demanding enough. On the matter of a summer reading list for sixth graders, he wrote to Shedd in July 1968: "I personally think that whoever got this list up must have watched too much TV.... It would seem to me that when a child reaches the age of 12, his reading should not be confined to *Gentle Ben*, *What the Gulls Are Singing*, *Pageboy of Camelot* and *The Picture Life of George Washington*." Dilworth, who was a voracious reader himself, told Shedd that "at the age of 12, children should at least be starting to read things like Dickens, Kipling, etc. instead of the mish-mash of porridge in the present reading list."

As for the increasingly virulent criticism of the way they were running the city schools, Dilworth and Shedd were victimized by their own candor. It would have been safer to operate a closed system as the old board had done, using homemade tests rather than nationally standardized ones, and refusing to release the results. In opening up the district to public inspection, they invited citizens to examine problems that had been swept under the rug for decades. Somehow Rizzo, in his relentless criticism, succeeded in pinning the blame on the housecleaners for the mess they had inherited.

There was a curious kind of double-think at work in Philadelphia. While Rizzo could blame Shedd for low test scores and other problems bedeviling the school system, he escaped responsibility for the city's increase in street-gang killings, drug abuse, and rape. It was largely a matter of style. As something of a staid New Englander, Shedd lacked the warmth and, ultimately, the credibility of the tough cop who was popular with the press and was always available to favored reporters.

In some respects, the educational reformers brought problems on themselves. "We were Kennedy-style liberals who ignored the white ethnics," Rick de Lone recalled. "This was a real flaw." He believed that the Dilworth board's "basic thrust"—making the schools more responsive to the needs of the majority black enrollment—was critically important. But "Rizzo's people," who resented the thrust, were vocal in their opposition, while the city's black population failed to rally in support of Dilworth and Shedd. Nor was the school board itself reflective of Philadelphia's social class structure. Five of the nine board members were millionaires. They were decent, well-intentioned, public-spirited millionaires, but millionaires nonetheless. They had little in common with Rizzo's working-class white followers in the row houses of Kensington, Tioga, and Southwark.

For all their efforts to strengthen Philadelphia's system of public education, for all the remarkable innovations that won praise nationally, the reformers searched in vain for a true constituency. One would have expected the city's formerly underpaid teachers to have supported them for raising faculty salaries dramatically. But even that didn't happen. Celia Pincus, the president of the Philadelphia Federation of Teachers, AFL-CIO, had grown up in the trade union movement. She had always admired Dilworth's courage and candor, and she had been among the civic leaders who pleaded with him to take the school board presidency. Over time, however, Pincus concluded that the policies he espoused were undermining the authority of teachers and damaging the system.

By 1971, Frank Rizzo's popularity had risen to the point that he decided to run for mayor. In his campaign against Republican Thacher Longstreth, Dilworth's old opponent, Rizzo pledged to fire Mark Shedd "within eight seconds" of becoming mayor. Celia Pincus and her teacher unionists backed Rizzo, and he won by 48,000 votes, taking 53 percent to Longstreth's 46 percent. Knowing he would be fired, Shedd resigned before Rizzo took office. Dilworth retired at the end of his term in December 1971, and he was succeeded as board president by William Ross, a Rizzo sycophant.

On August 16, 1971, Dilworth presided over his final meeting as president of Philadelphia's Board of Education. Impeccably attired in his usual double-breasted, dark-blue pinstripe suit, he drew out a yellow legal pad and delivered his farewell address.

The previous six years, he said, had been "exciting, stimulating, challenging, and, at times, frustrating." He had "learned a lot," and some of the most important of those lessons had been "splendidly expressed" many years earlier by Henry David Thoreau. "First, that the savage in man always lurks just beneath the surface. Second, there is 'no more encouraging fact than the unquestionable ability of man to elevate his life by conscious endeavor.' And, finally, that 'if a man does not keep pace with his companions, perhaps it is because he hears a different drummer. Let him step to the music he hears, however measured or far away.' "

Referring to Philadelphia, the 72-year-old memorably remarked: "This grand old city, which has been my adopted home for 45 years, has been wonderfully good to me. . . . I shall sorely miss serving her. But one of the most important things in public life is to know when to quit. So I say many thanks to all of you Philadelphians for having given me the opportunity to serve you these many years." And then, with a smile forming at the corners of his mouth, he concluded by saying, "God bless you all—even Jim Tate."

Epilogue
The betterment of the people

R ichardson Dilworth died of a malignant brain tumor on January 23, 1974. He was 75 years old. At his funeral three days later, warring Republicans and Democrats united in tribute to the remarkable champion of urban reform, the only Philadelphian ever to hold four city offices—one after another—as treasurer, district attorney, mayor, and school board president.

Hundreds of people filled Holy Trinity Church on Rittenhouse Square and thousands gathered outside on a damp, chilly, winter day for the funeral service. Dilworth's flag-draped mahogany casket was carried in and out of the historic Episcopal church by six Marines flanked by two officers of the corps that Dilworth proudly represented in two world wars. Among the 26 honorary pallbearers was W. Sheffield Cowles, Dilworth's Yale classmate, who enlisted in the Marine Corps with him in 1918.

On the day of the funeral, Philadelphia's newspapers published salutes to Dick Dilworth that spanned the political spectrum. Republican William W. Scranton, who defeated Dilworth in the 1962 race for governor, said the city and the state had lost one of its most outstanding citizens, who "accomplished as much as anyone for the betterment of the people." Congressman William J. Green, whose late father, the former Democratic city chairman, was so often at odds with

Dilworth, termed him "a giant...who made a tremendous impact on the city of Philadelphia."

Another Democratic leader, Peter J. Camiel, called Dilworth "a stirring human being," and said, "It was a privilege to have known him." Dick's longtime running mate, Joseph S. Clark, spoke of his "spontaneous gaiety," and Republican Thacher Longstreth, who lost the 1955 mayoralty to him, said that Dilworth had "the best sense of humor I ever saw in a politician."

*   *   *

In the years since Dilworth's death, Philadelphia has resumed its struggle over his legacy. Two months after he died, the Philadelphia City Council passed legislation naming the area adjacent to the west side of City Hall Richardson Dilworth Plaza. But Mayor Frank Rizzo refused to recognize the designation honoring his foe. Instead, he had a large sign erected on the site proclaiming it "City Hall West Plaza." Only after Rizzo left office five years later was the plaza's new name seen in public.It was fitting that the plaza be named for Dilworth, since he had often spoken of developing a park on the west side of City Hall. The space had opened up in the 1950s after the old Broad Street Station was closed and the elevated tracks that served it were demolished. "We are committed," the mayor wrote in 1961, "to making this plaza a really attractive setting." But the commitment never turned into effective action. Even after extensive "improvements" in the 1970s, the plaza remained an inhospitable concrete landscape that commuters hurried through.

Now, more than a half century after he first expressed it, Dilworth's idea for the plaza is finally wending its way toward realization. The private partnership Center City District/Central Philadelphia Development Corporation, having secured more than $50 million in federal, state, and local grants, is overseeing the last phases of construction on a parklike Dilworth Plaza, one that will feature lawns, shade trees, fountains and a café while incorporating new entrances to the subway below. With luck, the plaza will be a fitting capstone to the transformation of Philadelphia's central business district, begun under Clark and Dilworth, from a "hotbed of inertia," as the critics labeled it, into a locus of social, artistic, and commercial vitality.

*   *   *

Even as Dilworth Plaza nears completion, Dilworth's legacy is being battled over on another front. In moving into Philadelphia's Society Hill in 1957, Dick and Ann Dilworth helped spark the development of what became the nation's most successful urban renewal effort, one that restored a wealth of 18th- and

19th-century houses while incorporating modern buildings like I.M. Pei's Society Hill Towers. To many Philadelphians, the house they built at 223 South 6th Street is a potent symbol of the mayor's personal commitment to that extraordinary project.

To others, however, the reproduction Georgian house, designed for the Dilworths by George Edwin Brumbaugh, an architect best known for creating faux-18th-century mansions for clients in the suburbs, is little more than an impediment to progress. For the past decade, the difference of opinion has been quite pointed. Developer John Turchi bought the Dilworth house for $1.75 million in 2001, and in 2005 he unveiled plans to replace it with a 15-story condominium building—Dilworth Tower—designed by Philadelphia's most prominent architect, Robert Venturi. Acclaimed for sensitive restorations of historic buildings and imaginative work on historic sites as well as for groundbreaking modern buildings, Venturi argued that the Dilworth house was true neither to its own period nor to the one it imitated, and therefore was not worth saving. He and Turchi petitioned the Philadelphia Historical Commission to change its designation as a "significant contributing building" within the Society Hill Historic District so that it could be demolished. Part of a small courtyard in the new building would be dedicated to Dilworth and Society Hill.

There was immediate and vociferous pushback from the Historical Commission and from a broad array of Philadelphians. As a result, Turchi and Venturi returned to the Commission in early 2006 with a new plan, one in which the façade of the Dilworth house would be saved and incorporated into the new high rise. This concept was received with equal hostility, and a month later, the developer and the architect presented yet another idea. They now proposed that the Dilworth house be left mostly intact at the foot of the new tower. In 2007, the Historical Commission approved a version of this plan and granted permission for the demolition of the rear portion of the Dilworth house to make room for the erection of the new tower behind it. The Dilworth house would serve in part as a lobby for the tower. But the story didn't end there. The development plan was successfully challenged in court on various grounds, and in 2012, the Historical Commission's demolition approval was overturned for a second time by the Board of Licenses and Inspections Review. As of 2014, the Dilworth house had been vacant for over a decade and was beginning to show signs of neglect.

The question of the architectural merit of the Dilworth house may be a murky one, but the power of the building as a piece of history is quite clear to those who joined the Dilworths in Society Hill early on. For a 2005 article about the house, *Inquirer* reporter Stephan Salisbury interviewed Carter Buller, who moved to Society Hill and renovated a house in the early1960s. Buller remembered seeing the Dilworths frequently in the neighborhood, out walking their dogs, "stopping to chat, encouraging and welcoming new residents and old. The mayor actually

lived there…. When we pass the Dilworth home today, we know it tells a story—
and the story it tells is of a strong civic leader who was willing to take a risk so that
others would follow."

*   *   *

Dilworth was always willing to take a risk. Through the ups and downs of his
tumultuous career, even through the combustible 1960s, he never lost his passion
and affection for cities, and especially for Philadelphia. At a forum in the city in
1958, moderated by Walter Cronkite, Dilworth spoke after remarks by Frank
Lloyd Wright. The legendary architect favored spreading the population across
the countryside rather than concentrating it in the cities, and he held out no hope
for Philadelphia. It had been "doomed at birth" for failing to adapt to new ways
of life.

Dilworth felt differently: "I think our cities are perfectly wonderful. It is the
city which sharpens men's wits, concentrates their skills, provides for the inter-
change of their best goods and their finest services. There is nothing to equal the
dignity and elegance of a properly developed city or the richness and variety of its
life. I wouldn't live anywhere else."

Bibliography

Adams, Carolyn, et al. *Philadelphia: Neighborhoods, Division, and Conflict in a Post-Industrial City.* Philadelphia: Temple University Press, 1991.

Bartlett, Merrill L., and Jack Sweetman. *Leathernecks: An Illustrated History of the United States Marine Corps.* Annapolis, MD: Naval Institute Press, 2008.

Beers, Paul B. *Pennsylvania Politics Today and Yesterday: The Tolerable Accommodation.* University Park, PA: Pennsylvania State University Press, 1980.

Benson, Albert Emerson, ed. *Saint Mark's School in the War Against Germany.* Privately printed, 1920.

Birger, Jon S. *"Race, Reaction and Reform: The Three R's of Philadelphia School Politics, 1965–1971." Pennsylvania Magazine of History and Biography,* July 2008.

Brannen, Carl Andrew. *Over There: A Marine in the Great War.* College Station, TX: Texas A&M University Press, 1996.

Burk, William Herbert. *Historical and Topographical Guide to Valley Forge.* Philadelphia: John C. Winston Company, 1912.

Burt, Nathaniel. *The Perennial Philadelphians: The Anatomy of an American Aristocracy.* Boston: Little, Brown & Company, 1963.

Clark, Dennis J., ed. *Philadelphia, 1776–2076: A Three-Hundred-Year View.* Port Washington, NY: Kennikat Press, 1975.

Cooney, John. *The Annenbergs: The Salvaging of a Tainted Dynasty.* New York: Simon & Schuster, 1982.

Daughen, Joseph R. *Fearless: The Richard A. Sprague Story.* New York: The American Bar Association, 2008.

Davenport, Walter. *Power and Glory: The Life of Boies Penrose.* New York: G.P. Putnam's Sons, 1931.

Day, Sherman. *Historical Collections of the State of Pennsylvania.* Philadelphia: G.W. Gorton, 1843.

Decade of Progress: The Story of Philadelphia, 1952–1961. Philadelphia: The Office of the City Representative.

Edwards, Bob. *Edward R. Murrow and the Birth of Broadcast Journalism.* New York: John Wiley & Son, 2004.

Fonzi, Gaeton. *Annenberg: A Biography of Power.* New York: Weybright & Talley, 1969.

Fussell, Paul. *The Great War and Modern Memory*. New York: Oxford University Press, 1975.

Guinther, John. *Direction of Cities*. New York: Viking, 1996.

Halberstam, David. *The Best and the Brightest*. New York: Random House, 1972.

History of the Browning School, 1888–1988. New York: The Browning School.

Hobart, Frank, and William Archer. *Pictorial History of the Machine Gun*. New York: Drake, 1971.

Ickes, Harold. *The Secret Diary of Harold L. Ickes*. New York: Simon & Schuster, 1953.

Jones, EMIly Lewis, ed. *Walter M. Phillips: Philadelphia Gentleman Activist*. Bryn Mawr, PA: Portraits on Tape, 1987.

Jordan, John W., ed. *A Century and a Half of Pittsburgh and Her People*. Pittsburgh: Lewis Publishing, 1908.

Kennedy, David M. *The American People in World War II: Freedom from Fear, Part Two*. New York: Oxford University Press, 2003.

Killikelly, Sarah H. *The History of Pittsburgh: Its Rise and Progress*. Pittsburgh: B.C. & Gordon Montgomery Company, 1906.

Klemek, Christopher. *Urbanism as Reform: Modernist Planning and the Crisis of Urban Liberalism in Europe and North America, 1945–1975*. Philadelphia: University of Pennsylvania Press, 2004.

Kuklick, Bruce. *To Every Thing a Season: Shibe Park and Urban Philadelphia, 1909-1976*. Princeton, NJ: Princeton University Press, 1991.

Leeney, Robert J. *Elms, Arms and Ivy: New Haven in the Twentieth Century*. Montgomery, AL: Community Communications, 2000.

Libros, Harold. *Hard-Core Liberals: A Sociological Analysis of the Philadelphia Americans for Democratic Action*. Cambridge, MA: Schenkman, 1975.

Longstreth, W. Thacher, with Dan Rottenberg. *Main Line Wasp: The Education of Thacher Longstreth*. New York: W.W. Norton & Company, 1990.

Lowe, Jeanne R. *Cities in a Race with Time: Progress and Poverty in America's Renewing Cities*. New York: Vintage Books, 1968.

Morris, Joe Alex. *The Richardson Dilworth Story: Candidate for Greatness*. Philadelphia: Mercury Books, 1962.

Nevins, Allan. *John D. Rockefeller: The Heroic Age of American Enterprise*. New York: Charles Scribner's Sons, 1940.

Ogden, Christopher. *Legacy: A Biography of Moses and Walter Annenberg*. Boston: Little, Brown & Company, 1999.

Pederson, William D. *The FDR Years: Presidential Profiles*. New York: Facts on File, 2006.

Pepper, George Wharton. *Philadelphia Lawyer: An Autobiography*. Philadelphia: J. B. Lippincott Company, 1944.

Peters, Charles. *Five Days in Philadelphia: The Amazing "We Want Willkie" Convention of 1940 and How It Freed FDR to Save the Western World.* New York: Public Affairs, 2005.

Petshek, Kirk R. *The Challenge of Urban Reform: Policies and Programs in Philadelphia.* Philadelphia: Temple University Press, 1973.

Rishel, Joseph F. *Founding Families of Pittsburgh: The Evolution of a Regional Elite, 1760–1910.* Pittsburgh: University of Pittsburgh Press, 2005.

Siracusa, Joseph M. *The Kennedy Years: Presidential Profiles.* New York: Facts on File, 2004.

Stern, J. David. *Memoirs of a Maverick Publisher.* New York: Simon & Schuster, 1962.

Tarbell, Ida M. *The History of the Standard Oil Company.* New York: McClure, Phillips & Company, 1905.

Taylor, Frank H. *History of the Alan Wood Iron and Steel Company, 1792–1920;* published for private circulation.

Taylor, Frank Hamilton. *Valley Forge: A Chronicle of American Heroism.* Philadelphia: James W. Nagle Company, 1905.

Treadway, Jack M. *Elections in Pennsylvania: A Century of Partisan Conflict in the Keystone State.* University Park, PA: Pennsylvania State University Press, 2005.

Weber, Michael P. *Don't Call Me Boss: David L. Lawrence. Pittsburgh's Renaissance Mayor.* Pittsburgh: University of Pittsburgh Press, 1988.

Weigley, Russell F., ed. *Philadelphia: A 300-Year History.* New York: W.W. Norton & Company, New York, 1982.

Wisden's Cricketer's Almanac for 1910. London, John Wisden & Company, 1910.

Index